The Emperor and the Gods

Harvard Dissertations in Religion

Editors

Margaret R. Miles
and
Bernadette J. Brooten

Number 28

The Emperor and the Gods
Images from the Time of Trajan

Daniel N. Schowalter

The Emperor and the Gods

Images from the Time of Trajan

Daniel N. Schowalter

Fortress Press   Minneapolis

THE EMPEROR AND THE GODS
IMAGES FROM THE TIME OF TRAJAN

Copyright © 1993

The President and Fellows of Harvard College

Internal design and typesetting: Chiron, Inc.

Library of Congress Cataloging-in-Publication Data

Schowalter, Daniel N., 1957–
    The emperor and the gods : images from the time of Trajan / Daniel N. Schowalter
        p.   cm.—(Harvard dissertations in religion ; no. 28)
    Includes bibliographical references.
    ISBN 0-8006-7082-5
    1. Emperor worship, Roman. 2. Christianity and other religions --Roman. 3. Rome--Religion. 4. Christianity--Origin. 5. Church history--Primitive and early church, ca. 30–600. I. Title. II. Series.
DG124.S33 1993
292.2'13—dc20

90-40141
CIP

The paper used in this publication meets the minimum requirements of American National Standard for Information Sciences—Permanence of Paper for Printed Library Materials, ANSI Z329.48-1984.   ∞™

Manufactured in the U.S.A.   AF 1-7082

97   96   95   94   93   1   2   3   4   5   6   7   8   9   10

For Diane, Jeremy, Ryan, and Melanie

Contents

Acknowledgments

I wish to thank all of the people who made this thesis possible by providing tangible and intangible support. These include my parents and other relatives, colleagues and students at Wellesley College, and friends at North Prospect Church, especially Ikey Spear. Fellow students at Harvard and elsewhere provided insightful advice. I acknowledge the contributions made by members of the New Testament Doctoral Seminar at Harvard Divinity School; the important conversations I had with Steve Friesen, Judy Haley, and Kimberly Patton; and the careful reading and criticism of my work by Andy Overman and Greg Riley, who also assisted me with Latin translation.

The staff of Margaret Clapp Library at Wellesley College was of great help on numerous occasions. Guy Rogers of Wellesley College and Fergus Millar of Brasenose College, Oxford University, read parts of this thesis and gave me excellent criticism and encouragement. Dieter Georgi of the University of Frankfurt was instrumental in formulating many of the basic ideas. Bernadette Brooten, Gail Corrington, and John Strugnell of Harvard University read all or most of the work and their comments and advice were most helpful. My co-advisors, David Mitten and Helmut Koester, deserve my acknowledgment and my gratitude in countless ways. David was a constant source of the ideas, corrections, and words of good cheer that are essential to such a project. Helmut has given me insight, direction, and inspiration since I began my Master's program. I am deeply indebted to both of these men.

Finally, there is no way that I can express my appreciation to Diane, Jeremy, and Ryan. While the process of writing this thesis has put restrictions on the amount of quality family time we have been able to enjoy, they have continued to offer me loving support. To them I offer my thanks and my love.

Short Titles

Information appears here for frequently used works which are cited by short title. A few short titles do not appear in this list, but in each instance full bibliography is given on the page(s) preceding such references. Abbreviations used in this volume for sources and literature from antiquity are the same as those used in *HTR* 80:2 (1987) 243–60. Some abbreviations are not from that list and can be easily identified.

Beaujeu, *La religion*
> Jean Beaujeu, *La religion romaine a l'apogée de l'empire: I, La politique religieuse des Antonins* (Paris: Les Belles Lettres, 1955).

Berger, *Sacred Canopy*
> Peter Berger, *The Sacred Canopy: Elements of a Sociological Theory of Religion* (Garden City, NY: Doubleday, 1967).

Brunt, "Divine Elements"
> P. A. Brunt, "Divine Elements in the Imperial Office," *JRS* 69 (1979) 168–75.

Durry, *Panégyrique*
> Marcel Durry, *Pline le Jeune: Panégyrique de Trajan*, Préfacé, édité et commenté (Paris: Les Belles Lettres, 1938).

Fears, *PRINCEPS*
> J. Rufus Fears, *PRINCEPS A DIIS ELECTUS: The Divine Election of the Emperor as a Political Concept at Rome* (Papers and Monographs of the American Academy in Rome, 26; Rome: American Academy, 1977).

Fears, "Jupiter"
> J. Rufus Fears, "The Cult of Jupiter and Roman Imperial Ideology," *ANRW* (1981) 2/17.1, 3–141.

Gauer, "Bildprogramm"
> Werner Gauer, "Zum Bildprogramm des Trajansbogens von Benevent," *Jahrbuch des Deutschen Archäologischen Instituts* 89 (1974) 308–35.

Kenney, *Latin Literature*
>E. J. Kenney, ed., *The Cambridge History of Classical Literature*, vol. 2: *Latin Literature* (Cambridge: Cambridge University Press, 1982).

Hill, "Buildings and Monuments"
>Philip V. Hill "Buildings and Monuments of Rome, AD 96–192, Part 1," *Numismatic Chronicle* 144 (1984) 33–51; "Part 2," *Numismatic Chronicle* 145 (1985) 82–101.

Kennedy, *Art of Rhetoric*
>George Kennedy, *The Art of Rhetoric in the Roman World: 300 B.C.–A.D. 300* (Princeton: Princeton University Press, 1972).

Lepper, *Parthian War*
>F. A. Lepper, *Trajan's Parthian War* (Oxford: Oxford University Press, 1948).

Lepper, "Review of Hassell"
>Frank Lepper, "Review of Hassel, *Der Trajansbogen in Benevent*," *JRS* 59 (1969).

Liebeschuetz, *Continuity and Change*
>J. H. W. G. Liebeschuetz, *Continuity and Change in Roman Religion* (Oxford: Clarendon, 1979).

Mattingly, *BMC*, 3
>Harold Mattingly, *Coins of the Roman Empire in the British Museum*, vol. 3: *Nerva to Hadrian* (1936; reprinted London: Trustees of the British Museum, 1976).

Millar, "Emperor"
>Fergus Millar, "The Emperor, the Senate and the Provinces," *JRS* 56 (1966) 155–66.

Millar, *Emperor and the Roman World*
>Fergus Millar, *The Emperor and the Roman World* (Ithaca: Cornell University Press, 1977).

Price, *Rituals and Power*
>S. R. F. Price, *Rituals and Power: The Roman imperial cult in Asia Minor* (Cambridge: Cambridge University Press, 1984).

Price, "Noble Funerals to Divine Cult"
>S. R. F. Price, "From Noble Funerals to Divine Cult: the Consecration of Roman Emperors," in David Cannadine and Simon Price, eds., *Rituals of Royalty: Power and Ceremonial in Traditional Societies* (Cambridge: Cambridge University Press, 1987).

Radice, *Pliny*
>Betty Radice, *Pliny: Letters and Panegyricus* (LCL; Cambridge: Harvard University Press, 1969).

Richmond, "Arch"
> Ian Richmond, "The Arch of Beneventum," in idem, *Roman Archaeology and Art* (London, 1969).

Schuster, *C. Plini Caecili Secundi*
> Mauritius Schuster, ed., *C. Plini Caecili Secundi* (Berlin: Teubner, 1952).

Shochat, "Change in Roman Religion"
> Yanir Shochat, "The Change in the Roman Religion at the Time of the Emperor Trajan," *Latomus* 44 (1985) 317–36.

Sherwin-White, *Letters*
> A. N. Sherwin-White, *The Letters of Pliny: A Historical and Social Commentary* (Oxford: Clarendon, 1966).

Strack, *Untersuchungen*
> Paul L. Strack, *Untersuchungen zur römischen Reichsprägung des zweiten Jahrhunderts, Teil I. Die Reichsprägung zur Zeit des Traians* (Stuttgart: Kohlhammer, 1931).

Syme, "Review of Durry"
> Ronald Syme, Review of Durry, *Pline le Jeune: Panégyrique de Trajan*, in Ernst Badian, ed., *Roman Papers* (Oxford: Clarendon, 1979) 76–87.

Syme, *Tacitus*
> Ronald Syme, *Tacitus* (2 vols.; Oxford: Clarendon, 1958).

Talbert, *Senate*
> Richard J. A. Talbert, *The Senate of Imperial Rome* (Princeton: Princeton University Press, 1984).

Waters, "Traianus Domitiani Continuator"
> K. H. Waters, "Traianus Domitiani Continuator," *AJP* 90 (1969) 385–405.

1

Pliny and the *Panegyricus*
in Scholarly Context

Introduction

Gaius Plinius Caecilius Secundus had a long and illustrious career as a Roman orator, politician, and administrator.[1] He is best known today, however, as Pliny the Younger, a writer of letters. Since the pioneering work of E. G. Hardy in 1889,[2] Pliny's letters have been the subject of intensive scholarly inquiry.[3] Students of the ancient world have focused on various aspects of the entire corpus, but most of their efforts have been concentrated on the letter that Pliny wrote to the emperor Trajan concerning the proper procedure for handling people accused of being Christians.[4] At least since the time of

---

[1] *CIL* 5. 5262 (see Appendix 1).

[2] *C. Plinii Caecilii Secundi Epistulae ad Traianum imperatorem cum eiusdem responsis* (London: MacMillan, 1889).

[3] Certainly A. N. Sherwin-White's commentary on the letters (*The Letters of Pliny: A Historical and Social Commentary* [Oxford: Clarendon, 1966] 691–712) stands out as a classic reference. Sherwin-White does not include a full bibliography, but select titles are listed in the "Abbreviations" (pp. xi–xv). Bibliographic summaries can be found in *Jahresbericht über die Fortschritte der klassischen Altertumswissenschaft*, vols. 153 (1911) 1ff. (K. Burkhard); 221 (1929) 1–64 (M. Schuster); 242 (1934) 9–40 (M. Schuster); and 282 (1943) 38–77 (R. Hanslik). See also Hanslik, "Forschungsbericht über Plinius d. J.," *Anzeiger für die Altertumswissenschaft* 8 (1955) 1–18; Jean Beaujeu, "Pline le Jeune 1955–1960," *Lustrum* 6 (1961) 272–303.

[4] Pliny *Ep.* 10.96–97. Pliny was serving as *legatus* ("governor" or "representative") of the emperor in the provinces of Pontus and Bithynia. In an appendix Sherwin-White (*Letters,*

Tertullian, who discusses the letters in his *Apology*,[5] this letter and the response from Trajan[6] have been analyzed by adherents and students of Christianity for what they reveal about Roman perceptions of the Christian movement during the early second century. Recently Dieter Lührmann has reviewed the passages in the Pliny/Trajan correspondence and the historical writings of Suetonius and Tacitus that discuss the Christians. He has concluded that these Romans viewed Christianity as a *superstitio* or false faith, rather than a form of criminal heresy or atheism.[7]

Lührmann's comments on the Roman perception of Christianity focus on passages where Christians are mentioned specifically. Robert Wilken has sought a broader perspective by considering material from Pliny's letters concerned with organizations other than Christian communities.[8] For example, he notes that when Pliny requests permission to organize a company of workers (*collegium fabrorum*) to fight fires in Nicomedia (*Ep.* 10.33–34), Trajan refuses on the grounds that they could develop into a *hetaeria* (Wilken translates "political club.")[9] In another case, the emperor reluctantly permits

---

772–87) integrates his findings with other evidence on relations between Christianity and the empire to discuss "The Early Persecutions and Roman Law." See also idem, *Roman Society and Roman Law in the New Testament* (Oxford: Clarendon, 1963); Th. Mayer-Maly, "Der rechtsgeschichtliche Gehalt der 'Christenbriefe' von Plinius und Trajan," *SDHI* 22 (1956) 311–28; G. E. M. de. Ste. Croix, "Why Were the Early Christians Persecuted?," *Past and Present* 26 (1963) 6–38; W. H. C. Frend, *Martyrdom and Persecution in the Early Church* (Oxford: Blackwell, 1965) 162–66, and passim; R. Freudenberger, *Das Verhalten der römischen Behörde gegen die Christen im 2. Jahrh., dargestellt am Brief des Plinius an Trajan usw.* (Munich: Beck, 1969); Fergus Millar, "The Imperial Cult and the Persecutions," in Willem den Boer, ed., *Le culte des souverains dans l'Empire romain* (*Entretiens* 19; Geneva: Fondation Hardt, 1973) 147–75, 152–57; L. F. Janssen, "'Superstitio' and the Persecution of the Christians" *VC* 33 (1979) 131–59; Stephen Benko, *Pagan Rome and the Early Christians* (Bloomington: Indiana University Press, 1984) 4–14 and passim; Dieter Lührmann, "SUPERSTITIO—die Beurteilung des frühen Christentums durch die Römer," *ThZ* 42 (1986) 193–213.

[5] *Apol.* 2.6. Sherwin-White (*Letters*, 691–92) dismisses the claim that Christian interpolations found their way into the letters by the time Tertullian mentions them. Eusebius (*Hist. eccl.* 3.33.128–29) knows the correspondence from Tertullian.

[6] Book Ten contains letters written by Pliny to emperors, as well as the responses he received from Trajan while serving as the emperor's legate in Bithynia and Pontus. It is assumed that Pliny died without completing his term of service there (Sherwin-White, *Letters*, 82), and therefore, that Book Ten was published posthumously. Betty Radice (*Pliny: Letters and Panegyricus* [LCL; Cambridge: Harvard University Press, 1969] xvi) suggests that Book Ten was released by "Suetonius or another of Pliny's literary friends after Trajan's death."

[7] Lührmann, "SUPERSTITIO," 194–95.

[8] Wilken, *The Christians as the Romans Saw Them* (New Haven and London: Yale University Press, 1984) 1–30. Wilken's work is not a technical treatment of Pliny's letters, but rather a lucid introductory presentation of the ideas of Pliny and other Graeco-Roman thinkers of the second century CE.

[9] Ibid., 11–13.

the formation of "benefit societies" (*erani*) in the free city of Amisus, only because a local ordinance allows for such organizations (*Ep.* 10.93 – 94).[10] Wilken's illucidation of Pliny's dealings with other associations supports the contention that the suppression of the Christians which is described in *Ep.* 10.96 – 97 should be understood in the context of Trajan's general apprehension about social organizations in the area, rather than as reflecting a particular aversion to Christianity.[11]

Wilken has been especially enlightening in the formulation of this dissertation. His success in looking beyond *Ep.* 10.96 – 97 suggests that further exploration of Pliny's writings might contribute to a better understanding of Pliny's response to the Christian problem in Pontus, and also to the attitudes encountered by Christian communities around the world.[12] Specifically, the purpose of my study is to analyze how the relationship between the emperor and the gods is portrayed in Pliny's writings, to compare that portrayal with other images of the same relationship, some of which can be associated with Trajan,[13] and to consider how these various images might have informed the symbolic world of the early second century CE.

This approach is informed by S. R. F. Price's work on the imperial cult in Asia Minor.[14] Price insists that the imperial cult must be seen as an integral part of a complex "web of power" by which the inhabitants of the empire understood themselves to be connected with Rome and the emperor. Price believes that in order to study this web it is essential not to separate consideration of imperial rituals from either the traditional religious system or the traditional political power relationships of the empire.[15] In this approach, Price follows Fergus Millar who urges those considering the imperial cult

---

[10] Ibid., 14 – 15. Trajan's response includes the command that "in the rest of the cities, which are constrained under our laws, this type of thing is to be prohibited" (*Ep.* 10.93). (Translations are my own unless otherwise indicated.)

[11] Wilken, *Christians*, 22 – 24.

[12] The writings of Pliny will not provide data on all areas of Roman society. Pliny is speaking from the perspective of a member of the Roman Senate whose views on religion, politics, and culture would not necessarily represent the experience of the majority of the Roman population. His writings can, however, offer a glimpse of the conflict between Christianity and the empire from Pliny's perspective as an orator and senator in Rome, and an imperial representative in the provinces of Pontus and Bithynia (the two northernmost provinces in Asia Minor).

[13] That Pliny and Trajan did not necessarily share the same perspective of this relationship, and that neither of them was consistent in their descriptions of it is discussed at length below.

[14] Price, *Rituals and Power: The Roman Imperial Cult in Asia Minor* (Cambridge: Cambridge University Press, 1984).

[15] Ibid., 234 – 48. Price follows Foucault (*La volonté de savoir* [1976] 123; cited by Price, *Rituals and Power*, 241 – 42) in considering power not to be "an institution, a structure, or a certain force with which certain people are endowed." Rather, "it is the name given to a complex strategic situation in a given society."

to confine ourselves to an exact comparison of its external manifestations—cult-acts, dedications, prayers, oaths, erection of temples or whatever—with the external manifestations of the worship of the pagan gods. In this way it would be possible to arrive at limited, but factual, results.[16]

While Price focuses on evidence from the provinces,[17] I believe that his "web of power" model can also be applied to the city of Rome, and to Pliny's evidence for how his segment of Roman society used "their traditional symbolic system" to represent "the emperor to themselves in the familiar terms of divine power."[18] I do not intend to probe the minds of either Pliny or Trajan in an attempt to determine what they truly thought or believed.[19] Rather, I hope that this study will elucidate how the images that were used to describe the relationship of the emperor to the gods grew out of the social context of their time, and attempted to shape that context in specific and sometimes divergent ways.

The scene described in Pliny's letter concerning the Christians is the best-known example of a social context in which images of the emperor and the gods are central. Here Pliny discusses how he determined the innocence of those who denied being Christians:

> I decided to release those who denied that they were or that they had been Christians, after they addressed the gods repeating after me, and made an offering of incense and wine to your image, which I had ordered to be brought into the court with the statues of the gods, and after they had sworn a curse against Christ, things, it is said, which no one who is really a Christian can be forced to do.[20]

In this passage Pliny does not make a formal statement concerning the relationship between the emperor and the gods, but he juxtaposes invocation of

---

[16] Millar discussing Elias Bickerman, "Consecratio," in den Boer, *Le culte des souverains,* 37.

[17] Again, he follows Millar: "The Republic, it may be, can be seen from Rome outwards. To take this standpoint for the Empire is to lose contact with reality. Not only the pattern of the literary evidence, or the existence of an immense mass of local documents, but the very nature of the Empire itself, means that it can only be understood by starting from the provinces and looking inward" ("The Emperor, the Senate and the Provinces," *JRS* 56 [1966] 166).

[18] Price, *Rituals and Power,* 248. Millar has shown that Pliny's outward looking perspective does not capture the true scope and intricacy of the empire (see preceding n.). Yet in the *Panegyricus,* Pliny tried to convince his emperor, his readers, and probably himself that it was still the only perspective that mattered.

[19] Millar (Discussion of Bickerman, "Consecratio," 37) warns against "attempting to reach the 'psychology' of ancient pagans."

[20] *Ep.* 10.96.5. It was likewise with those who confessed to having been Christians, but claimed to have broken with the group—some up to twenty years earlier (10.96.6).

the gods and offerings to the image of the emperor. The emperor's statue is brought in with those of the gods, and is used in what might be called a ceremonial test of devotion.[21] While the gods are called on verbally, the emperor's statue is petitioned with incense and wine. Pliny describes this test without any explanation.[22] Trajan approves of the test *supplicando dis nostris* ("by offering prayers to our gods"), but does not mention the sacrifice to his own image (10.97.2). Presumably this implies that the practice is acceptable to Trajan, but not something he wants to emphasize. Since Pliny presents the test as something which he had improvised, it would be helpful to know more about the background for this connection of the emperor and the gods.[23] Further consideration of how the relationship between the emperor and the gods was portrayed during Trajan's reign is one way to enhance understanding of this particular passage in the letter. Such consideration can also provide information about the growing conflict with the Roman Empire that Christians were experiencing in the early second century CE, a conflict in which tests of devotion similar to Pliny's became an important factor.

In order to begin this consideration, it is necessary to follow Wilken and go beyond *Ep.* 10.96 and 97. In fact, it will be useful to range farther than the correspondence between Pliny and Trajan to the wider corpus of Pliny's letters,[24] and to Pliny's other surviving work, the *Panegyricus*.[25] This document is a speech of thanks (*gratiarum actio*; *Ep.* 3.13; 18.1; *Pan.* 1.6; 90.3) that Pliny delivered in the Senate when he took office as consul in 100 CE.[26]

---

[21] I use the term "devotion" here instead of "loyalty" in response to Price's arguments against making the imperial cult a strictly political phenomenon (*Rituals and Power*, 15–16, 239–48).

[22] Pliny does make a distinction between the *simulacra* of the gods and the *imago* of Trajan. The use of *simulacrum* for a statue usually refers to the image of a divinity; see Tacitus, *Hist.* 5.5; and Suetonius, *Div. Jul.* 88, where a *simulacrum* is used for a statue of the deified Julius.

[23] Sherwin-White (*Letters*, 701) thinks that for the offerings to the emperor's statue Pliny took as example the cult of "the *numen Augusti* which had republican precedents at Rome itself. Cf. the story of Gratidianus in 86 BCE: Cicero *Off.* 3.80." Sherwin-White also points out that "the gods were not mentioned in other trials of the second century, but the Christians were generally regarded as 'godless' by their opponents" (ibid.).

[24] The explicit religious content of the letters has rightly been downplayed. "Religion whether private or public only occupies a marginal place in the letters" (J. H. W. G. Liebeschuetz, *Continuity and Change in Roman Religion* [Oxford: Clarendon, 1979] 185). There is, however, much helpful information in the letters which will be incorporated as applicable.

[25] Edition and commentary by Marcel Durry, *Pline le Jeune: Panégyrique de Trajan*, Préfacé, édité et commenté (Paris: Les Belles Lettres, 1938). Edition in Mauritius Schuster, ed., *C. Plini Caecili Secundi* (Berlin: Teubner, 1952); R. A. B. Mynors, ed., *XII Panegyrici Latini* (Oxford: Oxford University Press, 1964); and in Radice, *Pliny*.

[26] The course of Pliny's public career is discussed by Sherwin-White, *Letters*, 72–82 (see Appendix 1 below).

In the remainder of this Chapter I shall attempt to resolve an initial question which complicates any study of the *Panegyricus*: a dispute over whether the *Panegyricus* represents the views of Pliny its author, or whether it should be understood as reflecting the policy of the emperor Trajan who is the subject and recipient of this speech of thanks. It is my contention that the *Panegyricus* can be understood most accurately if it is read as reflecting Pliny's perspectives as a member of the Roman Senate.

Having proposed this hypothesis in this Chapter, in the next Chapter I shall present evidence from the *Panegyricus* which demonstrates the prevalence of Pliny's senatorial perspective in the document. In the third Chapter I shall examine the picture of the relationship between the emperor and the gods which Pliny the senator presents in the *Panegyricus*, and in the fourth Chapter I shall investigate other pictures of this relationship that can be associated more or less with Trajan. These other pictures come from literary[27] as well as nonliterary sources, especially numismatic evidence and monumental art.[28] In concluding, I shall discuss how the insights gained from this study might inform further consideration of the practical situation described in *Ep.* 10.96 and 97 and the broader context of developing Christian communities in the early second century CE.

The Panegyricus: Preliminary Issues

As with any document from antiquity, there are several basic questions about the *Panegyricus* that must be addressed, but that cannot always be answered with certainty. These concern the text of the document, the length and form of the speech as it was delivered and later published, and the date of publication of the speech.

The Text of the Panegyricus

Pliny's *Panegyricus* has had a textual life of its own, circulating separately from his better known work, the *Epistles*.[29] The *Panegyricus* is preserved as part of a corpus of *XII Paengyrici Latini*. The other eleven speeches are much shorter encomia for emperors, written by various authors in the late-

---

[27] Specifically Trajan's responses found in the correspondence with Pliny.

[28] The difficulties and benefits of studying visual evidence are discussed briefly at that point.

[29] On the text of the *Epistles* see Sherwin-White, *Letters*, 82–84; S. E. Stout, *Scribe and Critic at work in Pliny's Letters* (Bloomington: Indiana University Press, 1954); idem, "The Basis of the Text in Book X of Pliny's Letters," *TAPA* 86 (1955) 233–49; R. A. B. Mynors, *Letters 1–10* (Oxford Classical Texts; Oxford: Oxford University Press, 1963); and Radice, *Pliny*, xxvi–xxvii.

third and fourth centuries.[30] Mason Hammond suggests that the *Panegyricus* was originally part of a published volume of Pliny's speeches, but that because it served as a model for the the later panegyrics, it was incorporated into the extant collection.[31]

Except for references in his letters,[32] Pliny's *gratiarum actio* was unknown until a manuscript of the *XII Paengyrici Latini* was discovered in Mainz in 1433 CE. This MS (M) is now lost, but it is thought to be the source for an Italian MS group (X), and the Harley MS (H).[33] According to Radice the text of the lost (M) as provided by (X) and (H) is the evidence on which the text rests.[34] Given the limited MS base, there are few significant text-critical problems found in the passages discussed below. Those that are encountered will be analyzed in the notes.

The Length and Form of the Speech

The composition of the *Panegyricus* took place in at least two stages: the actual speech delivered to the Senate, and the expanded published version.[35] In the extant document, Pliny claims to be unconcerned with making his *gratiarum actio* too long, since it is the good fortune of his listeners to owe the emperor so much gratitude (*Pan.* 25.1). Because the extant work is an edited and expanded version, however, it is impossible to determine the length of the original speech. In a letter to Vibius Severus (*Ep.* 3.18.4), Pliny reports that his friends were able to sit through a private reading of the speech which included sessions on three days. He does not specify whether this was the shorter original or longer revised version of the speech, but Durry, Syme, and Sherwin-White all understand it to be the expanded edition. The first two commentators estimate that the reading would have been accomplished in three hours total,[36] while Sherwin-White, claiming that three hours is an underestimation of the "toughness of the Roman audience," suggests that

---

[30] The speeches break down as follows: II for Theodosius (Augustus from 379–395); III for Julian (360–363); IV, V, VI, XII for Constantine (306–337); VII for Constantine and Maximian (286–305, given in honor of Constantine's marriage to Maximian's daughter, Fausta); VIII for Constantius (305–306); IX for the Tetrarchs (Diocletian [284–305], Maximian, Constantius, and Galerius [305–311]); X and XI for Maximian. See Lester K. Born, "The Perfect Prince according to the Latin Panegyrists," *AJP* 55 (1934) 20–35.

[31] Hammond, "Pliny the Younger's Views on Government," *CP* 49 (1954) 115–40, esp. 120.

[32] *Ep.* 3.15 and 18.

[33] Discovered by E. Baehrens in 1875.

[34] Radice, *Pliny*, xxvii. Radice claims that the editions of Puteolanus (1482) and Livineius (1599) are used for spot corrections. Cf. Mynors, *XII Panegyrici Latini*, v–xii.

[35] See discussion in Syme, *Tacitus* (2 vols.; Oxford: Clarendon, 1958) 1. 94–95.

[36] M. Durry, *Panégyrique*, 8; Syme, *Tacitus*, 94.

three sessions of 1 1/2 to 2 hours would have been required for complete delivery.[37]

In *Ep*. 3.18.6, referring to the original speech, Pliny compares his work with previous such addresses, which could scarcely have attracted a voluntary audience, since after the first minute they were tedious to those who were forced to listen to them in the Senate.[38] The questions as to how much of the published speech was original, and how much was added during the editing process cannot be answered exactly. Syme comments that certain sections are "probable additions," but "the process of deflating the *Panegyricus* would have to be very drastic and could not escape being arbitrary."[39] In spite of this uncertainty, it is important to remember the possibility that certain passages were added or expanded some time after the original presentation. In the volatile environment of Rome, even a short interval allows plenty of time for changes that would affect the content.[40]

Pliny may have been reluctant to say things in the first presentation that he felt were appropriate in the later written form. Perhaps increased familiarity with Trajan made Pliny more confident of his position in the imperial regime. This would have allowed him additional freedom not only for offering lavish praise, but also for reminding the emperor of the high calling to which he had

[37] Sherwin-White, *Letters*, 252. George Kennedy (*The Art of Rhetoric in the Roman World: 300 B.C.–A.D. 300* [Princeton: Princeton University Press, 1972] 545) says of the *Panegyricus* (made up of nearly 100 pages of Latin text): "If recited in an imposing manner [including appropriate gestures], with pauses for effect, it could easily take five hours to deliver, whereas the original form may well have taken less than an hour."

[38] "Even in the Senate, where it was necessary to endure, we were accustomed to be bored after only a short time, but now both someone to read (such a speech) and some to listen to it for three days running can be found, not because it is written more eloquently than before, but because it is written more freely, and on account of that with more enjoyment" (*Ep*. 3.18.6).

[39] Syme, Review of Durry, *Pline le Jeune: Panégyrique de Trajan*, in Ernst Badian, ed., *Roman Papers* (Oxford: Clarendon, 1979) 77; first published in *JRS* 27 (1938) 218. Syme follows J. Mesk ("Die Überarbeitung des Plin. Pan. auf Traian," *Wiener Studien* 22 [1910] 239–60) in concluding that the extent of the original speech is not discernible. Syme ("Review of Durry," 77) cites Durry's suggestions of probable additions: "the strenuous military career of the young Trajan (*Pan*. 13–15), the purple patch about famine in the land of Egypt (30–31), the horrid and deserved fate of the delators (55)," and "the unexceptionable family life of the new Emperor (81 ff)." Kennedy (*Art of Rhetoric*, 545) agrees that certainty is unattainable, but he feels that the passages prophesying a triumph and those showing influence from the *Dialogus* (of Tacitus) should be seen as additions. On the Tacitean influence on the *Panegyricus*, cf. Durry, *Panégyrique*, 60–66; Richard T. Bruère, "Tacitus and Pliny's *Panegyricus*," *Classical Philology* 49 (1954) 161–79; Rudolf Güngerich, "Tacitus' *Dialogus* und der *Panegyricus* des Plinius," *Festschrift Bruno Snell: zum 60. Geburtstag am 18. Juni 1956 von Freunden und Schülern Überreicht* (Munich: Beck, 1956) 145–52.

[40] The time period between the original speech and its final publication is discussed in the next section.

ascended.[41] Pliny may also have used the publication of an expanded version of the *gratiarum actio* to reiterate and reinforce the good beginnings of Trajan's rule which he had praised in the original.[42] In spite of the extravagant praise that comprises the bulk of this document, the full spectrum of motivations behind Pliny's speech, or behind his written version of the *Panegyricus*, cannot be known. Mingled with flowery commendation of the emperor, however, the advice and cautious concern of the senatorial author can be detected.

The Date of Publication

Although Pliny delivered his address of thanks in September, 100 CE,[43] there are different opinions about when the speech was actually published. Durry, followed by Syme, dates the publication of the *Panegyricus* to the year 101 CE.[44] R. Paribeni has argued for a date as late as 103 CE,[45] while Jerome Carcopino has suggested that after an initial publication in 103 CE, the piece was reworked for successive editions throughout the remainder of Trajan's reign.[46] Pliny reports (*Ep.* 3.13) that he is sending to Voconius Romanus a copy of the speech (*Liber*) which he has recently (*nuper*) presented as an expression of gratitude to the *optimus princeps*. In this letter, Pliny does not mention a specific plan to publish the work, but an intent to publish may be implied by Pliny's request that Voconius criticize the piece. In the afore-

[41] In a situation involving an oration of blame instead of praise, Cicero, who was denied the opportunity to deliver his second speech against Verres, elected to publish the work anyway, presumably with expansions (my thanks to Gail Corrington for this observation).

[42] This view is shared by Kennedy (*Art of Rhetoric*, 545): "He [Trajan] had begun well as emperor in the view of Pliny and his friends, but so had other emperors including Nero and Domitian, who had both ended badly. Enough time had elapsed so that some uneasiness had begun to build up about the difficulty of maintaing the felicity of the times: Tacitus' *Dialogue* and *Histories* betray a little of the same feeling."

[43] *Pan.* 92.2 confirms that Pliny and his friend Tertullus became consuls during a year which started with Trajan holding the consulship. This must be Trajan's third consulship in 100 CE, since it is the first time he held the office as emperor, and also the first time he held it while resident in the city. The month of the term is revealed in *Pan.* 92.4 where Pliny announces the good fortune that he and Tertullus shared in being consuls during the same month in which Trajan was born, Domitian was assassinated, and Nerva became emperor, i.e., September.

[44] Durry, *Panégyrique*, 9–15; Syme, "Review of Durry," 77–78.

[45] Paribeni, *Optimus Princeps: saggio sulla storia e sui tempi dell'Imperatore Traiano* (2 vols.; Messina: Principato, 1926) 1. 221.

[46] Carcopino, *Les étapes de l'impérialisme romain* (Paris: Hachette, 1961) 108. This is the ultimate extension of Durry's theory that the *Panegyricus* was "un instrument de la propagande gouvernementale" (Durry, "Les Empereurs comme historiens d'Auguste à Hadrien," in *Entretiens sur l'antiquité classique*, vol. 4: *Histoire et Historiens dans l'Antiquité* [Geneva: Fondation Hardt, 1956] 231–34).

mentioned letter to Vibus Severus *(Ep.* 3.18) Pliny seems to speak of the expanded version as finished. Since it is unclear when the letter was written, this reference does not provide any clue as to the date of completion.[47]

Several internal issues such as a possible mention of Trajan's construction of a new harbor complex at Ostia,[48] and an allusion to Trajan's first Dacian Triumph,[49] have not proved to be fruitful for dating the revision,[50] and as such, it is not possible to establish a firm date for final publication. The earliest date of 101 CE, offered by Durry and Syme, is supported by the lack of any mention of Trajan's fourth consulship which began in that year.

The Use of the Panegyricus by Scholars

Pliny mentions that a *senatus consultum* required him as a newly elected consul to deliver an address of thanks so that "good *principes* should recognize what they have done, and bad ones what they ought to do."[51] Since no panegyrics from the imperial period before Pliny survive, it is difficult to speak about development of the form, but it is obvious that in Pliny's speech, praise of the emperor has become the central focus. At the same time, it is impossible to read the *Panegyricus* without being struck by frequent allusions to and mention of the gods. Starting with a reminder that all speech and action should begin with prayer, the work proceeds on the basis that the good fortune of having Trajan for a ruler is due to the fact that he was divinely ordained and chosen by the gods.[52] Further, Trajan regularly intercedes with the gods on behalf of the people, and he refuses to have a seat with the gods in any temple.[53]

Given Pliny's concern about the divine, it is surprising that the *Panegyr-*

[47] Sherwin-White (*Letters*, 250) dates *Ep.* 3.18 "some months later than his consulship, and some time later than *Ep.* [3.]13, where the speech is still being trimmed for publication."

[48] "In fact, this one (Pompey the Great) is not any more an exemplary citizen than our parent who by authority, with consultation, and loyalty, opened roads, opened up harbors, restored roads to the land, sea to the shore, and shore to the sea, and thus he mixed by commerce different peoples, so that whatever thing is produced (in a particular place), now appears to be native to all" (*Pan.* 29.2).

[49] *Pan.* 16–17.

[50] Durry, *Panégyrique,* 110–12; Syme, "Review of Durry," 77–78.

[51] *Pan.* 4.1. William Stuart Maguinness (*OCD,* 774) claims that this *senatus consultum* was enacted under Augustus. Richard J. A. Talbert (*The Senate of Imperial Rome* [Princeton: Princeton University Press, 1984] 228) points out that although the consul regularly was called upon to make such a speech in the Augustan period (Ovid, *Ex Ponto,* 4.4.35–39), there is no other evidence for the dating of a *senatus consultum* on the subject. Cf. Radice, "Pliny and the *Panegyricus,*" *Greece and Rome* 15 (1968) 166.

[52] *Pan.* 1.4; 5.2.

[53] *Pan.* 52.1–2; 78.5.

icus has not been consulted more frequently by scholars discussing various aspects of the religious milieu of the early-second century CE.[54] Due to its nature and style, however, not only historians of religion, but also classicists and ancient historians have been reluctant to deal with this document.[55] F. R. D. Goodyear has described it as "couched in the grand style, being elaborately expansive, patterned in phrase and clause, and full of florid conceits and rhetorical artifice of every kind." He further suggests that Pliny "would have been wiser if he had not expanded and developed the more simple version actually delivered to the Senate."[56]

There have been some attempts to penetrate the difficult style of the *Panegyricus* in order to gain insight into Pliny's time. Recently, Klaus Wengst has discussed the concept of the *Pax Romana* in the early-second century CE, using passages from the *Panegyricus* in which Pliny mentions the emperor's relations with conquered nations and the army, his generosity and equity, and the emperor's concern for his subjects and the gods.[57] Other scholars have read the *Panegyricus* as a statement of Trajan's policy, and have used it to support broader theories of "religious ideology." Unfortunately, this approach tends to read too much meaning and authority into Pliny's words. This tendency becomes clear in a review and analysis of three scholars who use the *Panegyricus* to support theories of so-called imperial theology.[58]

---

[54] Liebeschuetz (*Continuity and Change*, 183–92) is heavily dependent on Pliny's letters when he discusses the "Breakdown and Reconstruction" of Roman religion. In this section, however, he draws only five references from the *Panegyricus* to support a brief paragraph on the morality of the gods in Pliny's understanding.

[55] Syme praised Durry for the scholarship and courage he showed in producing his edition and commentary of the *Panegyricus* in 1938. Syme ("Review of Durry," 77) says of Pliny's work: "The style of the orator, technically perfect and palatable in small doses, soon becomes tedious through preciosity and unrelenting pursuit of the pointless epigram and forced antithesis."

[56] Goodyear, "Pliny the Younger," in E. J. Kenney, ed., *The Cambridge History of Classical Literature*, vol. 2: *Latin Literature* (Cambridge: Cambridge University Press, 1982) 660. Goodyear adds that the work "has fallen, not undeservedly, into almost universal contempt," and that "while the antitheses and epigrams which Pliny readily excogitated are often as wearisome as they are vacuous (see e.g. 61.4, 62.9, 67.3, 84.5), it is probably his woolly repetitiveness, rather than misplaced ingenuity, which in the end reduces most readers to despair." Goodyear's charge is balanced by the fact that repetition was an important part of rhetorical practice and was used effectively by Cicero, for example. The sharp criticism of the *Panegyricus* by Goodyear and others should be viewed in light of the general disdain shown by scholars for "Silver Latin" literature (my thanks to Gail Corrington for the two previous observations). Introducing the section on "Early Principate" in the *Cambridge History of Classical Literature*, D. W. T. C. Vessey identifies this traditional scholarly bias, and discusses what he sees to be the response of "Silver Latin" to the challenge of the "Golden Age" (497–502).

[57] *Pan.* 12, 25–27, 29, 51, 68, 72, 93. Klaus Wengst, *Pax Romana and the Peace of Jesus Christ* (Philadelphia: Fortress, 1987) 16, passim.

[58] Jean Beaujeu, *La religion romaine a l'apogee de l'empire: I, La politique religieuse des Antonins* (Paris: Les Belles Lettres, 1955); J. Rufus Fears, *PRINCEPS A DIIS ELECTUS: The*

Jean Beaujeu's "Théologie jovienne du principat"

The earliest of these figures is Jean Beaujeu, the historian of religions who compiled a detailed survey of second-century CE Roman religion. In this study Beaujeu suggests that under Trajan there developed a "theology of imperial power" which had two aspects. The first was the promotion of the emperor's virtues and his military victories,[59] and the second was a "Jovian theology of the principat."[60]

Beaujeu uses evidence from the *Panegyricus* of Pliny to support the idea of an imperial theology based on the emperor's relationship to Jupiter. In the *Panegyricus* Pliny states that Trajan is as worthy to be called *Optimus Maximus* as is Jupiter,[61] suggests that in legal matters the emperor serves as the earthly representative of the King of the Gods,[62] and affirms that Jupiter is the guardian of the emperor.[63] Beaujeu also cites abundant material evidence to demonstrate Trajan's piety toward Jupiter.[64] This evidence ranges from a triumphal arch featuring a dedication to Jupiter Optimus Maximus[65] to a bronze medallion honoring Jupiter as part of the Capitoline Triad. Beaujeu suggests that the medallion was associated with the tenth anniversary of Trajan's accession in 108 CE.[66] Beaujeu effectively integrates literary and

---

Divine Election of the Emperor as a Political Concept at Rome (Papers and Monographs of the American Academy in Rome, 26; Rome: American Academy, 1977); idem, "The Cult of Jupiter and Roman Imperial Ideology," ANRW (1981) 2/17.1, 3–141; and Yanir Shochat, "The Change in the Roman Religion at the Time of the Emperor Trajan," *Latomus* 44 (1985) 317–36.

[59] Beaujeu, *La religion*, 59–69.

[60] Ibid., 69–81. Beaujeu also considers Trajan's promotion of the cult of Hercules from Gades in Spain (pp. 81–87), his concern for traditional piety and divinities (pp. 87–97), the refusal of divine honors, an affinity for the image of Alexander the great (pp. 98–101), and his attitude toward Eastern religions and especially Christianity (pp. 101–9).

[61] *Pan.* 88.8; Beaujeu, *La religion*, 72.

[62] *Pan.* 80.4; Beaujeu, *La religion*, 73–76.

[63] *Pan.* 1.6; Beaujeu, *La religion*, 76–78.

[64] Beaujeu, *La religion*, 78–80.

[65] The arch is attested only on sestertii reverses from Rome (*BMC* 3. pp. 177–78, nos. 842–46, pl. 31. 6–9). The abbreviated dedication *IOM* is clearly visible, as is a pediment scene over the passageway which pictures Jupiter. A six-horse chariot group being led by two Victories crowns the elaborate construction (fig. 1.C). Beaujeu (*La religion*, 78) associates the arch with the triumph celebrated after the victory in the first Dacian war, and dates the coin to 103–4 (on the first Dacian triumph see *Pan.* 17 and Chapter Two below). Philip Hill ("Buildings and Monuments of Rome, AD 96–192, Part 1" *Num Chron* 144 [1984] 42–43) follows Paul L. Strack (*Untersuchungen zur römischen Reichsprägung des zweiten Jahrhunderts: Teil I Die Reichsprägung zur Zeit des Traian* [Stuttgart: Kohlhammer, 1931] 114–16) in arguing that the monument is not a triumphal arch, but a gateway, possibly a *porta Areae Capitolinae* ("entrance to the courtyard of the Capitoline temple").

[66] Beaujeu, *La religion*, 79–80; see also Strack, *Untersuchungen*, 197.

nonliterary evidence in order to demonstrate the important role that Jupiter played in Trajan's imperial theology. As mentioned above, however, he is not concerned with Jupiter alone, but with evidence for several different aspects of the relationship between Trajan and the gods.

The "Jovian Theology" of J. Rufus Fears

In the case of J. Rufus Fears, *la théologie jovienne du principat* becomes the central focus of an imperial policy associating the emperor with the king of the gods. Fears has attempted to demonstrate that the relationship between the emperor and the gods is best considered in light of a long association between Jupiter and Roman rulers, culminating in the institution of what he calls a "Jovian theology" under Trajan and his successor Hadrian.[67] Fears contends that attempts to institutionalize the emperor's special connection with Jupiter can be seen under Nero, but they began in earnest during the reign of Domitian.[68] Although Domitian was especially devoted to the goddess Minerva, he did not allow her worship "to usurp the supreme position of Jupiter Optimus Maximus." Domitian is seen to be in direct contrast to Augustus, who subordinated Jupiter to his patron deity Apollo Actiacus.[69]

The coinage of Domitian is replete with images which honor Jupiter as *Conservator*, *Custos*, and *Victor*. Examples from Domitian's reign also portray the *princeps* drawing his power from Jupiter. One such image is the repeated coin reverse type which features Domitian dressed for battle and armed with a spear and a thunderbolt, being crowned by Victory (fig. 1.B).[70] This image combines the theme of Jupiter as *Victor*, and the emperor as Jupiter's representative and mediator between humanity and the supreme god.[71] It is a theme that is found both in the "official" propaganda of the regime and in the "metaphorical language" of some contemporary authors.[72]

---

[67] Fears (*PRINCEPS*, 111–16) points out that Livy (1.6–7, 1.34) and Dionysus of Halicarnassus (2.3–6, 3.47) record that special omens indicated that the early Roman leaders, Romulus and Tarquinius Priscus, were selected by the gods. Fears ("Jupiter," 9–16) marks the beginning of the association of the ruler with Jupiter at the establishment of the Temple of Jupiter Optimus Maximus by Tarquin (Cicero, *Rep.* 2.24.44; Livy 1.38.7, 55.1). He traces the development of the concept through the Republican period and into imperial times.

[68] Fears ("Jupiter," 74–77) notes that under Domitian "this Jovian theology of power fully emerged as a central element in official imperial ideology."

[69] Ibid., 59–65, 78.

[70] Ibid., 79. Fears cites *BMC* 2. p. 372 *; p. 377 †; p. 381, no. 381, pl. 75. 8 (sestertius); p. 386 ‖; p. 389, no. 410, pl. 77. 5 (sestertius); p. 399, no. 443, pl. 79. 6 (sestertius); p. 403, nos. 465–66, pl. 80. 5 (sestertius); and p. 406, no. 476, pl. 80. 11 (sestertius).

[71] Fears "Jupiter," 79–80. Fears also says that the emperor is like Hercules in this mediatory role, and that like Hercules he "will win deification for his labors" (p., 79).

[72] Statius (*Silv.*, 4.3.128–29; 1. praef.; 1.6.39–50; 4.4.58; 1.1.79–81), Silius Italicus (*Pun.* 3.570–629, 625–26), Quintilian (10.1.91), and Martial (4.8.12; 7.99) are mentioned as

Therefore it can be described as an "autocratic political concept" in which "the emperor and his policies are above human criticism because his power is rooted not in human institutions but in his election by the supreme god of the state."[73] In Fears's analysis, however, Domitian is not successful in promoting his "Jovian theology" because he cannot convince some of his subjects—specifically the members of that human institution, the Senate—to accept the concept that his rule is mandated by Jupiter.[74]

Fears credits the "magic of Trajan" with transforming "Jovian theology" from an unacceptable "autocratic principle" associated with Domitian, to an appropriate understanding of the basis for imperial power under Trajan.[75] Fears believes that upon his appointment as co-ruler with Nerva, Trajan began a concerted effort to reestablish the "Jovian theology" which Nero and Domitian had been unable to maintain.[76] As mentioned above, his evidence for this claim is drawn initially from the *Panegyricus* of Pliny, which Fears understands to be the perfect propaganda statement for Trajan.[77] The document vilifies Domitian, and allows Trajan to distance himself from the *damnatio memoriae* of Domitian while actually continuing the latter's program of "Jovian theology." The *Panegyricus* also "praises the constitutional qualities of Trajan's reign, and emphasizes that Jupiter, not the Senate or Nerva, is the source of Trajan's imperial power."[78] Specific references to Jupiter in the document are numerous, including the opening prayer which states that Trajan was selected as emperor because of the intervention of the king of the gods, and an affirmation that Jupiter can concentrate on heavenly matters since he has set up Trajan to preside over human affairs.[79] Pliny

---

represeuatives of the panegyrical literature of the period (Fears, "Jupiter," 80). For a discussion of Fears's distinction between "official propaganda" and the metaphorical language of authors at the time see below (pp. 24–27).

[73] Fears, "Jupiter," 80–81.

[74] Ibid., 81.

[75] Ibid. Fears discusses Nerva's tenure (96–98 CE), the transitional period between Domitian and Trajan, as a time in which the Senate was "ostentatiously portrayed" as the source of the ruler's *imperium*, and Jupiter was "conspicuously absent from the coinage." This is true of coinage of all metals. Coin types commemorating LIBERTAS PVBLICA, FORTVNA POPVLI ROMANI, and SALVS PVBLICA are mentioned, but without citation of specific examples. Nerva's emphasis on the Senate is understandable, since unlike the Flavians, or Trajan, he did not have a military powerbase for his regime, and he was dependent on the Senate's authority.

[76] Fears (ibid., 77) claims that although present under Vespasian and Titus, "it was only with Domitian that this Jovian theology of power fully emerged as a central element in official imperial ideology."

[77] Fears (ibid., 82) incorrectly calls the *Panegyricus* "an official publicity notice of the new regime."

[78] Ibid., 81.

[79] Pan. 1.5, 80.4; Fears, "Jupiter," 81.

presents the idea that Trajan has "made a pact with Jupiter; the god will preserve him as long as he governs the commonwealth well and for the benefit of all."[80]

Fears points to other evidence of Jovian theology in what he describes as "official sources."[81] He cites the revival under Trajan of the sestertius reverse type featuring the emperor holding a thunderbolt (fig. 1.A).[82] The Trajanic version of this coin differs from the similar type found under Domitian in that it includes the legend SPQR OPTIMO PRINCIPI. Fears feels that this legend is Trajan's way of indicating that his position as representative of Jupiter is recognized by the Roman Senate and people.[83]

For Fears, another official statement of "Jovian theology" was the triumphal arch erected at the starting point of the *via Traiana* at Beneventum in southern Italy. The relief program of this arch features a collection of scenes from the reign of Trajan. Fears claims that the arch was dedicated in 114 CE, and that the attic reliefs are especially effective in portraying the emperor as the emissary of Jupiter.[84] The left attic relief on the side of the arch facing toward the city depicts Jupiter and the other members of the Capitoline Triad standing along with Hercules, Liber Pater, Ceres, and Mercury (fig. 15.A). The king of the gods is holding a thunderbolt in his right hand, extending it to his left, in a gesture of passing it on toward the other panel. In that other scene (fig. 15.B), Trajan is dressed in a toga and he stands with lictors facing the figure of the goddess Roma, two Penates (deities of the household and family) and two smaller male figures who are identified as consuls.[85] Fears asserts that the imagery "thus presents a visual official statement of Trajan's divine election and a clear parallel to the verbal proclamation in Pliny's 'Panegyric.' "[86]

---

[80] Fears (ibid., 82) cites *Pan.* 67.

[81] Ibid., 82–85.

[82] *BMC* 3. p. 174, no. 825, pl. 30. 4 (sestertius); p. 190, no. 899, pl. 34. 7 (dupondius). For the Domitian coin see n. 70 above. On both coins see pp. 110–11 below.

[83] Fears, "Jupiter," 82. The difficulties of assigning responsibility for minting coins is discussed below in Chapter Four.

[84] Ibid., 83–85. Fears states: "The arch was an official statement of the program and achievement of the principate of Trajan, and its reliefs form a visual 'Res Gestae Traiani' " (p. 83).

[85] Studies of the Arch by other scholars, and the difficulties with Fears's interpretation of this scene and his general understanding of the message and history of the Arch are discussed below (pp. 114–22).

[86] Fears ("Jupiter," 84) cites *Pan.* 56.3 and 80.4, and maintains that "the actual investiture of Trajan by Jupiter never appeared on the coinage but was reserved for the arch at Beneventum." It seems unlikely that a major religious propaganda policy would be announced in a speech at the beginning of the reign, and then kept hidden in reserve for at least 14 years.

Fears sees a special significance in the cautious way in which Trajan established the Jovian theology as an ideological basis for his rule. The idea is initially presented by the Senator Pliny to an audience of his peers, it eventually appears on bronze coinage, which Fears classifies as "traditionally a senatorial prerogative," with the legend SPQR OPTIMO PRINCIPI, and finally it is spelled out in full on an arch dedicated by the Senate and Roman People.[87] Fears understands this caution to be Trajan's attempt to give his "Jovian theology" a constitutional appearance, the lack of which had meant failure for the programs of Nero and Domitian,[88] and although he cites other evidence, Pliny's *Panegyricus* is presented as a major component of that effort.

Critique of Fears: The Limits of Ideology

The view of the *Panegyricus* which Fears takes is problematic in several ways. Before detailing those problems, however, it is necessary to comment upon some general difficulties with his discussion of "Jupiter and Roman Imperial Ideology" and his use of the term "theology."[89] The material which Fears has assembled in this study is indeed valuable and informative. Given the scope of his task, however, Fears begins with an artificially monolithic picture of imperial ideology. It is not surprising, therefore, that his

[87] Fears, "Jupiter," 84. On the dedicatory inscription for the Arch, see pp. 202–6 below.

[88] Ibid. Fears also argues that Trajan did not exaggerate his association with the king of the gods, and cites as an example an aureus reverse (*BMC* 3. no. 493) from the start of the Parthian war (113 CE). The type shows a small figure of the emperor standing under a thunderbolt held by a Jupiter figure two times larger than the emperor (fig. 8.A). Fears (p. 85) claims that the image complements the idea that the emperor is Jupiter's equal on earth in that it shows that "at critical moments the supreme god materializes on earth to aid his vicegerent." This type appears on coins of all metals, and is discussed below in Chapter Four.

[89] Fears's study continues with a brief look at "Hadrian and the Hellenization of the Jovian Theology of Imperial Power" (ibid., 85–89); a summary discussion of "Jupiter and the Evolving Image of the Principate," which considers how Fears perceives "Roman national ideology," "popular philosophy and literature," and "the religious currents of the imperial age" to have influenced the "'resuscitation' of Jupiter" as the primary divinity supporting the principate (pp. 89–97); an analysis of how evidence from the Latin provinces for public and private *vota pro salute imperatoris* indicates that Jupiter was perceived as "a personal deity who intervened as a saviour not merely in state affairs but also in the private life of his individual worshippers," and further that "the central role of Jupiter in the imperial ideology of the Antonine Age was not a mere political fabrication devoid of any real religious feeling" (pp. 97–107, esp. 100); a review of how the Jovian Theology of imperial power played a role in the social and political crises of the third century (pp. 107–19); an epilogue which emphasizes a continuity between paganism, as he has described it, and Christianity in associating the emperor and the "high god" (pp. 120–22); and a bibliographical survey of research on "The Cult of Jupiter and Roman Imperial Ideology," covering 1918–1978 (pp. 122–38).

attempt to portray a single line of development of a dominant "Jovian theology" is unconvincing in some places.[90]

No one would contest the fact that Jupiter is a pivotal figure in much religious and political thinking throughout the imperial period; given this it is striking that Jupiter appears to be less prominent during the reigns of some emperors. The difficulties arise in trying to prove that any single understanding of the relationship between the emperor and the gods (or specifically Jupiter) was ever defined enough or dominant enough to be labeled as the 'ideological basis' for imperial power. It is not at all clear that the emperors attempted to develop the kind of unified "theological basis" that Fears posits. In most cases, an abundance of deities in a variety of forms promoted in diverse ways can be attested under each emperor. The use of divine imagery by an emperor varied depending on the place it appeared, the audience for which it was intended, and the point during the emperor's reign that it was employed.

Fears cites several sociological discussions of the importance of ideology in governing and the necessity for any leadership group "to provide the appropriate political myth for its society."[91] Further he adopts Talcott Parsons's definition of ideology as "a system of beliefs held in common by the members of a collectivity, a system of ideas that is oriented to the evaluative integration of the community."[92] While these definitions provide categories for understanding the composition and interaction of different societies, they cannot be expected to formulate an all-encompassing picture of a society. This is especially true in the case of an ancient society from which only a small percentage of the total evidence is available, and that portion is composed of extremely diverse and fragmentary kinds of material. As more information becomes available about how the empire was administered, it becomes more difficult to speak of any single monolithic imperial policy.

Millar has demonstrated that although the emperors had rules by which they sought to administer the empire, making exceptions to the rules was a matter of course. Any rigid and dogmatic policy which did not allow for flexibility in its interpretation and implementation would have had disastrous consequences. Millar aptly states this need for flexibility when he describes

---

[90] In spite of its shortcomings, Fears's developmental theory is adopted by other scholars. "Under the influence of Trajan and Hadrian and later emperors, the [capitoline] triad became an essential element of the imperial ideology and propaganda" (Peter Garnsey and Richard Saller, *The Roman Empire: Economy, Society and Culture* [Berkeley: University of California Press, 1981] 167).

[91] Fears, "Jupiter," 7–9.

[92] Ibid., citing Talcott Parsons, *The Social System* (Glencoe, IL: Free Press, 1956) 354–59.

how the whole nature of the imperial entourage, with its remarkably limited resources and increasingly peregrinatory character, was shaped by the pressure to respond to initiatives from below, ranging from requests or consultations by senators, to formal embassies from cities or associations, and to *libelli* from individuals or groups of low status seeking protection, justice or rulings on points of law.[93]

In view of the flexibility that was required of the emperor, the limits of Parsons's "system of beliefs held in common" by members of the Roman empire could never be defined as sharply as Fears attempts to do. Yet by tracing the development of "Jovian theology" as the central ideological element over a vast chronological and geographical spectrum, Fears is promoting the illusion that such a defined system did exist. This criticism is tempered by Fears's publication on other aspects of imperial ideology,[94] nevertheless, the tone of the "Jupiter" article presents his "Jovian theology" with such vigor that it can mask the many different gods which the emperors related to, and the many ways in which that relating took place. The rulers provided or adopted a number of different political myths from all over the empire which they hoped would assist in the integrative process upon which their successful rule depended.[95]

In order to lay a foundation for his monolithic picture of a "Jovian theology" beginning under Nero and developing until the reign of Hadrian, Fears begins by showing the limited role that Jupiter played under the previous emperors.[96] He contends that for the reign of Augustus there is a remarkable lack of evidence for Jupiter in the so-called official propaganda. Fears highlights the "polite way in which the Capitoline cult was pushed into the

---

[93] Millar, *The Emperor and the Roman World* (Ithaca, NY: Cornell University Press, 1977) 617. Millar ("The Imperial Cult and the Persecutions," in Willem den Boer, ed., *Le culte des souverains dans l'Empire romain* [*Entretiens* 19; Geneva: Fondation Hardt, 1973] 155) makes the same point in discussing how the emperor would respond to questions about and challenges to the imperial cult: "Most Emperors would make these responses in the light of some coherent general principles or policies. But it is necessary to the understanding of the function of an Emperor, and indeed of the nature of the Roman empire, that the *application* of any such general principles by an Emperor normally depended on the form, nature and occasion of communications to him by his officials or his subjects."

[94] Fears, "The Theology of Victory at Rome: Approaches and Problems," ANRW (1981) 2/17.2, 736–826; idem, "The Cult of Virtues and Roman Imperial Ideology," ANRW (1981) 2/17.2, 827–948; and idem, "Indices to Contributions by J. Rufus Fears in : ANRW II. 17.1 and 2," ANRW (1981) 2/17.2, 1201–55.

[95] A classic example of introducing and promoting myth is Hadrian's attempt to promote the cult of the deified Antinoos, and to assimilate him to Dionysos.

[96] Fears ("Jupiter," 72) mentions associations of Gaius with Jupiter, and appellations of Claudius as Optimus, but his main concern is with the Augustan period.

background'' because of the preeminence of Apollo and Diana for the first *princeps*.[97] While this importance cannot be denied, Augustus continued to show interest in other divinities as well, including Jupiter. His initiation into the Eleusinian Mysteries was not related either to Apollo or to Diana.[98] Jupiter's role may have been reduced, but he continued to play an important part in the religious reforms enacted by Augustus. The *Res Gestae Divi Augusti* mentions construction of the temple of Apollo on the Palatine as one of the sacred building projects of Augustus in Rome, the list also includes four temples of Jupiter which Augustus built or repaired.[99] This demonstrates one of the dangers in attempting to reconstruct ''Imperial ideology'': the tendency to generalize about the way an emperor did or did not use images of the gods in his propaganda and thereby to omit or minimize important evidence.

The same is true in the case of Fears's comments about Trajan, where his concentration on evidence for the importance of Jupiter omits a vast spectrum of divine imagery which Trajan used, and which may have been more important than Jupiter at certain points during Trajan's reign.[100] As mentioned above, Jean Beaujeu also discusses *''la théologie du pouvoir impérial''* under Trajan, and he too includes *''la théologie jovienne du principat''* as part of Trajan's understanding of his relationship to the gods. It is clear, however, that for Beaujeu, there are other facets of this relationship. Beaujeu stresses Trajan's concern with the cult of Victory and the emperor's association with Hercules as well as with Jupiter.[101] While Fears would not dispute the importance of these other divinities for Trajan, his narrow focus on Jupiter obscures their importance by streamlining the vast and variegated spectrum of divine imagery used by the emperors and others. This attempt to

[97] Ibid.

[98] See Dietmar Kienast, ''Hadrian, Augustus und die eleusinischen Mysterien,'' *Jahrbuch für Numismatik und Geldgeschichte* 10 (1959/1960) 61–69.

[99] *Res Gestae* 4.19–20: the temples of Jupiter Feretrius, Jupiter Tonans, Jupiter Libertas, and the Capitolinum of Jupiter Optimus Maximus. Fears (''Jupiter,'' 59) cites Seutonius's report (*Div. Aug.* 29.3) that Augustus built the Jupiter Tonans (''the Thunderer'') temple in honor of his close call with a lightning bolt in Cantabri. Even if the Seutonian account is true, and if the temple therefore celebrates ''Augustus and his *felicitas*,'' rather than ''Jupiter as supreme god of the *res publica romana*'' (Fears, ''Jupiter,'' 59) this is still evidence of attention paid to Jupiter by Augustus.

[100] See Chapter Four below.

[101] Beaujeu, *La religion*, 59–87. Pliny's *Panegyricus* (14.5) is also cited as evidence of Trajan as the *''empereur 'herculéen'''* (ibid., 86). This passage compares Trajan's obedience to the military commands of Domitian with the willingnes of Hercules (*genitus Iove*: ''offspring of Jupiter'') to carry out the tasks assigned by King Eurystheus. Hercules is also alluded to in *Pan.* 82.7.

create a neat package of "imperial theology" reflects more about a modern fascination with ideology than it does about the different ways in which the gods were portrayed throughout the Roman world.

Diverse use of divine imagery is even more pronounced during the reign of Hadrian, who Fears argues went beyond Trajan and Domitian in integrating the "Jovian theology" into the "official ideology" of the principate.[102] This may be true, but concentrating only on Jupiter/Zeus as a deity important for Hadrian's propaganda fails to do justice to his diverse religious interests. Fears describes two temples that Hadrian built for Zeus in Athens,[103] but he fails to mention that like Augustus, Hadrian was initiated into the mysteries of Eleusis, and that according to Pausanias Hadrian also set up a temple "to all the gods" in Athens,[104] and that he was responsible for a major reconstruction of the Pompeion, the building associated with the Panathenaic procession in honor of Athena, and that Hadrian also sponsored renovations and ornamentation for the Theater of Dionysos.[105] Everywhere he went, Hadrian demonstrated his interest in and support for a wide variety of divinities.

In Rome as well, Hadrian was busy building. Although he did not spend much time in the Capitol, he allocated much money for the construction and renovation of its religious complexes and monuments.[106] Of these, the Pantheon is probably the most famous project,[107] but Hadrian also constructed a temple for his divinized predecessor[108] and built or rebuilt the quarters of many other gods. Among those buildings in Rome, however, that were affected by Hadrian's beneficence, there is a dearth of evidence for works dedicated to Jupiter.[109] This absence raises questions about focussing too narrowly on Jupiter as the most significant deity for Hadrian's propaganda. When talking about the "theological" interests of Hadrian or any

---

[102] Fears, "Jupiter," 85.

[103] The Temple of Zeus Olympios and the temple of Zeus Panhellenios. The latter is actually dedicated to Zeus and Hera Panhellenios (Pausanias 1.18.9).

[104] Pausanias 1.5.5; 1.18.9.

[105] Wolfram Hoepfner, *Das Pompeion und seine Nachfolgerbauten* (Berlin: De Gruyter, 1976); for the Hadrianic stage front (usually refered to as the Bema of Phaidros reliefs) in the theater, see Mary C. Sturgeon, "The Reliefs in the Theater of Dionysos in Athens," *A JA* 81 (1977) 31 – 53.

[106] Mary Taliaferro Boatwright, *Hadrian and the City of Rome* (Princeton: Princeton University Press, 1987) catalogue pp. 263–72.

[107] Pantheon was dedicated as a rebuilding of a structure first erected by Marcus Agrippa, a close associate of Augustus. On the Pantheon, see William L. MacDonald, *The Pantheon: Design, Meaning, and Progeny* (Cambridge: Harvard University Press, 1976).

[108] Gellius, *Noctes* 11.17.1; *Scriptores Historiae Augustae, Hadrian* 19.9. Cf. Paul Zanker, "Das Traiansforum in Rom," *Archäologischer Anzeiger* (1970) 537 – 44.

[109] Cf. Boatwright, *Hadrian*, catalogue pp. 263 – 72.

emperor, it seems unwise to depend on evidence of only one divinity or one geographical area.

A related difficulty arises in applying a particular ideology such as "Jovian theology" to a succession of Roman emperors. While there may be similarities in the way that the divinity's image is used, those similarities do not necessarily prove that different rulers were using divine symbolism in similar ways. Fears claims that Hadrian's use of Jupiter/Zeus imagery "marks the culmination of a conscious policy, initiated under Nero and conscientiously developed by Domitian and Trajan ... which centered upon the image of the emperor as the divinely elected vicegerent of Jupiter-Zeus."[110] While it cannot be denied that Hadrian used images of Jupiter/Zeus as an important part of his propaganda, this does not mean that he used those images in the same way that Domitian and Trajan had.

For example, Jupiter imagery did play an important role in Hadrian's coinage. An aureus reverse type depicts the king of the gods handing Hadrian the globe as a sign of divine investiture.[111] This scene reflects the king of the gods taking a central role in Hadrian's justification of his rule. Fears himself points out, however, that this image is not part of the extant numismatic evidence for the reigns of Domitian and Trajan.[112] Hadrian's portrayal of this investiture by Jupiter, or his portrayal of other Jovian involvement in his reign was not necessarily the same as Trajan's. Since Hadrian ended the campaigns of conquest undertaken by Trajan in the east and elsewhere, he did not need to represent his ordination by Jupiter as a military charge. In this regard the absence under Hadrian of the coin type showing the emperor dressed for battle, holding a thunderbolt is striking. As mentioned above, this image was used by both Domitian and Trajan to portray the emperor as what Fears calls "the warrior vicegerent."[113] The divergence of Jupiter images used by different emperors is also apparent in Hadrian's use of Zeus imagery in Athens. Fears cites the Athenian evidence for Hadrian's promotion of Zeus worship as reflective of his further integration of the "Jovian theology" of Domitian and Trajan.[114] The Zeus cults that Hadrian supports in Athens, however, were not identical with the Roman cult

[110] Fears, "Jupiter," 89.

[111] *BMC* 3. p. 269, no. 242 pl. 51. 8; cited by Fears, "Jupiter," 86. Given the controversy over Trajan's selection of Hadrian as successor (*SHA* 4.9–10), it is not surprising to see this affirmation of divine support for Hadrian's accession.

[112] Fears, "Jupiter," 86. A scene with the personified Senate handing a globe to the emperor is attested under Nerva and Trajan (see p. 90 below).

[113] Fears, "Jupiter," 79, 82. For the Domitian coins see n. 70 above, and for those from Trajan's reign see n. 82 above.

[114] Ibid., 87–89.

of Jupiter Optimus Maximus in either form or function. Hadrian was responsible for the completion of the temple to Zeus Olympios and for the new construction of the sanctuary for Zeus Panhellenios. Fears himself describes these temples in Athens as symbolic of the unity of all Greek people under the one god Zeus, and by association, under the one *autokrator* Hadrian.[115] This is different, however, from Trajan's focus on Jupiter as divine protector and sponsor of military victories. Zeus Olympios and Zeus Panhellenios are symbolic sources of power for Hadrian, not as conqueror, but as unifier and consolidator of the empire. The difference is obvious in one point of detail. Domitian and Trajan stressed the original Homeric picture of Zeus/Jupiter bearing the thunderbolt,[116] but Hadrian's Zeus Olympios in Athens is a copy of the statue of Zeus made by Phidias for the temple of Zeus at Olympia (ca. 430 BCE), a statue without a thunderbolt.[117] Hadrian's use of Zeus as a symbol for his reign is a promising topic for study,[118] but such study should give sufficient consideration to Hadrianic activity in its own right, not as the culmination of his predecessor's policy.

Given the difficulties associated with formulating a sweeping conception of "imperial ideology," it seems wise to narrow the study and ask instead what imagery of the gods was used by individual emperors in promoting their ideas, their actions, and themselves. This approach concentrates on how the emperors presented themselves as related to various divinities. It also accounts for diversities in the way that different emperors interpreted the significance of a given divinity. Most of all, it does not require the piecing together of evidence into an overarching ideology or theology which invariably will reveal only a limited and in some cases contrived picture of how an emperor used divine imagery.

Critique of Fears: the Term "Theology"

In the ancient Greek world, "theology" could refer to discussion of the gods and the cosmos which was regarded as an intellectual activity.[119] Today,

[115] Ibid., 88.

[116] Ibid., 94.

[117] J. G. Frazer (*Pausanias's Description of Greece* [London: MacMillan, 1913] 182) reports that Athenian coins from the Roman period show an enthroned Zeus holding out a Victory in his right hand and a scepter in his left, and suggests that this image represents the statue from the Olympieion in Athens. Further study of both Athenian and imperial coinage is needed to prove this suggestion.

[118] Cf. Anna S. Benjamin, "The Altars of Hadrian in Athens and Hadrian's Panhellenic Program," *Hesperia* 32 (1963) 57–86; A. J. Spawforth and S. Walker, "The World of the Panhellenion. I. Athens and Eleusis," *JRS* 75 (1985) 78–104.

[119] Aristotle, *Metaph.*, 983^{b}29.

theology can be understood in the sense of intellectual or academic study of the gods and the cosmos, or it can refer to what an individual believes about the gods and the cosmos. As such, when looking at the ancient world, it is appropriate to use the term "theology" in the first sense when reading a learned study of the gods such as Cicero's *De Natura Deorum*, or in the second sense when when discussing the letters of Paul or the *Meditationes* of Marcus Aurelius. Given the different nature of the evidence, however, it is not consistent to talk about the "theology" of Trajan.

The available evidence for most of the emperors does not consist of discourses on the gods, or personal statements of faith. Rather it consists of fragments of the immense structure of divine imagery with which the emperor chose to illustrate and promote his reign to the people of the empire. No doubt each emperor had a personal understanding of the gods which influenced his reign and his propaganda, but given the vast spectrum of images that were used in the promotion of the reign, it is impossible to be certain of the "theological" meaning of each. The imagery also had "theological" meaning for the people who experienced it,[120] but again most of that meaning is inaccessible for modern students of antiquity. Price has argued that because scholarship has focused exclusively on individuals and their mental states—their theologies—which are generally inaccessible, the ritual and images of the gods in the Graeco-Roman world have been interpreted as devoid of true religious meaning.[121] Price maintains that ritual should be treated as a "public cognitive system" that can have genuine religious meaning without manifesting the kind of personal dimension for which scholars have traditionally looked.[122]

The use, by Fears, of the phrase "imperial theology" leads to confusion about the evidence that is available. It is a term that is too closely associated with the consideration of "interiorized beliefs" and "individual emotion" to be helpful in analyzing how the emperor portrays himself as related to the gods. It also seems to violate an important principle in study of the Graeco-Roman world which Fears himself mentions. He admits that the category of "religious" policy or activity is very difficult to isolate in the ancient world. Unlike the sharp distinctions (at least theoretically) made between church and state in modern society, people in the Graeco-Roman world did not draw such a clear line between religious and secular matters.

---

[120] The diversity of evidence in different regions indicates that images were chosen because of their local popularity, not because of an overarching ideology emanating from Rome.

[121] Price, *Rituals and Power*, 9–11.

[122] Price (ibid., 10) labels this fixation on interiorized beliefs and individual emotions as "Christianizing."

The modern dichotomy between sacred and secular is of questionable validity in approaching the theme of ideology in the ancient world. For the ancient, religion permeated every aspect of the state's life, providing the very basis of the socio-political order. Of necessity political ideology was formulated in theological terms and expressed through cult and ritual. Religious imagery defined the ancient's conception of his socio-political structures and the cult life of the state mirrored each transformation in those structures.[123]

In apparent contradiction to his own observation, Fears attempts to distinguish separate political and religious dimensions of his theory.[124] The confusion and difficulties which accompany the term "theology" in this context seem to make it a less-than-productive concept. For that reason, I avoid generalization about the "theology" of Trajan or the ideology of his reign. Instead, I focus on evidence for how the relationship between the emperor and the gods is portrayed in various and sometimes divergent sources during Trajan's reign.

Critique of Fears: Use of the Panegyricus

Fears uses a narrow range of evidence in discussing his picture of the development of "Jovian theology." Initially, he considers only evidence involving Jupiter that can be dated securely to a given emperor's reign. Then he attempts to classify the evidence as either relevant or not relevant to the "official ideology" of the emperor. Some evidence is regarded as officially related to the *princeps*, while others are tangentially related, or not related at all. As a standard for making this determination, Fears adapts A. D. Nock's advice that

we must distinguish sharply between (a) the normal working theory of the principate, and the implication of what the princeps officially says or does, and (b) the metaphorical language used by men of letters, or the corresponding expressions in art.[125]

In order for Nock's distinction to work, some definition of "official actions of the *princeps*" must be established. Fears provides such a definition by completing the phrase, ". . . what the princeps officially says or does," with

[123] Fears, "Jupiter," 8.

[124] Fears (*PRINCEPS*, xi) claims that in his book he deals with the "political implications" of his theory of divine election, while his article ("Jupiter") is concerned with "religious aspects" of the theory.

[125] Nock, "*A Diis Electa*: A Chapter in the Religious History of the Third Century," in Zeph Stewart, ed., *Arthur Darby Nock: Essays on Religion and the Ancient World* (Oxford: Clarendon, 1972) 262 (first published in *HTR* 23 (1930) 263–64); cited by Fears, "Jupiter," 58.

the words: "... as evidenced in such sources as the imperial coinage or imperial inscriptions and official monuments." This "official" material is distinguished from "the metaphorical language used by men of letters, or the corresponding expressions in art."[126]

Fears applies these standards for classifying the evidence rigorously. His reviewers praise his adherence to the second part of Nock's principle.[127] The clearest application of this principle occurs in Fears's discussion of Augustan "ideology." After identifying the "official" elements of Augustus's "theology" which, after the first few years of the reign, centered around Apollo, Diana, and Mars Ultor to the exclusion of Jupiter, Fears cites the evidence of authors from the Augustan period who utilized Jupiter imagery in relation to the princeps.[128] In order to resolve this seeming contradiction, Fears relegates the literary evidence to a secondary "unofficial" position, suggesting that Horace's concern for Jupiter (*Od.* 3.1.5–8) is in fact the poet's warning to Augustus that the king of the gods should not be ignored.[129]

Fears consistently separates the "official" and "unofficial" sources of evidence except in the case of Pliny's *Panegyricus*.[130] Here Fears chooses to read a work of literature, rich in "metaphorical language," steeped in the same "Hellenistic encomiastic tradition" that served as evidence of the "unofficial" nature of Augustan poetry, as an "official publicity notice" of Trajan's regime.[131] Fears claims that the *Panegyricus* differs from "panegyrical passages in such authors as Vitruvius, Horace, Vergil, Statius, Silius Italicus."[132] While the latter group is to be classified as the "metaphorical and non-official language of the *literati*," Pliny's speech of thanks is an exception because it is "a public oration spoken before the emperor and court by Pliny in his official capacity as consul." According to Fears, "like the coinage, public panegyrical orations of this form can be regarded as publicity notices of a reign."[133] In support of this point, Fears cites several studies of

[126] The extent to which numismatic, epigraphical, and architectural evidence can be regarded as reflecting "official policy" is taken up in Chapter Four below.

[127] See P. A. Brunt, "Divine Elements in the Imperial Office," *JRS* 69 (1979) 171–72; Millar, "Review of J. Rufus Fears, *Princeps a diis electus*" *Gnomen* 51 (1979) 406–7; and S. R. F. Price, "The Divine Right of Emperors," *Classical Review* 29 (1979) 277.

[128] Fears, "Jupiter," 66–68. He (p. 66) states that "Ovid and Manilius celebrated Augustus as the earthly counterpart of Jupiter"; and (p. 67) that "in Horace there is a subtle emphasis on the subordination of Augustus to Jupiter, supreme ruler of gods and men (*Od.* 3.1.5–8)."

[129] Ibid., 68–69. A complete review of the political connections of the Augustan poets is beyond the scope of this study. For perceptive comments and additional bibliography see E. J. Kenney, "Uncertainties," in idem, ed., *Latin Literature*, 297–300.

[130] Brunt, "Divine Elements," 173.

[131] Fears, "Jupiter," 82.

[132] Fears, *PRINCEPS*, 151.

[133] Ibid.

panegyrical literature,[134] and he emphasizes the traditional assumption of a close relationship between Pliny and Trajan as an indication that Pliny would have been "well aware of Trajan's official program."[135] Fears does allow for some nuance in his understanding of how the speech reflected the emperor's policy. He carefully points out that

> this is not to suggest that the panegyrist was given an official outline from which to draw upon in his speech. His composition was free, but he was aware of the policies and the image of himself which the emperor wished to project.[136]

At one point, Fears is willing to admit that other motivations—such as concern for the status of the Senate—may have influenced Pliny as he wrote. Fears cites G. Downey who suggests that "Panegyrics had a real significance as popular statements of what was expected of the emperor and what the limitations as well as the possibilities of the office were conceived to be."[137] Fears states that this view is not mutually exclusive with his own,[138] but in further discussion, his view of the *Panegyricus* as a policy statement from Trajan is predominant.[139]

There is a circularity to the reasoning which Fears employs to "prove" his thesis. First, he makes the assumption that, unlike other panegyrical

---

[134] See Martin Schanz and Carl Hosius, *Geschichte der römischen Literatur bis zum Gesetzgebungswerk des Kaisers Justinian, III. Die Zeit von Hadrian 117 bis auf Constantin 324* (Handbuch der Altertumswissenschaft 8.3; Munich: Beck, 1922) 150–52; J. A. Straub, *Von Herrscherideal in der Spätantike* (Forsch. zur Kirchen- und Geistesgesch. 18; Stuttgart: Kohlhammer, 1939) 146–59; Dietmar Kienast, "Nerva und das Kaisertum Trajans," *Historia* 17 (1968) 55–56; D. Romano, "Per una nuova interpretazione del panegirico latino in onore dell' imperatore," *Annali del Liceo classico G Garibaldi di Palermo* 2 (1965) 327–38; and S. Dabrowski, "O panegiryku," *Przeglad Humanistyczny* 9 (1965) 101–10.

[135] Fears, *PRINCEPS*, 151–52. Trajan did offer the consulate to Pliny (*consulatum obtulisti* [*Pan.* 91.1]) and approximately ten years later appointed him as legate to the provinces of Pontus and Bithynia (*CIL.* 5. 5262). Trajan also appointed Pliny to the Augurate (*Ep.* 4.8) in response to Pliny's request that he do so (*Ep.* 10.13), and asked Pliny to serve on an advisory board investigating the gymnastic games at Vienne in Gallia Narbonensis (*Ep.* 4.22). Trajan's willingness to make use of a given senator's talents is not conclusive proof that Pliny was "closely associated" with the emperor. It certainly does not prove that Trajan confided in Pliny regarding his "official program," if such a concept ever existed. Millar (*Emperor and the Roman World*, 114) suggests that "Pliny was certainly an *amicus* of the emperor, but equally certainly not an intimate friend in our sense."

[136] Fears, *PRINCEPS*, 151–52.

[137] Downey, "Justinian and the Imperial Office," *Lectures in Memory of Louisa Taft Semple* (Cincinnati: University of Cincinnati, 1968) 9; cited by Fears, *PRINCEPS*, 152.

[138] Ibid.

[139] This is especially true in Fears's article ("Jupiter"), where Downey's argument is cited without any indication that he disagrees with Fears's interpretation on this point (p. 82).

material, Pliny's speech of thanks should be classified as imperial propaganda. Then he finds evidence in the *Panegyricus* to support his thesis that
Trajan is promoting his rule as mandated by the gods. Finally, he insists that
the emphasis on the divine institution of Trajan's reign in the *Panegyricus* is
the "clearest evidence" that it is to be read as "an instrument of imperial not
senatorial propaganda."[140] I believe that Fears is not able to prove this point,
and that in fact, if the document is read without an eye to particular theories
of "imperial theology," the senatorial concerns of Pliny are predominant.
By putting too much emphasis on the supposed value of *Panegyricus* for
understanding imperial propaganda, Fears obscures other valuable data it
contains, specifically Pliny's portrayal of the relationship between the
emperor and the gods. The same criticism can be directed against the use of
the *Panegyricus* by Yanir Shochat.

Shochat and "The Change in Roman Religion"

Yanir Shochat begins from the same premise as Beaujeu and Fears, that the
Panegyricus represents a statement of "religious policy" made by Trajan's
regime,[141] and carries that premise to its extreme position by suggesting that
Pliny's *gratiarum actio* provides evidence of an "essential change that took
place in the Roman religion during the time of Trajan."[142] Shochat claims
that under Trajan, the traditional Roman religion based on sacrifice and other
rituals became "a religion whose fundamental principle was moral conduct."[143] Shochat points to evidence from *Panegyricus* 3 which suggests that
"what is important to the gods is the moral conduct of men rather than observance of ritual":

> I have noted that the gods themselves delight in the innocence and purity of
> their worshippers rather than in the elaborate preparation of the prayers they
> offer, and prefer the man who brings a chaste and sinless heart to their shrines
> to one who comes with a practiced incantation.[144]

Shochat draws a parallel between this sentiment and the writings of the

---

[140] Fears, *PRINCEPS*, 153.

[141] Shochat ("Change in Roman Religion," 324) states: "It is almost certain that the religious
attitude expressed by Pliny in the *Panegyricus* reflected the opinions of the Roman aristocracy
and the Emperor at its head. . . ." He points out that while Beaujeu's idea of a Jupiterian theory
of government is based in part on the *Panegyricus*, he misses the evidence for the "change in the
Roman Religion" that Shochat finds there (p. 317). Shochat does not mention the work of Fears.

[142] Ibid., 317.

[143] Ibid., 319.

[144] *Pan.* 3.5; cited by Shochat, "Change in Roman Religion," 325.

Jewish prophets.[145] He suggests that the similarity could be the result of Jewish influence on the Romans during the first century of this era.[146]

Shochat misses the point of this quotation from the *Panegyricus*, however, by ignoring its context. Pliny is attempting to show his humility in the face of the great task of praising the Emperor. He introduces the above comment by saying: "And I do not even fear that I seem either grateful or ungrateful, depending on if I say enough or too little" (*Pan.* 3.5). Pliny's concern is over how one delivers the speech and how long it is. Contrary to Shochat's interpretation, Pliny does not suggest in any way that the speech should not be delivered.

In order to support his point, Pliny introduces the hyperbolic example of the gods' desire for a proper attitude on the part of worshippers. The gods prefer the person who comes to worship in innocence and purity over the one who comes with a carefully thought-out prayer. In either case the gods want people to worship. This passage does not suggest (as Shochat assumes) that the gods want people to give up worshipping in favor of living more moral lives. Pliny is trying to emphasize that he is unpretentious about praising the emperor, just as people should be unpretentious about worshiping the gods. The second example makes the same point. The gods prefer the person who comes to the *delubrum* ("temple") with a chaste and sinless heart, over the one who comes with a practiced incantation, but in either case the gods expect the person to come to the temple. Pliny is using proper cultic behavior as an analogy for his modesty in presenting his speech, rather than making a general statement that morality has superceded the importance of the cult.

Shochat attempts to be even more specific in saying that the gods' protection of the empire is based on the moral conduct of the emperor. He claims that in *Panegyricus* 67 Pliny refers to a specific statement of Trajan that

[145] Esp. Hosea 6:6: "I desire steadfast love and not sacrifice, the knowledge of God rather than burnt offerings."

[146] Shochat, "Change in Roman Religion," 325. There is no way to test Shochat's suggestion that "it is not impossible that he [Pliny] was acquainted with Josephus Flavius, who at that time lived in Rome, and whose religious orientation was obviously a historio-moral [one]" (ibid., n. 25), except to say that other than Shochat's questionable reading of this passage, Pliny gives no evidence of any contact with or knowledge of Judaism. Mention of Josephus serves as a reminder that Jews and Romans did communicate in Rome during the late-first century CE. Shochat also points to "a deep bond of love that binds man, the Emperor and the gods to one another," as an important concept for Pliny (*Pan.* 72.3–4; 74.4; 85.7) and calls this a Judeo-Christian theme. He mentions in passing the much more likely hypothesis that the influence of Stoicism and Seneca "may have been at work as well" (Shochat, "Change in Roman Religion," 326–27). Durry (*Panégyrique*, 29, 35–39) cites Seneca as an important source of Pliny's ideas.

indicates that the emperor expects the gods to judge his reign on the basis of his conduct, and that he has authorized the people to hold him to this arrangement.

> At your instigation, Caesar, the State has struck a bargain with the gods that they shall preserve your health and safety as long as you will have done the same for everyone else.[147]

Shochat sees this agreement as a significant change in Roman religion under Trajan.[148] This seems to put too much weight upon the text of Pliny, again based on the assumption that the *Panegyricus* is a policy statement of Trajan. This passage also can be understood as a literary device employed by Pliny to remind Trajan of his responsibility to be a virtuous ruler.[149]

In Shochat's argument the difficulties with this "official" reading of the *Panegyricus* are even more severe than with Fears. Since Shochat cannot produce any other evidence to support the religious changes which he sees announced in the *gratiarum actio* of Pliny, he is forced to offer the explanation that

> in its religious content the Roman religion underwent conspicuous transformation, although outwardly nothing had altered: the Romans continued to worship the same gods as before and in the same temples, the same ceremonies were observed and the same priests officiated over them.[150]

Unfortunately, the *Panegyricus* is the only place where this transformation of content is conspicuous.[151] It seems highly unlikely that Pliny is the only surviving evidence of such a major shift in policy.

---

[147] *Pan.* 67.5. There is no evidence of what Trajan did or said to instigate this attitude, but whatever it was, it seems highly unlikely that he intended it to be taken as a call for radical reform of the religious system. In fact it may be an adaptation of the very traditional *do ut des* statement for Roman leaders.

[148] Shochat, "Change in Roman Religion," 329–30.

[149] Pliny could have built on a model provided by Cicero who discusses in *Somnium Scipionis* 12 the important part that the character, ability, and wisdom of Scipio Africanus plays in his decision to choose the right path and restore the order of the commonwealth.

[150] Shochat, "Change in Roman Religion," 319.

[151] Shochat (ibid., 325) argues that "the religious ideas referred to by Pliny in the *Panegyricus* are consistent with both the contract between the State and the gods, and the words of the Emperor included in the oration." In other words, Pliny agrees with himself, since both "the contract with the State and the gods" and the relevant "words of the Emperor" are attested only in Pliny's writing, and could be the result of his own literary embellishment.

Conclusion

Therefore, Shochat serves as an extreme example of misusing the evidence from Pliny's speech in order to attribute a theological position to Trajan. Beaujeu had started this movement with *la théologie jovienne du principat*. Fears followed by making the *Panegyricus* the lynchpin of his argument for the reign of Trajan as the pinnacle of "Jovian theology." Finally, Shochat bases his reconstruction of a "major change in the Roman Religion" on a document that at best must be understood to represent mixed influences. Even if Pliny was writing with some knowledge of Trajan's religious ideas, his own attitudes and presuppositions cannot be ignored. In fact, once the evidence for Pliny's individual motives has been examined, one must conclude that the effusive praise of Trajan and the seemingly endless attention given to his policies in the *Panegyricus* are to be understood as rhetorical devices framing Pliny's presentation of his own perspective on the direction of Trajan's reign: the perspective of a senator who was highly dubious of the office of *princeps* which Trajan had come to hold.[152]

---

[152] Sir Ronald Syme responds to Marcel Durry ("Les Empereurs comme historiens d'Auguste à Hadrien," in *Entretiens sur l'antiquité classique* vol. 4 [Geneva: Fondation Hardt, 1956] 238) who has come to believe that the *Panegyricus* was representative of "*la propagande impériale*, rather than "*un écrit sénatorial*": "As a senatorial writing, clearly it is the speech of a good senator, and part of what the senator knows is what is pleasing for the government. I do not believe that we deviate to think of a very indirect influence from Trajan. Pliny knows what is necessary to say."

2

The Senatorial Perspective
in the *Panegyricus*

Introduction

P. A. Brunt has suggested that Fears is wrong to read the *Panegyricus* as a policy statement of Trajan instead of "a statement of the senatorial ideal which the good Princeps should fulfil."[1] While delivering a *gratiarum actio* was an opportunity to gain the attention of the ruler, and while the speaker would, if at all possible, present his ideas in a form the emperor wanted to hear,[2] the ideas came from the author and not the emperor.[3] In fact, it would seem that the presentation of a panegyric would be the ideal occasion for the author to bring concerns and ideas before the emperor. In the case of Pliny, he is delivering his speech at the outset of Trajan's reign. Trajan had only

---

[1] Brunt, "Divine Elements," 172. Cf. Albino Garzetti, *From Tiberius to the Antonines: A History of the Roman Empire AD 14–192* (London: Methuen, 1974). Garzetti describes the *Panegyricus* as "the senatorial manifesto of the theory of the good princeps" (p. 310).

[2] Fears, *PRINCEPS*, 151.

[3] Fears's contention that the author was concerned only with what the *princeps* wanted to hear portrays the author as an automaton who is incapable of independent thinking. As will be seen, this view is contrary to the long history of tension between the senators and the *principate* and the abundant evidence for independent senatorial concerns seen in the document itself. "To do him [Pliny] justice we should surely recognize that for all its prolixity and lapses into absurdity the expanded speech was his own creation, and the idea behind it was his only sustained piece of political thinking" (Radice, *Pliny*, xxv).

been present in Rome for a year; he had only begun to shape his policies and ideas. While Pliny affirms much of what he has seen of Trajan's style and attitude as *princeps*, he does not hesitate to bring up issues of concern, and to express his expectations for the continuation of Trajan's positive beginning.

In one letter, Pliny explains his reasons for publishing a "fuller and more elaborate" (*spatiosius et uberius*) written version of the speech.

> I hoped in the first place to encourage our Emperor in his virtues by a sincere tribute, and, secondly, to show his successors what path to follow to win the same renown, not by offering instruction but by setting his example before them.[4]

Of course, the public statement of the Emperor's virtues would have served not only to flatter Trajan, but also to make him aware of Pliny's high expectations for his reign.[5] Citing the emperor as an example for future rulers was a powerful form of praise, but it also stated formally the Senate's wishes for the current ruler.[6] Pliny makes these wishes obvious in the *Panegyricus* every time he praises one of Trajan's actions, and then urges him "to continue in this course."[7] Since the *Panegyricus* is read and published near the beginning of Trajan's reign, it should be understood as in part a show of loyalty, in part an attempt to flatter, and in part an expression of Pliny's hopes that the emperor will continue to demonstrate virtue throughout his reign.[8]

---

[4] *Ep.* 3.18.2 (trans., Radice).

[5] Lester K. Born ("The Perfect Prince according to the Latin Panegyrists," *AJP* 55 [1934] 20–35) has argued for this double purpose of the panegyrical literature. He cites the words of Erasmus defending his own panegyric of Philip of Burgundy in 1504: "No other way of correcting a prince is so efficacious as presenting, in the guise of flattery, the pattern of a really good prince. Thus do you instil virtues and remove faults in such a manner that you seem to urge the prince to the former and restrain him from the latter" (Allen, ed., *Opus Epistularum Erasmi* [Oxford: Oxford University Press, 1906] *Ep.* 179.42–45; cited by Born, "Perfect Prince," 35). Although Pliny emphasizes the good qualities of the present emperor, it seems reasonable that he may have had a similar double purpose in mind.

[6] Radice, *Pliny*, xxiv. There is a difference between this more subtle approach and the blatant flattery of a court poet like Martial, who rejoiced upon Domitian's death that the Flatteries (*Blanditiae*) would no longer be welcome in Rome because "this one [Trajan] is not a lord, but a commander, and the senator most just of all" (*Epig.* 10.72). In regard to the *Panegyricus*, Garzetti (*Tiberius to the Antonines*, 310) contends (re. *Pan.* 44) that "a completely shameless flatterer would have avoided touching, in the presence of the reigning emperor, on the theme of the succession."

[7] E.g., Tene, Caesar, hunc cursum (*Pan.* 43.4, regarding more liberal inheritance laws); Perge modo, Caesar (*Pan.* 45.6, regarding a virtuous life that serves as a model for people); Persta, Caesar, in ista ratione propositi (*Pan.* 62.9, regarding the Senate's involvement in governmental appointments); see also *Pan.* 60.7, 67.2, 72.3, 73.5, 75.6, 85.7.

[8] While previous emperors received accolades at the beginning of their rule, they would not necessarily have received the same approval at the end; cf. Kennedy, *Art of Rhetoric*, 544–46.

The Senatorial Perspective on the Principate

The conception of the senatorial ideal in Pliny's writing must be understood in terms of a longstanding tension between the Senate and the *princeps*. Although Pliny was no doubt grateful for the order which Trajan's reign had restored to Roman society, as a senator he had continuing misgivings about the Principate as a form of government valid and suitable for the Roman state.[9] Similar mixed feelings had been part of the Senate's reaction to the establishment of the Principate under Augustus, who brought an end both to the horrors of the civil wars and to the preeminent stature of the the Republican Senate.[10] While friction between the *princeps* and the Senate would continue, the Senate had come to tolerate the emperor's leadership because the only alternative seemed to be anarchy. Depending on the strength, will, and agenda of a given emperor, his relations with the Senate could be cordial or antagonistic.

In the *Panegyricus*, Pliny portrays the reign of Domitian as a time of the worst possible relationship between the *princeps* and the Senate. Recent scholarship has questioned this influential picture, and has come to believe that although Domitian's relationship with the Senate deteriorated near the end of his reign, the picture of this time of terror is certainly exaggerated by Pliny and Tacitus.[11] Pliny cites many of the evil acts of Domitian as foils for

---

E.g., Nero received the *damnatio memoriae* after his death, but his accession was greeted with excitement: "The Caesar who had to pay his debt to his ancestors, god manifest, has joined them, and the expectation and hope of the world has been declared emperor, the good genius of the world and source of all good things, Nero, has been declared Caesar. Therefore ought we all wearing garlands and with sacrifices of oxen to give thanks to all the gods. The first year of the emperor Nero Claudius Caesar Augustus Germanicus, the twenty-first of the month Neos Sebastos" (*P.Oxy.* 1021).

[9] "Let us then appreciate our good fortune and prove our worth by our use of it, and at the same time let us remember how unworthy it would be if we should show greater deference to rulers who delight in the service of their subjects than to those who value their liberty" (*Pan.* 2.5). As Pliny praises the actions of Trajan, he measures them against an ultimate good of *Libertas* (87.1), and a vision of the continuing glory of the Republic (57.5).

[10] Syme ("The Apologia for the Principate," in idem, *The Augustan Aristocracy* [Oxford: Clarendon, 1986] 438–54) discusses how the propaganda of the Augustan authors attempted to defend the move toward a monarchical system of government, opposed to the principles of the Republic.

[11] See Syme, "The Imperial Finances under Domitian, Nerva, and Trajan," *JRS* 20 (1930) 55–70; a response to Syme's article by C. H. V. Sutherland, "The State of the Imperial Treasury at the Death of Domitian," *JRS* 25 (1935) 150–62; Kenneth Scott, *The Imperial Cult under the Flavians* (1936; reprinted New York: Arno, 1975) 88–89; K. H. Waters, "The Character of Domitian," *Phoenix* 18 (1964) 49–77; and Brian W. Jones, *Domitian and the Senatorial Order* (Philadelphia: American Philosophical Society, 1979).

the good deeds of Trajan. Almost every act of Trajan, from his march to Rome (*Pan.* 20) to his building policies (51), to his attitude toward divine honors (52), to his military accomplishments (11, 14), is held up to the negative example of Domitian.

Negative comparison does not stop with Domitian, however. Except for Nerva, Pliny has few positive comments for any previous emperor. He tells Trajan, "previous emperors, except for your father [Nerva] and one or two more (and I have exaggerated) rejoiced more in the vices of their subjects than in their virtues" (*Pan.* 45.1). He also claims that "the first work of loyal citizens with respect to the best emperor is the duty to reproach those who are unlike him" (*Pan.* 53.2). In Pliny's opinion, nothing should be said about Trajan which could have been said about the emperors before him.[12] While the other *principes* were designated by normal omens and signs, Trajan received an extraordinary confirmation (*Pan.* 5.3). In his most stinging condemnation of Trajan's predecessors, Pliny states that though "we went through the motions" of showing affection to them, they knew they were not genuinely liked.[13]

Of course, it could be that by "evil predecessors" Pliny is referring only to the recent "bad emperors" like Nero and Domitian. It is striking, however, that except for Nerva, only Titus is cited as a positive example (*Pan.* 35.4), and Trajan is even more worthy of praise than is Titus.[14] The first *princeps*, Augustus, does not appear in the *Panegyricus* as a role model.[15] The only other Roman leader who serves as a positive example for Trajan is Pompey, who "pushed bribery from [elections] on the Campus Martius, drove pirates from the seas, and strode in triumph across East and West" (*Pan.* 29.1).[16] In spite of this impressive litany of Pompey's achievements, Trajan

---

[12] *Pan.* 2.1; cf. *Ep.* 3.13,2.

[13] *Pan.* 74.3, 5.

[14] In fact he is more worthy of being deified. Interestingly, an inscription (*CIL* 5.5667) from Fecchio records that Pliny served as the priest of the deified Titus. Radice (*Pliny*, 553) speculates that this office must have been held in Pliny's home town, Comum.

[15] In *Pan.* 88.10, reference is made to the way in which the title *Augustus* will forever bring to mind the first *princeps*, so the appellation *Optimus* will always be associated with Trajan. Augustus is mentioned here only as one who has long been identified by a title. There is no comment on his legacy, just the report that he has one. The deification of Augustus by Tiberius is mentioned in *Pan.* 11.1. Once again the purpose is not to laud Augustus; rather, it is to contrast the ulterior motives of Tiberius with Trajan's genuine act of sponsoring the deification of Nerva. In *Ep.* 5.3.5, Pliny cites Caesar and Augustus as examples in support of his enjoyment of light verse and other nonscholarly works.

[16] Pompey's title *"Magnus"* is also mentioned in a discussion of the proper appellation for Trajan (*Pan.* 88.5). It is rejected as being "more to be envied than beautiful." It is striking that the example of Julius Caesar is not mentioned.

is to be praised more for building roads and harbors, and thereby guaranteeing the food supply of the city (*Pan.* 29.2). In *Panegyricus* 88, Pliny reports that Trajan is known as *Optimus* because he is so clearly superior to the emperors who have gone before him.

Pliny's lack of regard for Trajan's predecessors should be understood as reflecting the longstanding friction between the senators and the *princeps*. To whatever degree Pliny was supportive of Trajan's regime, he was not about to endorse the Principate wholeheartedly. His words of praise for Trajan are often put in terms of reestablishing the power and prestige enjoyed by the Senate under the Republic.[17] Trajan appeared to be intent on restoring the proper order of society, and establishing congenial relations with the Senate. Tacitus reports that from his viewpoint as a writer of history, the situation had improved. He contrasts the days after Actium, "when the interests of peace required that all power should be concentrated in the hands of one man, writers of like ability disappeared; and at the same time truth was impaired in many ways,"[18] with the situation under Trajan, when "we may feel what we wish and may say what we feel."[19]

These positive words of Tacitus, and the strong sense of approval in the *Panegyricus*, should not be taken to mean that the senators were convinced that Trajan was the answer to their problems. Although Pliny was satisfied with Trajan's performance as *princeps* after a year in Rome, he had not forgotten how Trajan came to power. Following the death of Domitian, the Senate was able to establish the elder statesman Nerva as emperor, for whom they had high expectations. In one letter, Pliny describes Nerva as *optimus* and *amicissimus* ("best" and "most friendly" [*Ep.* 2.1.3]).[20] Tacitus even claims that Nerva was responsible for bringing together the opposites *principatus* and *libertas* (*Agric.* 3).[21] Although Nerva was highly qualified as a

---

[17] "Truly it is possible with this *princeps* for consuls to do as much as they did before the Principate existed" (*Pan.* 93.2). Pliny contends that playing an active part in the government is the senator's way of affirming that "we believe that the Republic still exists" (93.3). In response to Trajan's modesty over taking the consulship for a third time Pliny mentions two Republican leaders who had done so, and maintains that there is still a Republic and a Senate to call on Trajan for the office (57.5).

[18] Tacitus *Hist.* 1.1 (trans. Clifford H. Moore; LCL; Cambridge: Harvard University Press, 1980). Liebeschuetz (*Continuity and Change*, 183) remarks that Tacitus is critical of society in proportion to the degree that Pliny idealizes it. It will be shown that Pliny has his critical side, just as this passage reveals the idealism of Tacitus.

[19] *Hist.* 1.1; Pliny remarks that the same is true now in the Senate as well (*Pan.* 76.1–6).

[20] Dietmar Kienast ("Nerva und Das Kaisertum Trajans," *Historia* 17 [1968] 51–71) has argued that under the influence of Trajan's policy, Pliny downplays the importance of Nerva in the *Panegyricus*. Fears (*PRINCEPS*, 152) also holds to this position. Passages like this one and *Pan.* 45.1 seem to demonstrate that Pliny's portrayal of Nerva is positive in some places.

[21] Martial also has great expectations for the reign of Nerva (*Epig.* 11.3) and the restoration of

senator, he lacked the military connections and experience of either his successor Trajan, or his predecessor Domitian.[22] Pliny reports that Trajan came to power at a time when the Praetorian Guard had rebelled against Nerva, "the kindest of elderly men" (*Pan.* 6.1), and jeopardized the stability of the empire. Syme has suggested that the rebellion Pliny speaks of was actually a coup attempt instigated by soldiers who had been loyal to Domitian.[23] Kenneth Scott maintains that "Domitian stood high in the favor of the troops, was apparently not disliked by ordinary citizens and provincials, and was hated by the Senators alone."[24] While this is surely an oversimplification,[25] it is important to remember that, like Domitian, Trajan was a soldier, a different figure than Nerva, the man the Senate had installed as *princeps*.

While Trajan was also part of the senatorial order, unlike Nerva, he was a strong military leader who could assure the troops that control of the government had not fallen into the hands of bureaucrats like Nerva or Pliny. There can be no certainty about the amount of power Nerva retained after his adoption of Trajan. Syme says that in fact "the adoption was tantamount to an abdication."[26] Pliny's description of the transfer of power emphasizes not Trajan's actions, but rather divine actions and Nerva's orders that Trajan assume the *imperium* (*Pan.* 9.5). Again this could indicate an attempt to avoid mention of the actual chain of events. In the face of the reality of Trajan's power, Pliny, who had been a strong supporter of Nerva, now converted to being an outspoken partisan of the new Caesar.

This change of allegiance should not be surprising. Somehow—presumably by keeping his head low and his level of flattery high—Pliny had survived the terrible reign of Domitian during which time many senators

---

liberty and increased senatorial authority. "This our Chief preserve ye all, preserve ye the Senate; by its Prince's pattern may it live, he by his own!" (*Epig.* 11.4.6–7 [trans. Walter C. A. Kerr; LCL; Cambridge: Harvard University Press, 1919]). He voices approval of Nerva on behalf of Republican heroes (*Epig.* 11.5).

[22] Syme, "Imperial Finances," 10.

[23] Syme, *Tacitus*, 10–18. *Pan.* 9.2 describes the difficulty that posterity will have in believing that the great general, Trajan, was not made emperor by his troops, and received the title *Germanicus* from Rome. Following Syme's theory, this can be read as an attempt to remind Trajan of the Senate's opinion of the true source of his power.

[24] Scott, *Imperial Cult*, 189.

[25] Obviously, there is some evidence of provincial disdain for the policies of Domitian to be found in the book of Revelation, since "most modern scholarship is inclined to put Revelation in the Domitian persecution" (Norman Perrin and Dennis C. Duling, *The New Testament, an Introduction* [2d ed.; San Diego: Harcourt Brace Jovanovich, 1982] 116).

[26] Syme, *Tacitus*, 12. Syme also maintains that the legions were the true basis of Trajan's power (ibid., 17).

were executed or exiled.[27] At the end of the *Panegyricus*, Pliny goes to great lengths to assure his listeners/readers that he only advanced his career under Domitian until the *princeps* revealed his hatred for humankind.[28] Of course, the fact that Pliny has to defend himself so vigorously indicates that he was under suspicion of complicity with Domitian's reign of terror.[29] This explains why elsewhere Pliny is so insistent that displays of affection for Trajan's predecessors were not always genuine.[30] In any case, the *Panegyricus* supports Trajan and his regime, but not unreservedly, and not without proffering some suggestions about how the government should be run.

Like Tacitus, Pliny suggests that under Trajan his writing was better received than ever before because the present freedom made it more pleasant to write.[31] Above all, he extols "how our parent [Trajan] reformed and corrected the customs of the Principate depraved and corrupted by long standing practices" (*Pan.* 53.1). The senators knew that the Principate was a necessary part of ruling the empire,[32] and their desire was not to undermine the emperor, but to embrace the moderation that Trajan had shown, while pressing for more involvement in the governing process. As Syme puts it, "Above all, the speech is not merely an encomium of Trajan—it is a kind of senatorial manifesto in favour of constitutional monarchy."[33] Against the background of the oppression experienced under Domitian—that time of terror when many perished due to the "emperor's ferocity"[34]—the reign of Trajan held out the promise of more reasonable treatment, less fear of offending the emperor, and perhaps a greater degree of senatorial autonomy.[35]

---

[27] *Pan.* 35.2 acclaims the fact that those who were informers under Domitian are now exiled in the same way Domitian's victims were.

[28] *Pan.* 95.3. Earlier, Pliny made the claim that no advancement was possible under Domitian (90.6).

[29] Tacitus (*Hist.* 1) admits that his career progressed under the reign of Domitian. Goodyear ("History and Biography," in Kenney, *Latin Literature*, 659) suggests that Pliny "is not always honest with himself. He would like to believe, and have us believe, that he challenged dangers under Domitian: in truth he was a time-server, like most senators, and he would earn more respect if he admitted the fact." Goodyear is right, of course, but Pliny wanted to retain the respect of his peers, not to meet the expectation of future commentators.

[30] *Pan.* 74.3.

[31] *Ep.* 3.18.6.

[32] Liebeschuetz, *Continuity and Change*, 198.

[33] Syme, "Review of Durry," 86.

[34] Tacitus *Agric.* 3.

[35] Pliny contrasts the situation under Domitian when whoever was the Senate's friend was the emperor's enemy and vice versa (*Pan.* 62.4).

Evidence for the Senatorial Perspective

In the *Panegyricus*, Pliny applauds specific actions that Trajan has taken to support the senators. The *princeps* exhorts them "to recover their freedom, to undertake the administration of the power which they supposedly share."[36] As consul he makes a positive judgment of the Senate when he confirms their choices for election and promotion (*Pan.* 71.7). While Pliny commends Trajan on his handling of senatorial relations, he also makes suggestions for further improvement.

A large section of the *Panegyricus* (54–79) discusses various aspects of Trajan's relationship to the Senate. In chapters 54–55 Pliny stresses the modesty of the emperor in not accepting *adulatio* during theatrical performances, or as part of the oratory of the Senate. He even comments that Trajan's reluctance to accept praise will lead to a conflict between the *pietas* of the Senate and the *modestia* of the emperor (*Pan.* 79.4). This moderation, as well as a responsible fiscal policy, is said to insure for Trajan a positive reputation in the minds of his subjects and his successors.[37]

Pliny salutes Trajan for the elections which he ran as consul, and for promoting the proper senatorial role in the electoral process.

> Neither were you inactive in urging our young men that they should make the rounds of the Senate, entreat the Senate, and only hope for honors from the *princeps* if they had sought it from the Senate. (*Pan.* 69.2)

Trajan's emphasis on the Senate's role in filling public offices, leads Pliny to ask if anyone could ever show more respect to the Senate (*Pan.* 69.3). There is some question of how accurately Pliny's praise here reflects the reality of governmental life. Pliny later writes to Trajan asking for the emperor's personal attention to the advancement of a friend.[38]

Pliny also commends Trajan for giving preferential treatment to the sons

---

[36] *Pan.* 66.2; see also 66.4.

[37] *Pan.* 20.6. In fact, Trajan's reputation was remarkably positive for many years to come. See K. H. Waters, "Trajan's Character in the Literary Tradition," in J. A. S. Evans, ed., *Polis and Imperium: Studies in Honour of Edward Togo Salmon* (Toronto: Hakkert, 1974) 233–52.

[38] *Ep.* 10.26; Sherwin-White (*Letters*, 595–96) places this letter in the first year of Pliny's legateship in Bithynia. Millar (*Emperor and the Roman World*, 300–313, esp. 302) points out that although "the electoral assemblies of Rome (the *comitia centuriata* and *tributa*) . . . continued, in form at least, until the third century," emperors since Augustus had been in control of the selection of consuls, and had been influential in filling lesser positions in the cursus. In *Pan.* 63.2 Pliny remarks with irony to Trajan "you became consul as one of us whom you make consul." Juvenal, in discussing the plight of the plebs, (Satires 10.78–81) notes the irony that "the ones who once elected are now reduced to bread and games." Cf. Talbert, *Senate*, 341–46.

of noble families by promoting them to offices ahead of schedule (*Pan.* 69.4). As a *novus homo*, Pliny was not heir to the privileges due to descendants of the venerable Republican patrician families,[39] but he views Trajan's preferential treatment of the *nobilitas* as a positive support for the Senate and a link with the pre-Principate past. The young appointees are referred to as "those grandsons of noble men, those decendants of liberty" (*Pan.* 69.5).[40]

Behind each of the many good things that Pliny has to say about the relationship between Trajan and the Senate, lies an expectation that Trajan will continue to restore honor and power to the neglected and long maligned body. Language and images recall the past glories of the liberty experienced before the coming of the Principate. Trajan receives lavish praise in the *Panegyricus* because at this initial stage in his reign he has avoided the anti-senatorial tendencies of Domitian. In his *gratiarum actio*, Pliny expresses hope that this trend will continue.

Trajan's Reluctance to Accept a Third Consulship

Pliny does show concern about several aspects of Trajan's relationship with the Senate, especially his refusal of certain senatorial duties and honors.[41] The office of *consul* was the position of highest authority in the Senate. During Republican times the consuls had been the chief Magistrates of Rome. During the Principate, consular power had been reduced, but the office continued to have enormous prestige and influence, some of which was due to the emperor's regular assumption of the office.[42] After serving his second consulship *in absentia*,[43] Trajan is reluctant to assume a third. Pliny addresses this issue in chapters 56–62. While he praises Trajan's humility, Pliny is concerned that refusal to hold the consulship could be interpreted as a lack of regard for the dignity of this traditional position and also a lack of respect for the Senate.[44] Pliny does not want Trajan to follow the excessive

---

[39] Like Trajan's father he had ascended to the Senate and even to the consulate from equestrian lineage. Trajan's father is mentioned in *Pan.* 8.2 as "senator, consul, and triumphator."

[40] Syme (*Tacitus*, 2. 578) contends that elsewhere (*Ep.* 5.17) Pliny speaks of the *nobilitas* with "a tone of smug and possessive condescension," which indicates their lessening importance since "Trajan supplanted Nerva, and 'virtus' conquered pedigree." In *Panegyricus* 69 Pliny's regard for the *nobilitas* and their improved status under Trajan seems to be genuine.

[41] It is not accidental that Pliny chides Trajan for refusing the Senate's election, and being more modest than the great Republican leaders (*Pan.* 57.5).

[42] Talbert, *Senate*, 20–22. Cf. *Pan.* 93.2.

[43] *Pan.* 58.3. According to Pliny (*Pan.* 60.1), Trajan's reason for refusing the third consulship in 99 was because of his absence from the city.

[44] Pliny (*Pan.* 76.5) draws an explicit connection between respect for the Senate and holding the consulate when he refers to emperors who showed some reverence to the Senate while present as consul, but who abandoned all consular duties as soon as they left the office.

example of Domitian who was Consul seventeen times and was nominated
for a ten-year term (*Pan.* 58.1), but neither should he ignore the office alto-
gether.

In chapter 59, Pliny states frankly that refusing the consulship too many
times will give the impression that Trajan values it too little. While he understands Trajan's modesty in refusing arches, trophies, and statues, refusing to
accept the third consulship is not a matter of personal preference (*Pan.* 59.2).
Rather, it is a matter of respect and honor for the Senate to have the emperor
duly serve his proper terms as consul. With obvious rhetorical intent, Pliny
asks if Trajan's second consulship has caused him to become haughty, and
ironically inquires how long the Senate must rejoice over him while he is
absent (*Pan.* 59.3–4). These were not meant to be harsh criticisms of the
emperor, but rather reminders that the Senate had certain expectations for his
conduct of government. If an emperor was secure enough in military support, he could afford to ignore such requests from the Senate. Trajan was
certainly secure in his power, but Pliny records that eventually he gave in and
accepted the consulship. Chapters 63–77 discuss the details of his election
and his third term of office.

It is important to note that since Trajan had already served his third consulship by the time the *Panegyricus* was presented, it would have been
natural for Pliny to avoid any mention of the controversy over its acceptance.
Instead, he actually elaborates on the dispute. The conflict between the *pietas* of the Senate and the *modestia* of the emperor is an important subject for
Pliny's *gratiarum actio*, not because he wants to flatter Trajan, but because
he wants to provide a vivid reminder of senatorial perspective.

Immediately after completing the report on the third consulship, Pliny
begins to repeat the theme, urging Trajan to accept the office for a fourth
time (*Pan.* 78–79).[45] This time he makes explicit the previously implied
value of the Consul as the symbol of the freedom of the Senate.

> We know that your intention is to recall and bring back liberty. What honor
> should you cherish more, what title should you bear more often than that which
> was the first created when liberty was restored? (*Pan.* 78.3)

The Title "Optimus"

Further evidence of the senatorial perspective can be detected in Pliny's comments regarding a second honor offered to Trajan by the Senate. As he is
praising Trajan early in the document, Pliny asks "What is more characteris-

---

[45] Trajan served his fourth consulship from 1–12 January 101. Pliny chose not to include
details of this term in his revision of the speech.

tic of a citizen, or of senators than that title *'Optimus'* added by us?'' (*Pan.* 2.7). The appellation *Optimus* (''best'') was one of the most enduring of Trajan's imperial titles. The legend *optimus princeps* was used on coins starting in 103 CE,[46] but *''Optimus''* did not appear as part of the emperor's official nomenclature in inscriptions and coinage until late in the year 114 or early 115 CE.[47] Why then does Pliny mention the title in the *Panegyricus* which is dated to 100 CE?

Some commentators have suggested that, in the *Panegyricus*, Pliny uses the term *''Optimus''* in an informal way which foreshadows the official adoption of the title.[48] Weighing against this suggestion, however, the tone of the passage referring to the addition of a *cognomen* is hardly unofficial.[49] Pliny is describing (and, I think, defending) an official action of the Senate, taken early in Trajan's reign, by which the title of *''Optimus''* was offered to the new emperor. Since Trajan does not take on the title until near the end of his reign, it is apparent that for some reason he refused the Senate's initial offer. As with the refusal of his third consulship, it makes good sense that Pliny's mention of the title in the *Panegyricus* is not an unofficial anticipation, but rather a senatorial plea for Trajan to accept the honor which had been conferred.

This is not the only example in the *Panegyricus* of Pliny pressing Trajan on his refusal to accept honors offered by the Senate. In addition to the postponement of the third consulate, there is another instance which involves nomenclature. While discussing Trajan's moderation in returning to Rome for the first time as *princeps* (*Pan.* 21–24), Pliny reminds the emperor of his initial refusal to accept the title *Pater Patriae* which had been voted to him by the Senate. Using vivid language, Pliny describes how the Senate was eventually able to overcome Trajan's reluctance. ''How long was our battle against your modesty, how slowly we conquered'' (*Pan.* 21.1).[50] It is true that this phrase is

---

[46] Mattingly, *BMC*, 3. lxx–lxxx.

[47] Durry, *Panégyrique*, 232 (Appendix 1). F. A. Lepper (*Trajan's Parthian War* [Oxford: Oxford University Press, 1948] 34–39, Table 1 on p. 34) has arranged the evidence in a convenient form. He also discusses the evidence for the title *''Parthicus,''* and states that in this case more precise dating is possible because of a fragment of the *Fasti Ostienses* which mentions that the Senate conferred the title *''Parthicus''* on 20 February 116 CE (ibid., 39–43). Dio's reference to the Senate awarding the title *''Optimus''* after the subjegation of Armenia in 114 (68.23.1) must indicate that either Dio did not know that it was offered much earlier, or that he did not care.

[48] Radice (*Pliny*, 326) calls it ''unofficial.'' Lepper (*Parthian War*, 38) refers to ''anticipations,'' and talks about a gradual ''conversion from an applicable compliment into an inseparable title.''

[49] Cf. *Pan.* 88.4.

[50] The following translation by Radice (*Pliny*, 369) muffles the tone somewhat: ''It was only after a prolonged struggle that you were persuaded.''

found in a context of praise for Trajan's modesty, but, as with the refusal of the third consulate, Pliny is careful to emphasize the importance of Trajan's proper regard for honors extended to him by the Senate. The same call for respect is found in the discussion of the title *"Optimus."*

By the time that Pliny published his *gratiarum actio*, Trajan had accepted the disputed third consulship, and also the title of *pater patriae*;[51] there is no indication, however, that the emperor was willing to be called *"Optimus"* until much later. In both instances when Pliny mentions the title in the *Panegyricus*, he appears to be defending the Senate's granting of the name.[52] Pliny introduces his speech by saying that it is not the *Divinitas* ("godlike qualities") of the emperor which is praiseworthy, but rather his *humanitas*, *temperantia*, and *facilitas* ("human character, self control, and aptitude" [*Pan.* 2.7]). Following this comment, Pliny asks what could better demonstrate that Trajan is a citizen and a senator than the title *"Optimus"* which the Senate had offered to him? This insistence on *"Optimus"* as a proper senatorial title may imply that in rejecting the title, Trajan was arguing that *"Optimus"* had divine connotations as one of the names of Jupiter Optimus Maximus.[53] Pliny responds by insisting that the title is an appropriate way of recognizing Trajan's human virtues, not an attempt to emphasize his divine nature.

Pliny answers this same concern again in the second, much longer, defense of the *cognomen*: "Were there not just causes for the Senate and people of Rome to add to your name the title *'Optimus'*?" (*Pan.* 88.4). It is possible to read this query as a rhetorical question, but, given the fact that Trajan had not accepted the title, it makes more sense as a straightforward appeal for the emperor to reconsider. The request consists of several arguments. First, Pliny suggests that although *optimus* may seem *medius* ("common"),[54] it is in fact a name that had not been merited by any previous ruler, although it had been available.[55] Next Pliny, comparing the title *"Optimus"*

---

[51] Mattingly (*BMC*, 3. xciv) dates the acceptance of *pater patriae* to autumn of 98 CE.

[52] *Pan.* 2.7b, 88.4–10. In each case the defense of the title interrupts the larger scheme of Pliny's argument.

[53] Pliny could also be answering the objections of other senators to the granting of the title. It is unlikely, however, that he would need to argue so strongly against the senatorial opposition, given that he claims the title had already been awarded. Perhaps Trajan's reluctance to accept the title is in response to doubts about its appropriateness voiced by an influential minority of senators. K. H. Waters ("Traianus Domitiani Continuator,"*AJP* 90 [1969] 396) asserts that the delayed acceptance of the title by Trajan is "another example of his diplomatic attitude." Any diplomacy implied in the refusal is lost on Pliny.

[54] Pliny uses *optimus* as a simple descriptive adjective in *Pan.* 7.4. Interestingly, he says that both Nerva and Trajan are "best."

[55] Suetonius (*Gaius* 22.1) reports that Gaius "took on many various surnames" including *optimus maximus Caesar*.

with two other possible names, *"Felix"* and *"Magnus,"*[56] asserts that the name *"Optimus"* defines the emperor as clearly as the name Trajan (*Pan.* 88.6). To state that he is *"Optimus,"* Pliny contends, means that Trajan is greater than all those who were known for having single virtues (*Pan.* 88.7). Further, because Trajan is better than all previous *principes*, he should add *"Optimus"* after his other titles of *Imperator*, *Caesar*, and *Augustus*.[57] What is more, Trajan is worthy of sharing the title with Jupiter:

> And for that reason, the parent of human beings and gods is worshipped by the name '*Optimus*' first, and then '*Maximus*.' How much more honored is your reputation, who are known to be no less *optimus* than *maximus*. (*Pan.* 88.8)

Having established the propriety of the title once again, Pliny returns to the uniqueness of *"Optimus,"* asserting that it will always be associated with Trajan, just as *"Augustus"* will always be a reminder of the first *princeps* (*Pan.* 88.9–10).

Pliny's purpose in this section consists of more than flattering Trajan with a list of the characteristics that make him eligible to receive the title *"Optimus."* It is a thoughtfully constructed argument aimed at convincing someone that the title was appropriate. Since the Senate has already voted the name, it would seem as though the only person to be convinced would be Trajan, who is known to have refused it until 114 CE. Trajan's reasons for refusing the title are not entirely clear, but, given his reluctance to accept divine honors elsewhere, and Pliny's attempts to show that *"Optimus"* is really a human appellation (esp. *Pan.* 2.7) it is likely that Trajan felt uncomfortable with such a close association with Jupiter Optimus Maximus.[58]

This issue cannot be resolved without consideration of the hybrid form of *"Optimus,"* *optimus princeps*. If Pliny's persistence in trying to justify the title *"Optimus"* is evidence of contention between the senate and the *princeps*, then perhaps the use of the phrase *optimo principi* on coinage is evidence of a compromise. As mentioned above, Lepper has chosen to see *optimus princeps* as "an unofficial anticipation" of the *cognomen* *"Optimus."* This is unlikely, however, given the copious production of coinage bearing the legend S P Q R OPTIMO PRINCIPI. Mattingly comments that the legend is to be found on all Roman coins of all metals beginning in

---

[56] *Pan.* 88.5. Pliny points out that the name *Felix* would be a comment on the good luck of Trajan, not on his exemplary character.

[57] Ibid. When *"Optimus"* finally appears in 114 CE, it follows immediately after Traianus (*BMC* 3. 108, 215).

[58] It is striking that by the end of his reign Trajan is apparently much more comfortable with it. See Chapter Four below.

late 103 CE, and that the dative form should be read as a dedication to Trajan "perpetually recorded on the official coinage."[59] Pliny hints that the adjective *optimus* was common (*Pan.* 88.4), and in fact, the appellation *optimus princeps* was not a unique creation for Trajan in 103. Pliny refers to a decree of the Senate in which Claudius is referred to as *princeps optimus* (*Ep.* 8.10). The adjective *optimus* and the phrase *optimus princeps* are used to describe Nerva several times in Pliny's writings.[60] The most telling occurrence is Pan. 88.5, where Nerva as *optimus princeps* confers his name on his successor, while the Senate offers to Trajan the name "*Optimus.*" In this juxtaposition, Pliny is distinguishing the two appellations: "*Optimus*" which the Senate offered but Trajan did not accept until 114, and *optimus princeps* which was used to designate other emperors. It is common for scholars to conflate these two expressions,[61] but Pliny wants to separate them. He calls Trajan *optimus princeps* only twice in the *Panegyricus* (1.2; 74.3), and makes a strong yet unsuccessful case for the Senate's chosen title "*Optimus.*" Perhaps the use of the more common appellation *optimo principi* (with the notation SPQR) on the coinage starting in 103 CE was intended to be a compromise incorporating the Senate's desire, but upholding Trajan's decision to shun "Optimus" perhaps because of its divine connotations. (This seems to be the most likely reason for his refusal of the title.) If Trajan resisted the "Optimus" title because he wanted to avoid comparison with Jupiter, he might have been convinced that *optimus princeps* was a more appropriate title since it implied a clear comparison not with the gods, but with his human predecessors.[62] In the *Panegyricus*, Pliny argued for this point from the senatorial perspective; perhaps his attempts to justify the title, along with additional senatorial pressure, eventually led to the adoption of *optimo principi* as an acceptable form of honor.

Military Issues

The significance of Trajan's military connections as a basis for his political power has already been mentioned. Since the civil wars following Nero's death, it had been clear that control of legions was a decisive factor in determining who would rule. Tacitus (*Hist.* 1.5–11) describes the situation in which would be successors to Nero aligned themselves and waited for their

[59] *BMC*, 3. lxx. *Aes* coins included the signature SC (*Senatus consultum*).

[60] *Ep.* 2.1.3; *optimus* (*Pan.* 7.4, in reference to both Nerva and Trajan) *optimus princeps* (*Ep.* 2.13.8); Sherwin-White (*Letters*, 173–74, 178) holds that the questions over the dating (of 2.13) can only be resolved if the emperor mentioned is Nerva. See also *Ep.* 9.13.23.

[61] See, e.g., Lepper (*Parthian War*, 38) and Sherwin-White (*Letters*, 178–79).

[62] In this light it is worth asking why the "*Optimus*" title became acceptable in 114.

chance to take power. First Galba came to power with support from his troops in Spain, then Vitellius whom Galba had put in control of lower Germany, and finally Vespasian returned from Judea and established the Flavian dynasty.[63] As Tacitus declared, the secret of the empire had been revealed, that is, "that it was possible to become *princeps* elsewhere than Rome" (*Hist.* 1.4). This revelation would have increased tensions between the Senate and the *princeps* as well as between the Senate and the armies. Given such tensions, it is not surprising that Pliny is very cautious about discussing Trajan's military background and connections.

Pliny (*Pan.* 16.1) is quick to praise Trajan for moderate actions, and especially so when the actions concern the military. "For this your moderation is even more praiseworthy, that nurtured on the glories of war, you love peace!"[64] In describing Trajan's first return to the city as emperor, Pliny (*Pan.* 23.3) emphasizes that the soldiers who were with him could not be distinguished by dress (*habitus*), calmness (*tranquillitas*), or moderation (*modestia*). Finally, when speaking of Trajan's second consulship held in Germany during January of 98 CE, Pliny imagines the glory of the senatorial office being exercised in front of the conquered tribes; with the enemy fearing the togate consul no less than the armed general (*Pan.* 56.7).

These indications of a senatorial concern about the emperor's military power, are reinforced by Pliny's comments on the impending conflict on the Dacian frontier. Reports of the uprising of the *barbarus rex* in *Pan.* 16.3–4 and the anticipated triumph in *Pan.* 17.1–3 are inserted between references to Trajan's *moderatio* in avoiding war (*Pan.* 16.1–3 and 17.4).[65] The references to moderation in resisting the taunting of the Dacians were probably part of the original *gratiarum actio* delivered in September of 100 CE. As

---

[63] Syme, *Tacitus*, ix–xi.

[64] Appreciation of Trajan's more peaceful tendencies is also evident in Pliny's comparison of the *optimus princeps* with Pompey the Great (*Pan.* 29.1–2). While Pompey is praised for ridding the sea of pirates, and celebrating triumphs from east to west, Trajan receives greater accolades for ensuring the food supply by peaceful means.

[65] In 16.1–3, Trajan receives praise for his *moderatio* in not pursuing the enemy across the Danube. This probably refers to Trajan's tour of the northern provinces during his extended return journey to the city after Nerva's death. A probable sequence of travels is reconstructed by Syme (*Tacitus* 17–18). He emphasizes that Trajan used this time to secure the northern frontier, and transfer command: "Trajan proceeded to Moesia. There he wintered at one of the camps, Viminacium or Singidunum, facing the land of the Dacians—and the strategic centre of the Empire, half-way between the northern ocean and the river Euphrates, on or beside the highway of empire that linked Italy and the West to the eastern provinces" (ibid.). Martial expresses the desire of the inhabitants of Rome for the return of Trajan: "O Rhine, father of Nymphs and of whichever rivers drink the Thracian snow . . . Lord Tiber asks you to send back Trajan to his people and city" (*Epig.* 10.7).

Pliny worked on the revision of the speech, the Dacian threat was increasing, and he might not have finished the final version until after the outbreak of hostilities in Dacia in 101 CE. Thus he inserts the reports on the uprising, and the prediction of a glorious triumph[66] into the speech in order to bring it up to date. He does not delete, however, his praise of Trajan's moderation as shown by his earlier refusal to attack the enemy and thereby seek glory and triumph for its own sake (*Pan.* 17.4). The *moderatio* of the emperor who avoids war serves as an *inclusio* for the report of his military success.

Pliny's tendency to minimize the military side of Trajan's rule supports the picture of senatorial apprehensions about the military basis for the power of the *princeps*. Pliny would not have wanted to glorify the fact that Trajan's power was firmly based in his control and effective use of the army. On the contrary, Pliny stresses that in spite of Trajan's military up-bringing and his own successful service, he does not become emperor on the basis of military strength (*Pan.* 9.2).[67] By the time he published the *Panegyricus*, Pliny had seen that the emperor had not been able to avoid conflict in future dealings with the Dacians. Contrary to Pliny's expectations, Trajan's reign is marked throughout by serious armed conflict. The Dacian wars proved to be great triumphs for the *optimus princeps*,[68] but his campaigns to conquer Parthia failed, and have been judged as "out of all proportion to their material advantages."[69] It seems clear that Pliny's hopes for the

---

[66] Complete with *spoila opima* which are awarded to the *triumphator* who himself kills the enemy king (Syme, "Review of Durry," 78). Since Trajan did not kill the Dacian king Decebalus, even at the end of the second Dacian war, Pliny's description of the triumph is clearly prophetic and optimistically so.

[67] It is also possible that, having served in several treasury posts (*CIL* 5. 5262 [see Appendix 1 below]; *Pan.* 92.1; *Ep.* 5.14.5), Pliny would be aware that, while secure border defenses were essential, an extensive foreign campaign would be a tremendous drain on the finances of the empire. Elsewhere, Pliny shows concern that Trajan's generous giving coupled with the remission of certain taxes might endanger the emperor's finances (*Pan.* 41.1). In contrast to what he saw as excessive foreign expenses of Domitian, Pliny exalts Trajan for publishing a statement accounting for his expenditures while returning to the city, and states that an emperor should become accustomed to settling accounts with the empire (*Pan.* 20.5).

[68] The story of the war and triumph is recorded in pictorial form on the magnificent Column of Trajan erected in his Forum in Rome (see pp. 122–23 below). Both projects were underwritten by Trajan using the spoils of the second Dacian campaign.

[69] C. H. V. Sutherland and Mason Hammond, "Trajan," *OxCD*, 1089. They propose that the Parthian fiasco was so great that Trajan's "judgement may have been warped by delusive megalomania." G. W. Bowersock (*Roman Arabia* [Cambridge: Harvard University Press, 1983] 82) presents a different picture, however, in which Trajan's plans for eastern expansion were carefully drawn from the earliest days of his reign, and informed by knowledge of the region gained during his father's tenure as governor of Syria under Vespasian. Lepper (*Parthian War*, 204) suggests that the negative view of the Parthian campaign, prominent even in antiquity, was

princeps ruling with *moderatio* and *modestia* in regard to military affairs were not realized.[70]

Conclusion

Given this evidence for the senatorial perspective of the the the *Panegyricus*, the view that the document constitutes an official policy statement of Trajan cannot be accepted uncritically. Communications between the Senate and the emperor were conducted with mutual respect, but it cannot be assumed that senators always represented the views of the *princeps*, or vice versa. Fears admits to this possibility in his book, and even suggests that the view of the *Panegyricus* as a document written from a senatorial perspective is not mutually exclusive from his own.[71] Once the material appears again in his article "The Cult of Jupiter and Roman Imperial Ideology," any compromise has vanished, and the view that the *Panegyricus* is a statement of Trajan's policy is assumed. Certainly Pliny takes his task seriously in writing this speech, and he is speaking in his official position as consul, but this does not necessarily imply that he is simply presenting Trajan's party line. The *Panegyricus* supports Trajan, but it does so from the senatorial point of view. Given the ambivalence that continued to characterize imperial-senatorial relations, Pliny's fulsome praise of Trajan must be understood as qualified and not without ulterior motive.

Pliny the Rhetorician and the Senatorial Perspective

In order to analyze Pliny's motivations and intentions in the *Panegyricus*, it is essential to recognize his background as an orator. As justification for his speech, Pliny cites a *senatus consultum* ("decree of the Senate" [*Pan.* 4.1]) compelling him to give thanks to the *princeps* (*Ep.* 3.18.1). The task is understood to be an extension of the rhetorical work he was accustomed to

---

started by Hadrian who had to justify his decision to withdraw from much of the "conquered" territory.

[70] Pliny was dead by the time the Parthian campaigns began. Since his testamentary inscription (*CIL* 5.5262 [see Appendix 1]) from Comum cites Trajan as a living emperor, it is certain that Pliny died before him. A more specific date is suggested from the fact that the inscription does not use Trajan's title of *Optimus* (assumed in 114). Sherwin-White (*Letters*, 80–82) claims that the last argument is suspect since the absence of *Optimus* cannot be proven due to lacunae. He further states, however, that the letters reveal Pliny spending parts of three calendar years in Bithynia before the correspondence ceases. Assuming that this break indicates his demise, Sherwin-White assigns Pliny's arrival in Bithynia to 109 and his death to 111 CE. The beginning of the Parthian Campaign is usually dated to 114 with the annexation of Armenia.

[71] Fears, *PRINCEPS*, 152, n. 57.

undertake in the Senate as well as in other parts of the Roman legal system.[72] As a student of Quintilian,[73] Pliny was part of a long line of Latin rhetorical tradition.[74] As a fervent admirer of Cicero, Pliny was proud to admit that he was not satisfied with the rhetoric of the the day, and that he tried to imitate Cicero's style.[75]

Pliny defends a more expansive and daring rhetorical touch at length in two of his letters (*Ep.* 1.20; 9.26). Sherwin-White, on the other hand, maintains that Pliny reveals his personal preference for a more simple style in his comments about the audience's reaction to his revision of the *Panegyricus*:[76] "For instance, I noticed that the more austere passages satisfied most" (*Ep.* 3.18.8). In his willingness to apply different styles, Pliny reveals himself to be a student of both Cicero and Quintilian. In his discussions of rhetorical style, Cicero charges that the best orator is the one with a wide basis of education and experience and a willingness to employ all kinds of style (*Orator*, 46). This perspective is very similar to Quintilian's admonition "to adapt one's style to the theme of the moment" (*Inst.* 12.10.69).[77]

There is another dimension of Quintilian's teaching which is important for understanding the *Panegyricus*. In Quintilian's *Institutio oratoria*, a massive guidebook for the education and training of an orator in the tradition of Cicero, he emphasizes the standard of Cato, that the orator be "a good man (*vir bonus*), skilled in speaking" (*Inst.* 1. praef. 9, 18).[78] That the speaker be good is essential to Quintilian's model, for he believes that by following his method of instruction, the *vir bonus* can become the perfect orator, who will

---

[72] *Pan.* 90.3; see also *Pan.* 1.6; *Ep.* 3.13.1, 18.1.

[73] *Ep.* 2.14.9. In 6.6.3 Pliny mentions that he had attended lectures of both Quintilian and the Greek rhetorician Nicetes Sacerdos.

[74] Durry (*Panégyrique*, 27–33) discusses the ideas and their sources, emphasizing the influence of Cicero's *Pro Marcello*, the elegy of Tiberius by Velleius, and Seneca's *De Clementia*.

[75] *Ep.* 1.5.11–12. Pliny's desire to emulate Cicero extends to areas other than oratory. He repeats the words of Arrianus, who was congratulating Pliny for being appointed *augur*, a position held by M. Tullius "whom I desire to imitate in my literary work" (*Ep.* 4.8.4). Pliny goes on to say that since he has been made consul and *augur* at a much earlier age than Cicero, he hopes he can also attain some of his genius. Pliny's dissatisfaction with the present state of oratory is evident from his letters. Pliny suggests that Quintilian's teacher Domitius Afer was premature in asserting that rhetoric was dead, but "now truly its destruction and annihilation are nearly complete" (*Ep.* 2.12.12).

[76] Sherwin-White, *Letters*, 87–88.

[77] Cited by Sherwin-White, ibid., 88. Kennedy (*Art of Rhetoric*, 533) describes Quintilian as "teaching that style should be suited to content, that Cicero was the best guide, but that style should change with the times."

[78] In criticizing his enemy Regulus, Pliny quotes a friend who described Regulus as "an evil man, unskilled in speaking" (*Ep.* 4.7.5).

be able to exert a strong influence on society, to "direct the counsels of the Senate and guide the people from the paths of error to better things."[79] It is hard to imagine that Pliny was not strongly influenced by his teacher's vision. As he presented the *Panegyricus* he did not regard himself as an eloquent puppet of the emperor, but rather as a *vir bonus* whose words had the potential for leading society, or at least the Senate, to better things. Pliny states that the *Panegyricus* was intended "to praise in truth the best ruler and moreover, through this to shine a light like a watchtower which can be followed by posterity" (*Ep*. 3.18.3).

[79] *Inst*. 1.1 cited in Thomas W. Benson and Michael H. Prosser, eds., *Readings in Classical Rhetoric* (Bloomington, IN: Indiana University Press, 1972) 121–22.

3

The Relationship between the Emperor and the Gods in the *Panegyricus*

Introduction

In his investigation of the imperial cult, Price has tried to avoid the "Romanocentric," "Christianizing," and "modernizing" tendencies of scholarship by considering the evidence on its own terms. He insists that "careful investigation of the parallels between imperial and divine rituals" limits the "imposition of our categories on the ancient world."[1] To whatever extent it is possible, I want to limit the imposition of my categories as well. Pliny did not write the *Panegyricus* as a treatise on the relationship between the emperor and the gods, but yet he was trying to describe and promote a certain picture of who the emperor should be in relation to the inhabitants of the empire, the people of Rome, and especially the Senate. In speaking of provincial imperial cult ritual, Price describes this process as creating "a relationship of power between subject and ruler."[2] As he presents his *gratiarum actio* to Trajan, Pliny also is trying to describe a similar relationship. In doing so, he draws from a "traditional symbolic system" which is replete with images of the gods.[3]

---

[1] Price, *Rituals and Power*, 7–22. He states: "While in the end we have no choice but to attempt to make some sense of the participants' perspective in our own terms, still we must start by looking at the subject, as far as possible, through their eyes" (p. 19).

[2] Ibid., 248.

[3] Ibid. As described above, Pliny's role in presenting the *Panegyricus* was to redefine the

In order to analyze the relationship of power that Pliny is describing, it is necessary to examine the "traditional symbolic system" he uses, and to determine how he uses it. The first step in this process will be to consider how Pliny discusses the gods. This involves looking at both the vocabulary employed, and the ritual activities described. Once this basis is established, I shall investigate how Pliny uses the symbolic system of the gods to incorporate deceased emperors who have been deified into his relationship of power. Finally, Pliny's portrayal of how the living emperor is related to the gods will be considered. In the conclusion I return to the question of how Pliny has used the "traditional symbol system" to create a picture of the "relationship of power" in Roman society which he hoped would be meaningful and transformative for that society.

Pliny Discusses the Gods

Vocabulary

In the *Panegyricus* Pliny uses three words to refer to gods: *deus*, *numen*, and *divus*. The first term, the one most commonly used in the document, often appears in the plural to refer to "the gods," usually as a nonspecific group.[4] For example, Pliny refers to the "assembly of human beings and gods" (*contio hominum deorumque*) present for the ceremony in which Nerva adopted Trajan (*Pan.* 8.3); "the foresight of the gods" (*Providentia deorum*) is credited with raising Trajan to the supreme position (*Pan.* 10.4); and the gods are given credit for the premature greying of Trajan's hair (*Pan.* 4.7).[5] Pliny also employs the common phrase *di immortales* referring to the "immortal gods" (*Pan.* 1.1; 4.4).[6] In a few cases the unspecified *deus* is used to refer to Jupiter.[7] In *Pan.* 5.4, Pliny describes a scene during Nerva's reign in which

---

relationship between the senators and the *princeps* after the horrible years under Domitian, and the short-lived hope offered by Nerva. Delivering this address at the beginning of Trajan's reign afforded Pliny the opportunity to promote a "relationship of power" that would be mutually acceptable to the two forces represented in his audience, the Senate and the emperor.

[4] There is not enough information to determine if Pliny might have had a subset of all the gods, such as the Capitoline Triad, in mind when he refered to *di/dei*. Presumably this term refers to both male and female gods. At one point Pliny, speaking about human beings who were somehow regarded as divine, mentions "husbands of goddesses and children of gods" (*Pan.* 82.7).

[5] A particular group of gods is mentioned in connection with Nerva's deferring the punishment of Domitian's informers "to the gods of the sea" (*Pan.* 35.1).

[6] Cf. Cicero *N.D.* 3.27.

[7] Jupiter is by far the most frequently named god. He is called, *Iuppiter* (*Pan.* 1.5), *Capitoline Iuppiter* (94.1), *Iuppiter Optime* (1.6), *Iove* (1.5; 8.3; 14.5), *Capitolino Iovi* (16.1), *Iuppiter Optimus Maximus* (8.1; 52.3, 6). He is also called *parens hominum deorumque* ("parent of

Trajan was entering the temple to Capitoline Jupiter, and the crowd called out an appellation which at the time was mistakenly thought to hail Jupiter (*deus*).[8]

The term *numen* is derived from the verb *nuto* which means "to nod with the head (as a signal of assent or command)."[9] Based on this connection, *numen* is used to indicate "divine power," "divine purpose," or "divine nature." Pliny praises Trajan for pausing "to consult with the auspices and to show respect for the admonition of the divine will (*numinum monitus*)" (*Pan.* 76.7).[10] *Numen* can also represent the divine element of a particular divinity, as in Pliny's report of Trajan's redirecting thanks to "the deity (*numen*) of Jupiter best and greatest" (*Pan.* 52.6). Pliny uses *numen* to indicate divine powers in nature,[11] and also the divine element of human beings, as when Pliny contends that Domitian interpreted insults to his gladiators "as offending his divinity (*divinitatem*) and his deity (*numen*)" (*Pan.* 33.4).[12]

Pliny also uses *numen*, in some cases, as a synonym for *deus*. This is seen in the letter to Trajan on the Christian problem (*Ep.* 10.96.5) when Pliny refers to the *simulacrum numinum* ("images of the gods").[13] In the *Panegyricus* he marvels that "having been successfully entreated, the gods (*numina*) finally gave [Trajan] to the earth" (*Pan.* 5.1). Toward the beginning of the work, Pliny uses *deus* and *numen* in parallel construction: "under no circumstances should we flatter him [Trajan] as a god, or a divinity" (nusquam ut deo, nusquam ut numini blandiamur [*Pan.* 2.3]).

The use of the term *divus* generates a different set of questions, since it is usually the word associated with deceased emperors who have been deified. Price provides a helpful summary of the usage of the term in this regard.

---

human beings and gods" [88.8]), and *mundi parens* ("parent of the world" [80.4]).

[8] Pliny maintains that the crowd's premature salute was an omen of Trajan's imperial destiny. *Pan.* 1.5 and 5.9 also use *deus* to refer to Jupiter.

[9] *OLD*, 1208.

[10] See also *Pan.* 11.2, where Trajan's deification of Nerva is seen "not as an insult to the gods."

[11] *Pan.* 81.1, in reference to the divinities inhabiting the sacred groves. Pliny mentions nature gods in another sense: "But if there are divinities in the earth, and spirits in rivers, I myself pray to that soil (Egypt) and that river (the Nile)" (*Pan.* 32.3).

[12] Pliny's disdain for Domitian's claims to divinity influence the reading of this passage. At the same time, the coupling of *divinitas* and *numen* leads to problems of both translation and interpretation. While it is possible to understand the construction as parallel use of the two terms for emphasis, Pliny might have understood a subtle difference between them. It is possible that the *numen* of Domitian in this case could refer to a sense of taboo or sacrosanctity which was violated when Domitian's supposed divinity was offended.

[13] Pliny uses *deus* in the same passage when referring to his insistence that the accused invoke the gods. The phrase *simulacrum numinum* is also used by the Elder Pliny (*Nat.* 12.5).

The term *divus* was originally not sharply distinguished from *deus* ("god") but from the consecration of Caesar onwards it was used almost exclusively (outside poetical texts) of properly consecrated members of the imperial family. This is not to say that *divus* and *deus* were two exclusive categories; rather, *divus* was a subcategory of *deus* and it was thus perfectly possible to refer to a consecrated emperor as *deus*.[14]

In most cases, Pliny confirms Price's guidelines in the use of the term *divus*. In several places Pliny discusses *divus Nerva* (*Pan.* 7.4; 38.6; 89.1; 90.6) and *divus Titus* (35.4).[15] As Price suggests, however, Pliny does not hesitate to use *deus* for both the rightfully consecrated dead emperor (*Pan.* 10.4–5, 11.2–3, 23.4 [deum ipsum tuum <patrem>, "the god, your <father>"]) and for the extraordinary claims to divinity made by Domitian during his lifetime (33.4). Pliny even substitutes *dei filius* for the more common *divi filius* in several places (*Pan.* 10.5 [Domitian], and 14.2 [Trajan]).

The one usage of *divus* which seems to be an exception to Price's standards is the application of the term in the plural to stand for "all the gods." The first chapter of the *Panegyricus* commences with mention of the gods[16] and moves to address a prayer specifically to *Iuppiter Optimus*. At the end of the speech, Pliny addresses a prayer to all the gods, and again focuses on Capitoline Jupiter (*Pan.* 94.1). In the latter case, however, the term *divus* is used to designate the gods. This is an instance where *divus* was employed to denote gods other than those whom Price calls "properly consecrated members of the imperial family."[17] While I shall say more about Pliny's discussion of consecration below, it is already clear that, at the level of terminology, a great deal of flexibility was possible. It is necessary to be cautious in classifying terminology about the gods, or about the relationship between the emperor and the gods. This need for caution is demonstrated most clearly by considering the terminology used in one paragraph on the consecrated

[14] Price, "From Noble Funerals to Divine Cult: the Consecration of Roman Emperors," in David Cannadine and Simon Price, eds., *Rituals of Royalty: Power and Ceremonial in Traditional Societies* (Cambridge: Cambridge University Press, 1987) 77.

[15] In the letters Pliny mentions *divus Iulius* (*Ep.* 5.3.5; 8.6.13 [statue]); *divus Augustus* (*Ep.* 5.3.5; 8.8.6; 10.65; 79; 83–84); for Claudius see *Ep.* 10.70.2 and *Pan.* 11.1; *divus Vespasianus* (*Ep.* 1.14.5; 10.65); *divus Titus* (10.65); and *divus Nerva* (4.11.14; 5.3.5; 7.33.9; 10.65; (cf. 10.4.2 [*divo patre tuo*, "your father the god"], 10.8.1 [*divus pater tuus*, "your father the god"], 10.58 c and d). Nerva is also called *imperator* in 4.17.8; 4.22.4; 7.31.4; and *imperator et parens generis humani* ("emperor and parent of the human race" [*Pan.* 6.1]).

[16] Note the mention of *Deorum immortalium* ("of the immortal gods" [*Pan.* 1.1]) and *munus deorum* ("gift of the gods" [1.3]).

[17] Price, "Noble Funerals to Divine Cult," 77. Helmut Koester suggests that in this passage Pliny may be imitating classical usage of *divus*.

Titus (*Pan.* 35.4) in which Pliny refers to him as *divus Titus, numinibus aequatus,* and *deus.*

Ritual Activity

In order to understand the context for Pliny's discussion of the relationship between the emperor and the gods, it is necessary to consider the ritual activities mentioned in the *Panegyricus*. Pliny drew upon the symbolic world of these rituals to construct his picture of the relationship of power between the emperor and the gods, and between himself (as a representative of his fellow senators) and the emperor. These aspects of ritual include, but are not limited to: prayer, sacrifice, and priesthoods. Pliny's comments on ritual should by no means be taken as a textbook theory of Roman religion, but rather as reflecting his understanding of how worship of the gods affected the power relationships that surrounded him.

> And then you entreated [the heavens], that this very ordering of the elections would result in goodness and happiness for us, for the state, and for you. Ought we not rather to reverse the order of the prayers, and to implore that everything that you do and everything that you will do turns out to benefit you, the state, and us, or if we ought shorten our prayer, to benefit you alone by whom both the state and we exist? (*Pan.* 72.1)

Prayer

Prayer is the most common ritual act mentioned in the *Panegyricus*. Pliny opens and closes his speech with a prayer. In doing so he is heeding what he calls ancient advice: "Take the beginning of a speech just like a course of action from prayer" (*Pan.* 1.1). Forms of the word *precari*, which means "to make a request or entreaty," often are used by Pliny for requests directed toward the gods.[18] In one case, however, a form of *precari* is used for entreaties directed to Trajan: "We see that he hastens to meet the desires of the provinces and also the requests (*precibus*) of each city" (*Pan.* 79.6).[19] *Opto* is also found frequently in the *Panegyricus* referring to prayers to the

---

[18] E.g., *Pan.* 1.3 and 94.1 (to Jupiter Optimus Maximus), 32.3 (to the Nile and the soil of Egypt), 72.1–3 (Trajan to the gods [*deus*]), and 75.6 (prayers of the whole senate).

[19] Cf. *Pan.* 60.7: "What ought I to pray (*precer*), except that you be obliged as you always oblige?" In most instances, requests to the emperor are described with the terms *rogo* and *postulo*. For *rogo* see *Pan.* 46.2 (people ask of Trajan), 12.2 (enemies ask of Rome), 78.1 (Senate asks Trajan to take a fourth consulate). *Rogo* is found frequently in the letters, e.g., *Ep.* 10.10 where Pliny asks for a letter from Trajan and for permission to meet the emperor as he returns to Rome. For *postulo* see *Pan.* 33.2 and 59.2 (the Senate asks Trajan to be an example for future emperors by assuming a third consulate).

gods.[20] As with *precari*, however, *optare* is also used to describe an entreaty to Trajan: "Agree to these requests (*optantibus*), Caesar" (*Pan.* 78.5). Pliny uses the terms *precari* and *optare* to refer to requests directed to either the emperor or the gods.[21]

In the case of the noun *votum*, however, the ambiguity disappears. Pliny reserves *votum* to signify only prayers, vows, or offerings addressed to the gods, whether they be the *vota* of Trajan, of all the people, or of the Senate seeking a better ruler.[22]

> Your (Trajan's) prayers were heard. (*Pan.* 10.4)
> The prayers of everyone were united for one man's (Trajan's) safety.
> (*Pan.* 23.5)
> The chief point of our prayers was for a *princeps* better than the worst.
> (*Pan.* 44.2)

Pliny's discussion demonstrates that *vota* normally included the promise to repay something to the god(s) for a favorable response to the request. The most commonly mentioned *votum* is the official entreaty for the health and safety of the emperor (*salus principis*).[23] "Since public welfare had come to depend so much on the well-being of the ruler, it was now the principal object of public religion to ensure divine support for him and his family."[24]

---

[20] See 30.3 (the Egyptians pray in vain for relief from the drought), 31.4 (sailors pray for a shortened journey), 44.1 (Pliny remembers Trajan praying for relief from evil emperors), 74.4 (pray that gods will love senators as much as Trajan does), and 94.1: "You (Jupiter Optimus Maximus) heard the things which we prayed (*precabamur*) under a bad *princeps*, now hear the things which we desire (*optamus*) on behalf of one very dissimilar."

[21] Cf. S. R. F. Price ("Gods and Emperors: The Greek Language of the Roman Imperial Cult," *JHS* 104 [1984] 91) who asserts that "personal prayers were made to the emperor, both living and dead."

[22] In the letters Pliny does use *votum* for a request directed to the emperor (*Ep.* 10.4.2). This letter was probably written prior to the *Panegyricus* (Sherwin-White, *Letters*, 563).

[23] *Pan.* 23.5, 67.3–4, 68.1, 94.2. This ritual often involved offering incense or wine, or sacrificing animals to the gods (*Pan.* 23.5). Images of *salus* and *vota* abound on Trajan's coinage, and are discussed in Chapter Four below. The *Res Gestae* (2.9) mentions a senatorial decree that sacrifices should be made for Augustus's well-being (*valetudine*) by the consuls and priests (these vows took the form of quadriennial games). In the *Res Gestae*, Augustus also reports that all citizens, both as individuals and as cities, joined together to make continued sacrifice for his health at all the couches of the gods (2.9). An inscription found in the Asklepion on the south slope of the Akropolis in Athens (*IG* II 2, 3181) petitions Asklepios and Hygeia for the good health of Tiberius Caesar, son of the god Augustus; see E. Vanderpool, "Athens Honors the Emperor Tiberius," *Hesperia* 28 (1959) 86–90. The concern for the emperor's health is closely connected with the general well-being of the empire, and the continuation of the reign. In this way the sentiment is similar to the expression, "Long live the king!"

[24] Liebeschuetz, *Continuity and Change*, 198.

A *votum* for the *salus principis* was made annually on the anniversary of the emperor's accession (*Pan.* 67.3 – 4: 92.5; *Ep.* 10.52, cf. 10.35; 102), but one could also be made at other times.[25] For instance, the crowds pray in unison for Trajan's *salus* when he returns to the city as emperor for the first time (*Pan.* 23.5).[26] Pliny also expounds on the idea that Trajan has added a further request to the standard prayer. He reports that Trajan included the condition that he should be kept safe by the gods only to the extent that he preserves the safety of the state (*Pan.* 67.6 – 68.1). While Trajan may have made such a statement early in his reign, it is doubtful that he meant it to be the firm standard which Pliny makes of it. Not surprisingly, there is no evidence of such a condition in any of Pliny's letters mentioning prayers on the emperor's behalf (*Ep.* 10.1; 14; 35; 88; 100; 102).

Pliny uses prayers on Trajan's behalf as an argument for receiving the position of priest: "So that by the right of priesthood I will be able to pray publically to the gods for you, which I now do as private devotion" (*Ep.* 10.13). Pliny did become a priest (*Ep.* 4.8, *CIL* 5. 5667), but whether his promise to pray for Trajan had anything to do with his appointment is impossible to know.

The act of praying to the gods is mentioned frequently in the *Panegyricus*. In some cases, it occurs in a situation of ritual prayer, while at other times Pliny mentions hopes and wishes which are directed to the gods without a set form but not without some hope for fulfillment.[27] Most of the requests that Pliny makes are concerned with Trajan's safety, and with the continuation of what Pliny perceives to be his enlightened rule. One can assume that Pliny remembers similar prayers offered under previous emperors which did not prove to be effective.[28] I believe that in the *Panegyricus*, Pliny is seeking the continued support and favor of Trajan, and he is using many different arguments to do so. He does not depend upon the gods alone to maintain Trajan's course, but he is willing to make the gods his allies in this task.

[25] Prayers were offered on the emperor's birthday (*Ep.* 10.88, cf. 10.17b.2), and at the time of a triumph (*Ep.* 10.14).

[26] Pliny sends a petition to Trajan from the people of Nicaea and tells the emperor that the senders charged him by his [Trajan's] immortality and safety (*Ep.* 10.83).

[27] In *Pan.* 5.1, Pliny refers to Trajan as the gods' answer to prayer (*exorata*). Elsewhere Pliny displays some confidence that the gods are in control and can be invoked. He refers to a wife's prayer for her sick husband (*Ep.* 1.22.9), and the fact that the doctors have a good prognosis for a friend (1.22.11), but it remains for the gods to confirm (*deus adnuat*). And Pliny expresses gratitude to the gods that his wife did not die during a miscarriage (8.10 – 11).

[28] The horrors of Domitian's reign stand as a constant reminder of this fact.

This city devoted to religion, and always deserving of the indulgence of the gods because of its loyalty, thinks it is able to add nothing more joyful to itself, except that the gods should imitate Caesar. (*Pan.* 74.5)

Sacrifice

Although Pliny frequently mentions *vota* which must have involved some type of sacrifice, he only refers to a specific act of sacrifice when describing Trajan's return to Rome in 99 CE. There, Pliny cites the enthusiasm of the people of Rome who set up so many altars that there were not enough victims to go around (*Pan.* 23.5). Unfortunately, he does not elaborate on the ceremonies except for mentioning that all *vota* were for Trajan's well-being. There is no indication of offerings made to Trajan as if to a god. Price identifies these two types of sacrifices (either "on behalf of" the emperor, or "to" the emperor), and argues that in the case of evidence for provincial imperial cult the distinction is sometimes intentionally blurred.[29]

Pliny is determined to avoid any such confusion, and in his comments he encourages Trajan to do the same. Pliny criticizes Domitian's attempts to be worshipped as a god, "being invoked on quite venerable altars with large numbers of victims" (*Pan.* 52.1), and deplores the fact that during Domitian's reign, large numbers of animals on the way to be sacrificed at the *Capitolinum* were diverted and sacrificed to the statue of Domitian in the Forum.[30] The fate of Domitian's golden statues serves as just punishment for his excesses, and as a graphic reminder to Trajan. Pliny describes the dismembered and melted images as being an acceptable sacrifice (*litaverunt*) for the public celebration following the tyrant's death (*Pan.* 52.4).[31] The importance of offering sacrifice on behalf of the emperor, but not to the emperor, is clearly stated.[32]

As mentioned above, Shochat has argued that the paucity of sacrificial imagery in the *Panegyricus* is part of a major shift in Roman religion under Trajan in which morality superceded the traditional importance of sacrifice.[33]

---

[29] Price, "Between Man and God: Sacrifice in the Roman Imperial Cult," *JRS* 70 (1980) 30.

[30] "Indeed in past times, enormous herds of victims were intercepted on their way to the Capitolinum, and large parts of them were forced to be diverted from their path, because to honor the statue of that atrocious master, as much the blood of victims had to flow, as exactly the amount of human blood which he had shed" (*Pan.* 52.7).

[31] Pliny uses sacrificial imagery elsewhere to chastize opponents. *Pan.* 34.4 describes how Trajan brought to justice those who had been informers under Domitian, "just as victims for the expiation of public anxiety." In *Pan.* 82.2, Domitian is mocked for being so afraid to travel by boat that "he was towed like some expiatory sacrifice."

[32] These passages also demonstrates that as much as Pliny urged Trajan to eschew excessive worship, sacrifices to the living emperor must have taken place in Rome under Domitian.

[33] Shochat, "Change in Roman Religion," 318–19.

The main problem with this view is the lack of any evidence outside of the *Panegyricus* for such a radical change. Although there are very few references to sacrifice in Pliny's letters, there is no indication there of decreased importance of sacrificial ritual. On the contrary, Pliny rejoices at the renewal of sacrificial activity following his measures against the Christians (*Ep.* 10.96.10), and goes to great expense to enlarge a temple of Ceres located on his property in light of the great crowd that gathers there for an annual festival (9.39), and to build a temple in Tifernum (3.4; 4.1; 10.8). Proper sacrifice at the appropriate time is expected and commended, but there is no tolerance for shifting the recipient of the sacrifice from the gods to the emperor.

Priesthoods

One of the clearest indicators of the intricate connection between government and religion in the Roman Empire is the way in which priesthoods had long been political appointments. The writings of Pliny provide eloquent confirmation of this phenomenon. In the *Panegyricus* Pliny applauds Trajan for rewarding good subjects with honors, including priesthoods (*Pan.* 44.7), and he also appreciates the diminished authority of imperial freedmen who formerly had de facto power to appoint priests (Pan. 88.1). The *Epistulae* bear witness to Pliny's own efforts to obtain a coveted priestly position for himself.[34] Accolades for the deceased Verginius Rufus include his regular but apparently unsuccessful recommendations of Pliny for a priesthood (*sacerdotium* [*Ep.* 2.1.9]).[35] Later, Pliny takes matters into his own hands when he writes directly to Trajan asking to be appointed either to the College of Augurs, who determined if the omens were favorable for various state actions, or to the *septemvirate*, which had control of the sacrificial feasts in the city. As mentioned above, Pliny cites increased ability to pray for Trajan as justification for his request. His appeal was successful, and in a letter dated to 103, Pliny expresses thanks to Maturus Arrianus for congratulating him on his appointment to the augurate (*Ep.* 4.8).[36]

---

[34] Seneca lists appointment to priesthoods (a single one is not enough) as one of the higher honors conferred by the *princeps* (*De ira* 3.31.2); cited in Millar, *Emperor*, 209, 356.

[35] Verginius, who died during Nerva's reign, was himself a priest, since Pliny describes "that day when the priests were accustomed to nominate those who they judged to be most worthy of the priesthood" (*Ep.* 2.1.9). Talbert (*Senate*, 345–46) wonders whether the nomination process by the priests led to a vote in the Senate, or they if it served only as a recommendation to the emperor.

[36] For the date of Pliny's augurate, see Sherwin-White, *Letters*, 79–80. In *Ep.* 4.8 Pliny tells Maturus Arrianus that he is taking the position of Julius Frontinus "who on the day of nomination during the past years has regularly nominated me for the priesthood." Apparently Pliny had the support of both Julius and Verginius, perhaps for different priesthoods. An interesting com-

As an augur, Pliny would have been involved in reading omens to insure favorable conditions for the conduct of state business. On several occasions in the *Panegyricus*, Pliny refers to omens. While praising Trajan for his swift and informal journey to the *curia* ("Senate house"), he mentions that "the one stop was at his threshold to consult the omens and to show respect for the admonition of the divine will" (*Pan.* 76.7). In addition, Pliny describes a procession "among favorable omens and competing vows" when listing the honors he and Cornutus Tertullus shared in being consuls during the same year as Trajan (*Pan.* 92.5). He also cites an unsolicited omen of Jupiter Optimus Maximus to explain the crowd's spontaneous cry when Trajan mounted the Capitolium (*Pan.* 5.3). This last sign, interpreted by Pliny as an indication that Trajan was destined to become emperor, is contrasted with the way in which previous emperors were designated: "For other *principes* were announced to those who consulted [the gods] by the abundant flow of blood from victims or by the flying of birds on the left" (*Pan.* 5.3). Although this statement is not meant as a criticism of the practice of consulting omens, it is an example of Pliny's extending the imagery of ritual practice to describe what he hopes will be a new form of the the the relationship between Trajan and the Senate and People of Rome.[37]

One additional aspect of priesthoods concerns the emperor as *Pontifex Maximus*. In this traditional role, which had been held by the *princeps* since Augustus, Trajan was the leader of one of the four major priestly colleges in Rome.[38] Latte describes the *Pontifices* as "politically the most important of the priestly colleges."[39] This is not surprising since the members of this group were responsible for "the solution of points of sacred law, relating to rituals, temples or sacred places."[40] In one letter (*Ep.* 10.68), Pliny, addressing Trajan in his role as *Pontifex Maximus*, inquires about granting permission to persons wishing to move the remains of deceased relatives.[41] In the

---

parison of Julius and Verginius and their approaches to fame is found in *Ep.* 9.19.

[37] Pliny is critical of some forms of consultation of omens; see the harsh words for Regulus who consulted *haruspices* ("soothsayers") on the outcome of his trials (Ep. 6.2.2). Pliny calls this action *superstitio*, but says it shows his dedication to his profession; cf. *Ep.* 2.20.5 and 13 on other consultations by Regulus. Pliny also mentions that he was told by a *haruspicium* to rebuild a temple of Ceres on his property near Tifernum.

[38] From Augustus on, the emperor was a member of all four colleges (Talbert, *Senate*, 345). The *augurate* and *septemviri epulonum* are mentioned above. The fourth was the *quindecimviri sacris faciundis* which was responsible for the Sibylline oracles, the *ludi saeculares* ("the sacred games"), and the regulation of foreign cults in Rome. See Latte, *Römische Religionsgeschichte* (Munich: Beck, 1960) 297–98; and Millar, *Emperor*, 357–59.

[39] Latte, *Römische Religionsgeschichte*, 400.

[40] Millar, *Emperor*, 359.

[41] Trajan responds that the rulings of the pontificate should not necessarily be applied to the provinces, and that Pliny himself should make decisions based on individual situations. In

Panegyricus, Pliny mentions the post of *Pontifex Maximus* casually several times as part of his praise of Trajan's modesty,[42] but he discusses priestly functions only once, and this in ambiguous terms. While arguing that Trajan should take on his third consulate, Pliny urges Trajan: "Assent to their desires, Caesar, and for whom you are accustomed to stand before the gods, fulfill their wishes which you yourself are able to fulfill" (*Pan.* 78.5). Pliny portrays Trajan as an intermediary between the gods and the senators who are beseeching him. "Standing before the gods" must be an allusion to one of Trajan's priestly roles, most likely that of *Pontifex Maximus*. Pliny creates a parallelism between the role of the emperor as a mediator who regularly intercedes with the gods for the people, and Trajan's ability to grant this particular request himself. Although Pliny carefully acknowledges the traditional ritual role of the *princeps*, he uses that role to persuade Trajan to honor the earthly request of the Senate that he take up his consulship.

Pliny Discusses the Gods: Deified Emperors

An inscription found in the village of Fecchio near Pliny's hometown of Comum attests that Pliny served as *Flamen Divi Titi Augusti* ("priest of the god Titus Augustus").[43] This is the only attestation that Pliny held this office

---

another case, although Pliny does not address him as *Pontifex Maximus*, Trajan makes a similar decision about relocating a temple to the Magna Mater in Nicomedia (*Ep.* 10.49).

[42] He asserts that Trajan's modesty in standing to take the consular oath is remarkable for one who is Caesar, Augustus, and *Pontifex Maximus* (*Pan.* 64.2), and he maintains that Trajan's wife Plotina is a suitable mate for the *Pontifex Maximus* (*Pan.* 83.5). Pliny attributes Trajan's Pontifex Maximus status to Jupiter: "You chose a son for him [Nerva imperator], a parent for us, and a Pontifex Maximus for yourself" (*Pan.* 94.4).

[43] C.I.L. 5. 5667:

    C· PLINI[O L·F·]
    OUF· CAEC[ILIO]
    SECUNDO· [C]OS·
    AUGUR· CUR· ALV·TIB·
    E[T RI]P· ET CLOAC· URB·
    P[RAEF· A]ER· SAT· PRAEF·
    AER· MIL·[. . .]Q· IMP·
    SEVIR· EQ· R· TR· M[I]L·
    LEG· III GALL· X·VIRO
    STL· IUD· FL· DIVI· T· AUG·
    VERCELLENS[ES]·

To Gaius Plinius Caecilius Secundus, son of
Lucius of the tribe of Oufentina, consul,
augur, curator of the bed and the banks of the
Tiber, and the sewers of Rome, overseer of

which was probably a local priesthood in Comum.[44] Worship of deceased emperors, however, was a widespread and important part of Roman religious ritual.[45] Instead of journeying to the underworld and being among the shades of the dead as was the lot of other human beings, good emperors were thought to rise up to the stars and join the gods of heaven.[46] The idea of the ascent of the good ruler was foreshadowed in the *Somnium Scipionis* ("the dream of Scipio") by Cicero (*Rep.* 6.16). Cicero resisted the concept, however, when it was first actualized by the heirs of Julius Caesar. Octavian claimed that a comet which appeared after Caesar's death was proof that he had ascended to the heavens,[47] and based on this evidence, the Senate voted to include Caesar among the gods. The funeral and deification of Caesar became a model that was to be followed with some variation until the fourth century CE.

Price states that from Augustus to Constantine "thirty-six of the sixty emperors . . . and twenty-seven members of their families were apotheosised and received the title of *divus* ("divine")."[48] Given the importance of the cult, Pliny's participation in it as attested in the inscription from Vercellae is to be expected,[49] as is the favorable attitude that Pliny expresses toward the deification of deceased emperors in the *Panegyricus*. Pliny uses similar astral imagery in describing Nerva "whom the gods have claimed for their heaven" (*Pan.* 10.4).[50] When addressing both *divus Nerva* and Trajan's natural father who was also deceased, Pliny proclaims to the latter: "For you

---

the Treasury of Saturn, overseer of the Treasury

of the military . . . quaestor of the Emperor,

official of the Roman knights, military

tribune of the Third Gallic Legion, on

the commission of ten for adjudicating disputes,

priest of the god Titus Augustus,

dedicated by the citizens of Vercellae.

[44] Radice, *Pliny*, 553.

[45] "It is normal Roman practice to deify emperors who die leaving behind children to succeed them. The name they give to this ceremony is apotheosis" (Herodian 4.2); cited by Price, "Noble Funerals to Divine Cults," 56.

[46] Manilius 1.799–804. Cited by Price, "Noble Funerals to Divine Cults," 76–77. For Manilius, the divinized emperors were "peers of the gods," but not fully gods. He placed the emperors in an astral level just short of the heavenly plateau of the gods.

[47] *Philippic* 1.13; 2.110.

[48] Price, "Noble Funerals to Divine Cult," 57.

[49] If the priesthood was held in Comum, his participation was probably in name only, since his responsibilities in Rome made it very difficult for him to travel; see *Ep.* 10.8 and 9; 3.4; 4.1.1–2.

[50] The reading *di ide<o>* is preferred by Schuester (*C. Plini Caecili Secundi*, 377) and Radice (*Pliny*, 2. 346). The reading of *dii de* is found in the oldest MS (M), and would yield a reading "whom the gods from heaven claimed." Either reading would support my point here.

also, if not the stars, nevertheless have obtained a seat/throne near to the stars'' (*Pan.* 89.2).[51] Further Pliny tells the two father figures, "the virtue of your son gave one of you a triumph, and the other heaven" (*Pan.* 89.3). In both the *Panegyricus* and the letters, *divus* is one of the titles which Pliny uses to refer to Nerva and others of Trajan's predecessors. Pliny describes Nerva's deification as involving temples, altars, couches, and priests (*Pan.* 11.1, 3).

In all these ways, Pliny accepts and embraces the deification of deceased emperors. As usual, however, Pliny's senatorial perspective in the *Panegyricus* leads him to point out the past excesses of the principate, and to caution Trajan lest they be repeated. Pliny reminds Trajan that in the past, emperors had deified their predecessors for the wrong reasons.

> Tiberius dedicated Augustus to heaven, only to introduce the crime of high treason; Nero deified Claudius only to make him a laughing stock; Titus deified Vespasian, and Domitian deified Titus, but only so that one would appear to be the son of a god, and the other the brother of a god. (*Pan.* 11.1)

Pliny contends that, unlike some of his predecessors, Trajan deifies Nerva without any ulterior motives: "You introduced your father to the stars not to put fear into your subjects, not as an insult to the gods, not for your own honor, but because you believe that he is a god" (*Pan.* 11.2).

Pliny accomplishes several things by stating that Trajan deified Nerva *quia deum credis*. In the first place, he affirms against ancient and modern critics the belief that the deceased emperor had in truth become a god. Elias Bickerman, following Minucius Felix (*Oct.* 21), contends that "the emperors were consecrated not because of the belief in their divinity, but in honor of power they had exercised."[52] On the contrary, Pliny states that there was a genuine belief in *divus Nerva*, and he praises Trajan because he was motivated to recognize Nerva's divinity by this belief, and not by desires similar to those that had motivated Tiberius and his other predecessors.

Pliny's emphasis on this genuine belief does not mean that he ignored the effects that Nerva's deification would have had on power relationships in Rome. It is not possible to separate spheres of political and religious

---

[51] An interesting division of the heavenly spheres, especially in light of the distinctions made by Manilius. On Trajan's earthly father see Durry, *Panégyrique*, 233–34. In spite of the fact that Pliny speaks of Trajan's father as deceased in 100 CE, Waters ("Traianus Domitiani Continuator," 397–98) argues that he did not die until 113 CE when coins to *Divus Traianus Pater* appear (see Chapter Four below). Mattingly (*BMC*, 3. lxxxi) refutes this idea as it was suggested by Strack, *Untersuchungen*, 199–202.

[52] Bickerman, "*Consecratio*," in Willem den Boer, ed., *Le culte des souverains dans l'Empire romain* 1–37 (Geneva: Fondation Hardt, 1972) 10.

influence in ancient society. Pliny knew that Trajan's belief in Nerva's deification had important implications for the way in which Trajan related to the Senate. This is to be expected since from the time of Augustus, senatorial recognition of the new *divus* had been an essential part of the process of deification.[53] Price describes how the ceremony of apotheosis combined funerary traditions of the Roman nobility with traditional worship of the gods.[54] Because the Senate was empowered to hear the testimony of witnesses who had seen the deceased emperor ascending, and to vote on official recognition of the new *divus*, the whole process entailed a mutually acceptable sharing of power.[55] The Senate refused Claudius's request for deification of Tiberius, and Antoninus Pius (138–161 CE) had to push the senate to recognize the consecration of Hadrian.[56]

Pliny's comments on deified emperors reflect a concern to maintain the balance of power found in the deification process. Given the imbalance of

[53] Bickerman ("Consecratio," 13) emphasizes that "the vote of the Senate was declarative and not constitutive." The Senate's vote was a recognition of the fact that the deceased emperor had become a god. One might also see deification of the deceased emperor as the ultimate vindication of Berger's "microcosm/macrocosm understanding of the relationship between society and cosmos" (Peter Berger, *The Sacred Canopy: Elements of a Sociological Theory of Religion* [Garden City, NY: Doubleday, 1967] 34–35). The emperor who had held the parallel function of the gods while part of the microcosm/earth, now departs from the earth and joins the gods in the macrocosm/heaven.

[54] Price, "Noble Funerals to Divine Cult," 57–58, 72–73.

[55] In the context of what he sees to be a decline in the Senate's authority, Price (ibid., 91) asserts that the vote of recognition and the ceremony of apotheosis "granted the senate symbolic supremacy over both populace and emperor." In Berger's terms the ritual ceremony was also an essential "reminder" that the social structure on earth was legitimated by a parallel structure in heaven (Berger, *Sacred Canopy*, 38–40).

[56] "The senate wanted to make his acts invalid, nor would he have been called divus had not Antoninus insisted" (*SHA* Hadrian 27.2). Cf. *SHA Antoninus Pius* 2.5, 5.1. Dio reports that it was only when the Senate realized that if they annulled Hadrian's acts, Antoninus would no longer be his adopted heir that they consented to honor Hadrian (70.1.2–3, cf. 69.23.2–3). Dio also contends that the Senate resisted Trajan's deification without success (69.2.5). The fact that an emperor could achieve his predecessor's deification against strong opposition shows that in the second century, the Senate's influence in this process had become secondary to the emperor's. Price ("Noble Funerals to Divine Cult," 91–92) maintains that in the course of the second and third centuries, whatever power the senate had had in the consecration process became inconsequential. He argues that it was the traditional practice that the Senate would meet after the funeral to hear evidence of the emperor's ascent (usually choreographed into the funeral service). Upon hearing satisfactory evidence, the Senate would then vote cult to the deceased emperor. When the Senate's vote is shifted to a time prior to the funeral service, Price (p. 92) sees the Senate's role reduced to a "political formality." Millar (*Emperor*, 350–54) discusses "the evolution of the complex, greatly changed, but still significant relations of senate and emperor." Talbert (*Senate*, 488–91) sees a diminishment of the Senate's role during the reign of Commodus.

power and disregard for traditional order which had marked Domitian's reign, Pliny, speaking from his senatorial perspective, wanted to remind Trajan that believing in *divus Nerva* also meant believing in the Senate's role in the consecration. This connection is not stated overtly in the *Panegyricus*, but I think it can be seen in the document in two ways. First, Trajan's belief that Nerva was a god constitutes implicit proof that the Senate acted wisely and properly in deifying him. Secondly, in talking about other deceased emperors, Pliny emphasizes the virtuous rule which led to their deification by the Senate. The implications for Trajan are obvious. It was necessary to continue in the virtuous character of his reign in order to ensure that he too eventually would be deified. Trajan might be motivated to have greater regard for the Senate during his lifetime, if he fully appreciated the importance of their support after his death.

Price comes to a similar conclusion in talking about Seneca's[57] *Apocolocyntosis* in which the deification of Claudius is questioned and overturned, not by earthly critics, but by the gods themselves.[58] The picture of a heavenly Senate arguing over the fate of Claudius makes it clear that Seneca was operating with a Stoic understanding that earthly reality was parallel to the heavenly reality.[59] The deliberations of the heavenly Senate were intended to show that any emperor who does not rule with a virtuous attitude will ultimately forego his chance to dwell with the gods in heaven, and instead will join the rest of humanity in the underworld.[60] A similar opinion can also be detected in the *Panegyricus*. When Pliny talks about divinized emperors, he emphasizes the positive acts that led to their deification, and he makes it clear that if Trajan continues to rule in a virtuous way, he too can follow in the same path.[61]

While discussing Trajan's punishment of those who had served as inform-

---

[57] F. R. D. Goodyear ("Prose Satire," in Kenney, *Latin Literature*, 633–34) points out that, although tradition and circumstantial evidence tie Seneca to the work, it could also have been written by someone else.

[58] Price, "Noble Funerals to Divine Cult," 87–89.

[59] This is another example of Berger's microcosm/macrocosm understanding of the religious legitimation of societal order (*Sacred Canopy*, 34–35).

[60] Price ("Noble Funerals to Divine Cult," 89) concludes his discussion of the *Apocolocyntosis* by saying that Seneca's argument expresses the opinion "that virtue alone entitled the emperor to a place in heaven." Price furthers his case by quoting from *De Clementia*, where Seneca attempts to influence Nero to be a just and wise ruler. Price does not say so explicitly, but I would argue that in the *Apocolocyntosis* Seneca does not care about the fate of the departed Claudius, but rather about the future under the present emperor. In the *Apocolocyntosis* he gives Nero the same message as in *De Clementia* , but he does so within a different literary genre.

[61] "No kind of expenditure is more fitting for a *princeps* destined for immortality as what is disbursed for posterity" (*Pan.* 26.4).

ers under Domitian (*Pan.* 34 – 36), Pliny mentions that *divus Titus* had enacted measures aimed at stopping informers (*Pan.* 35.4).[62] The results of Titus's efforts are clearly stated: "And because of this he was made equal to the gods," as are the prospects for Trajan, given his similar actions. "But at some future time, how much more will you be worthy of heaven, who has added many things to those on account of which we made that man god."[63] Pliny was very pleased that Trajan had acted against those who had devastated the Senate under Domitian. Introducing the parallel to *divus Titus* allowed Pliny to affirm what Trajan had done by a subtle reminder of the heavenly rewards for a virtuous reign.[64] The message to Trajan is clear: "Someday (if you continue to rule wisely and well) you will be even more deserving of heaven than Titus!"

In the case of *Divus Nerva*, Pliny's argument is more complicated. Since both Nerva and Trajan have benefitted from the other's actions, Pliny introduces mutuality into the relationship by giving Trajan credit for establishing Nerva as a god (*Pan.* 11) and giving Nerva credit for establishing Trajan as an *imperator* (*Pan.* 23.4). For the sake of Pliny's argument, the most important act of Nerva's short reign was the adoption of Trajan. It was so important that the gods decided to take Nerva to heaven shortly after the adoption so that "he should not do any mortal thing after this godly and immortal act" (*Pan.* 10.5).[65] Therefore while Nerva's act opened the door for Trajan's accession, it also led to Nerva's ascension, and was, from Pliny's perspective, an advantage for Nerva.[66] In the same way, Pliny viewed Trajan's proper conduct as a benefit for his predecessor, since it provided ample proof of Nerva's divinity.

> And indeed it is right that you honor this one with altars and couches and a priest; nothing else, however, produces and confirms his divinity than that you yourself are such. Certainly for a *princeps* who dies having selected his successor, the one best proof of divinity is a good successor. (*Pan.* 11.3)

[62] Suetonius *Divus Titus* 8.5.

[63] *Pan.* 35.4. Pliny adds that Nerva had also made additions to Titus's legislation (cf. Dio 68.1.2), making Trajan's accomplishments all the more remarkable.

[64] The fact that Pliny mentions actions of both Titus and Trajan that provided protection for senators against informers fits in with his senatorial perspective.

[65] The adoption is discussed at length in *Pan.* 7.4 – 8.6. To stress the importance of the adoption, Pliny predicts that posterity will wonder whether Nerva had done this great deed before or after he became a god (*Pan.* 10.5). Pliny's comment might reflect contemporary debate over whether previous rulers (e.g., Julius Caesar) received divine honors before or after death; see Price, "Noble Funerals to Divine Cult," 71 – 73.

[66] Nerva might have preferred to retire safely (*asphalōs idioteusai*) as suggested by Dio 68.3.1.

As he does so often, Pliny affirms the traditional ritual action of Trajan (altars, couches, and a priest) but then goes beyond it with an additional message. In this case Trajan is instructed that while Nerva's good deeds led to his deification, Trajan himself confirms his predecessor's divine status.

This mutual benefit is also demonstrated when Pliny reminds Trajan that, as he returned to the city as emperor and climbed the steps of the Capitoline temple: "Indeed you walked in the same footsteps which your father walked when he made known the vast secret of the gods" (*Pan.* 23.5). The secret, of course, was the adoption of Trajan, who should remember that it was by the efforts of his divine parent that he had come to such a glorious moment. Near the end of the speech, Pliny frames as a prayer his hope that the noble act of the adopting father would become a model for the adopted son. Pliny asks Jupiter Optimus Maximus to grant Trajan a natural heir, or, failing that, to direct his choice of an adopted successor (*Pan.* 94.5).[67]

Pliny Discusses the Relationship between the Living Emperor and the Gods

Having examined some of the language and ritual that Pliny used to discuss the gods and the divinized emperors, I shall now turn to Pliny's portrayal of the relationship between the living emperor and the gods. This task is complicated by the fact that Pliny did not have a fixed conception of how to describe this relationship, and that he was struggling to define such an understanding. Pliny realized that the perception of the Emperor's relationship with the gods would have a direct impact upon the relationships of power between the emperor and the rest of society. Pliny's main concern was with the relationship between the emperor and the Senate[68] but he discussed other groups especially as their relationships with the emperor affected the Senate's relationship with the emperor.

Relationships between Groups in Society

Pliny expounded on the danger of allowing imperial freedmen too much power. "While most *principes* were masters over their subjects, they were

---

[67] Trajan did not have a child, and ironically, after he died, a scandal arose over whether or not Hadrian was legally adopted (*SHA Hadrian*, 4.8–10). Dio reports that news of Trajan's death was delayed for several days until Hadrian's "adoption" was announced (69.1.1–4). Suetonius (*Divus Claudius*, 45) reports similar intrigue taking place after the death of Claudius.

[68] When Pliny praises Trajan for not confiscating land from people who had splendid houses (*pulcherrimas aedes*), and in fact for selling much of the land in his possession (*Pan.* 50), he is talking about a benefit that could have been realized only by the small minority of people who could afford luxurious real estate.

also slaves of their freedmen" (*Pan.* 88.1 – 3). The growth of the power of freedmen had no doubt affected the Senate's influence, and its relationship with the emperor.[69] Pliny was grateful that Trajan seemed to be rectifiying this aberration of the established social order.[70] Trajan's distaste for using charges of *maiestas* ("treason") as a weapon against political enemies, also wins approval from Pliny.[71] By doing this, previous emperors, especially Domitian, had opened up the possibility for slaves to accuse their masters of this charge. Now that this threat was eliminated; Trajan had corrected another dangerous imbalance in the social order.

> Trust has been restored to friends, loyalty to freedmen, and submission to slaves, who now respect and obey and retain their masters. Indeed now our servants are no longer friends of the *princeps*, but we are. Nor does the father of the country believe himself to be more dear to slaves of others than to his own citizens. (*Pan.* 42.2 – 3)[72]

Having endured an era of confused social relations in which the roles of slave and master were transposed (*Pan.* 85.2), Pliny is grateful to Trajan for restoring the proper social order.[73] Pliny's description of the restored social order was characterized by the return of the senators to the position of *principis amici* ("friends of the emperor").[74]

---

[69] Priesthoods, prefectures, and consulships were obtained through, or even from the emperor's freedmen (*Pan.* 88.1). Cf. *Ep.* 8.6 (a lengthy denunciation of the freedman Pallas, who had received honors from the emperor Tiberius and the Senate); and 7.29 (criticism of a monument to Pallas on the road to Tibur). Cf. Tacitus *Ann.* 12.60.

[70] Millar (*Emperor*, 80) posits that the reign of Trajan marked the end of freedmen and other members of the imperial *familia* ("household") having excessive influence with the emperor. Cf. *Ep.* 10.84, where Trajan tells Pliny to consult with the procurators in Nicea, one of whom is his freedman; and *Ep.* 10.85, where Pliny writes a letter of recommendation for one of Trajan's freedmen with whom he had worked.

[71] Pliny calls *maiestas* the only way of incriminating a person who had committed no crime (*Pan.* 42.1). Trajan dismissses without discussion what he interprets to be a charge of *maiestas* against Dio Chrysostom (Pliny *Ep.* 10.81), and indicates that this is his general policy. Cf. Dio Cassius 68.2, on similar actions by Nerva.

[72] This passage has implications for the study of Christian admonitions from the same period in which slaves are ordered to obey their masters (e.g., Titus 2:9).

[73] One could also add the excessive affection which Domitian showed for his gladiators (*Pan.* 33), and their corresponding inflated status to the list of social inequities which Trajan had eliminated.

[74] Millar (*Emperor*, 110 – 22) describes the *amici* of the emperor as a circle of advisors and friends which lacked official definition, but meant the possibility of both benefaction and harm for the *amicus*, depending on the emperor's "character or passing whim" (p. 112). According to Millar, "Pliny was most certainly an *amicus* of the emperor, but equally certainly not an intimate friend in our sense" (p. 114). Radice (*Pliny*, 2. 522) emphasizes the description of Trajan's

Pliny also applauds Trajan's gifts to poor children because such benefactions increase the stability of the social order.[75] "In vain he cares for the nobles if he neglects the masses, like a head that has been cut (*desectum*)[76] from a body, and being unstable of balance is about to tip" (*Pan.* 26.6).[77] Pliny assumes that the system of mutually dependent classes in society is good, and must be maintained since it works for the benefit of the society as a whole. "For whoever partakes in whatever is shared by all, he himself has as little as or as much as everyone else" (*Pan.* 27.4).[78] Pliny sees Trajan as a unifying figure, reestablishing the proper relationship between the different groups of the society.

In describing Trajan's first return to Rome as emperor, Pliny narrates a scene which reflected this unifying function. The streets and rooftops were packed with people waiting to get a glimpse of the *princeps* "so the same delight was felt by all upon your arriving, because you were coming for all" (*Pan.* 22.5). In spite of the crowds, there was a definite order to this reception: Trajan greeted senators first, then ranking *equites* ("knights"), then his own clients, and finally the crowds of spectators (*Pan.* 23.1 – 2). Pliny commended Trajan for not surrounding himself with a group of *satellites* ("attendants"), but for moving freely among those of the senatorial and equestrian orders. The same kind of praise is directed to the inconspicuous presence of the military on that day. "For the soldiers differed in no way from the masses, with regard to style of dress, calmness, or orderliness" (*Pan.* 23.3). Pliny's description of Trajan's arrival reflects his vision of the the reign of Trajan in which all elements of society were being restored to their rightful places and levels of influence. In the case of the senators, that ideal place

restoration of *amicitia* ("friendship") in *Pan.* 85.2, and suggests that the reference alludes to the "precarious position of the *amici principis*."

[75] Trajan is also praised for adding 5000 new seats to the Circus Maximus, and for placing his own box at the same level as the seats of the *populus* (*Pan.* 51.4 – 5). Pliny makes it clear that Trajan's gifts are from his own wealth, not from funds confiscated from accused nobles as was the practice of Domitian (*Pan.* 27.3 – 4; see Millar [*Emperor*, 189 – 201] on "imperial wealth and public wealth"). The poor (*pauperes*) are said to have only one motivation for having children, and that is *bonus princeps* ("a good *princeps*"), as opposed to the wealthy who receive tax advantages based on their procreative success (*Pan.* 26.5; see also *Pan.* 22.3).

[76] *Desectum* is a later reading, but *defectum* found in the witnesses to the oldest manuscripts does not make as much sense. Schuster (*C. Plini Caecili Secundi*, 390) and Radice (*Pliny*, 380) opt for the first reading, while Durry (*Panégyrique*) prints *defectum*.

[77] The use of body imagery to describe a social system was very common in the Graeco-Roman world; it is adapted by Paul (1 Cor 12:12 – 27; Rom 12:3 – 8).

[78] Pliny is referring to the impoverishment of Trajan who had given from his wealth to help the poor. Mason Hammond ("Pliny the Younger's Views on Government," *HSCP* 49 [1938] 127) sees this perspective to be based on "the doctrine derived by Cicero from the Stoics, that all good men should cooperate for the public weal."

included a strong relationship with the *princeps*, free from the distractions of overly powerful imperial freedmen, untrustworthy slaves, "consecrated" gladiators, or an overzealous military.

Relationships between the Emperor and Society

In the *Panegyricus* Pliny argues for revival of what he considered to be the proper social order in Rome. As part of this order, he attempts to reaffirm for Trajan that the Senate and the emperor had a shared responsibility for ruling the Empire. In order to support his picture of the proper relationship between the Senate and the emperor, Pliny appeals to his vision of the proper relationship between the emperor and the gods.[79] Pliny knew that balance and mutuality were the keys to both relationships, but he also knew from experience how difficult that balance was to maintain. The reigns of the two previous emperors had graphically demonstrated the dangers of unbalanced power relationships. Domitian presented himself as a god during his lifetime, and thereby tried to utilize improper symbols of his authority. An elder statesman, Nerva reacted against Domitian's excesses and avoided any suggestion that he was equal to the gods.[80] It is possible that he separated himself too far from the legitimation of his rule that could have come from a proper relationship between the emperor and the gods, and that this lack of legitimation left him unable to govern alone.[81] In attempting to rule while presenting an unbalanced relationship between themselves and the gods, both Nerva and Domitian created an unbalanced relationship between themselves and their subjects. Domitian had no accountability, Nerva had no legitimation, and both of their reigns ended in failure.[82]

As Pliny was writing the *Panegyricus* in 100 CE, he must have realized how important it was for Trajan to present a proper image of the relationship between the emperor and the gods, for he was very scrupulous in arguing against either of the extreme relationships described above. Pliny wanted Trajan to understand that, as a living emperor, he could not allow any suggestion that he was a god. At the same time, he wanted Trajan to realize that in

---

[79] For Berger's concept of "religious legitimation" see *Sacred Canopy*, 29–39.

[80] Dio (68.2.1) states that "he forbade the making of gold or silver statues in his honour."

[81] Berger (*Sacred Canopy*, 36) describes how the "religious legitimations, however, ground the socially defined reality of the institutions in the ultimate reality of the universe. . . . The institutions are thus given a semblance of inevitability, firmness and durability that is analogous to these qualities as ascribed to the gods themselves."

[82] Unlike Domitian, who was assassinated, Nerva died a peaceful death (Dio 68.4.2). Nevertheless, he was unable to withstand a coup attempt, and was forced to share his rule with Trajan.

his role as *princeps* he was uniquely connected with the gods in a relationship of mutual responsibility and accountability. Finally, as I have shown above, Pliny wanted Trajan to remember that if he followed the first two lessons and otherwise ruled in a virtuous way congenial to the Senate, his special relationship with the gods would be consummated after he had departed from the constraints of this world. In the remainder of this Chapter, I shall examine the first two lessons that Pliny tried to deliver: (1) "You are not a god!"; and (2) "Your relationship with the gods is unique." And I shall ask if a coherent picture of the relationship emerges from the document.

The Emperor Is Not a God!

In the *Panegyricus*, Pliny presents ample evidence that Trajan is a great man, but the emphasis in that phrase is on the word "man," as well as on the word "great." From the beginning of the speech Pliny presents this message with clarity and vigor.

> Never should we flatter him as a god or a divinity. We are speaking not of a tyrant but of a citizen, not of a master, but of a parent. He himself is one of us, and this is especially eminent and stands out, that he thinks he is one of us; no less though he presides over human beings, he remembers that he is a human being. (*Pan.* 2.3–4)

There can be no doubt that Pliny was concerned to make Trajan's humanity clear to all who would listen. There may have been a chance that Trajan would someday join the ranks of the gods, but that chance would be lost if he were to expect such honors prematurely. Domitian's insistence that he be worshipped as a god was of no use to him when *Poenea* ("Vengeance") swept through the halls of the palace and exacted the penalties for his crimes (*Pan.* 49.1). The reward for Domitian's evil ways was not deification, but death, and the dismembering of the golden statues depicting him as a god (*Pan.* 52.4). Pliny discusses the fate of Domitian with such relish that he is probably exaggerating both the emperor's crimes and their punishments, but in his enthusiasm he was also presenting a foil for the current emperor.

Trajan had acted nobly in setting up a cult to *divus Nerva*, but his acts were all the more meaningful since he himself did not demand such treatment.

> This claim means less when it is made by those who think themselves to be gods. (*Pan.* 11.3)

> Is there, therefore, a way that any kind of arrogance would come to you from your father's immortality? (*Pan.* 11.4)[83]

---

[83] Cf. *Pan.* 82.7.

Pliny's support for divine honors offered to deceased emperors and his aversion to similar treatment for the living emperor accords with the conventional scholarly understanding.

> Following the principle established by Augustus, and observed until the end of Roman religion, the provincials were free to worship a living emperor. In Roman religion he could become god only after his death.[84]

Three assumptions in this statement require further comment. First, I have already discussed the difficulty with proposing any ideology or policy that transcends the reign of more than one emperor, much less a principle that runs "from Augustus to the end of Roman religion."[85] Secondly, Price has challenged as "Christianizing" and "Romanocentric" the view that, in contrast to the modest restraint of the western Empire, people in the east engaged in non-Roman, overenthusiastic flattery of the emperor. Price demonstrates that the rituals involved in the imperial cult in Asia Minor were part of a complex "web of power" that should not be oversimplified.[86] Finally, one may also question the proposition that in Roman religion—by which Bickerman seems to mean religion in Rome—the emperor could not receive divine honors during his lifetime.[87] Pliny went out of his way to reinforce Trajan's moderation regarding divine honors, not because he was concerned about excessive honors offered in Athens, Ephesos, or Alexandria,[88] but because he had seen them offered in the city of Rome.

Since he had returned to the city as emperor, Trajan had refused to accept divine honors in Rome. In Pliny's eyes this was a great accomplishment because sacrifice to the living emperor as a god had taken place in the Roman Forum only a few years before Pliny delivered the *Panegyricus* (*Pan.* 52.7). For the modern reader such as Bickerman, this fact can be labeled as an aberration in the otherwise "normal" practice of Roman religion, and dismissed because of Domitian's madness. Pliny would have agreed with this assessment of Domitian's mental state;[89] whether or not the resultant sacrifice in the Forum was an aberration, for Pliny it was a reality that he had endured

---

[84] Bickerman, *"Consecratio,"* in Willem den Boer, ed., *Le culte des souverains dans l'Empire romain* 1–37 (Geneva: Fondation Hardt, 1972) 9–10.

[85] Ibid.

[86] Price, *Rituals and Power* , 17–18; idem, "Gods and Emperors: The Greek Language of the Roman Imperial Cult," *JHS* 104 (1984) 79.

[87] Cf. Duncan Fishwick, "The Development of Provincial Ruler Worship in the Western Roman Empire," ANRW (1978) 2/16.2, 1201–53; and idem, "AUGUSTUS DEUS and DEUS AUGUSTUS" in *Hommages à Martin Vermaseren* (Leiden: Brill, 1978) 1. 375–80.

[88] He does not mention imperial cult in the provinces.

[89] Pliny calls Domitian *demens* in *Pan.* 33.4.

too often. His description of "enormous herds of victims" being stopped and "great portions of them" being diverted indicates that this practice occurred more than once and on a grand scale (*Pan.* 52.7).

Pliny had probably been an observer, while Domitian's scandalous abuse of the divine ritual was going on in the Forum.[90] Without venturing into the realm of psychoanalysis, it is fair to say that Pliny knew first hand how powerful the imagery of the divine emperor could be.[91] He had seen and experienced the speed with which traditional beliefs and philosophical opinions about the absurdity of divine honors for human beings could evaporate under imperial pressure. Pliny was aware that even if restraint in accepting divine honors had been a principle of Roman religion under Augustus,[92] there was no guarantee that it would apply to the current emperor. The Panegyricus was written with the fervent hope that, at the beginning of his reign, Trajan's moderate tendencies could be encouraged,[93] and that those who had been pressured to give divine honors to Domitian could revert to praising the emperor as a human being: "Is it the divinity of our *princeps* or his humanity, his moderation, and his friendliness, that as love and joy have brought us, we are in the habit of celebrating?" (*Pan.* 2.7). Pliny underlines the point

[90] The fact that he was able to advance his career during Domitian's reign makes it likely that Pliny did not resist Domitian's policies overtly. Later he had to defend himself against charges of collaboration (*Pan.* 95.3–4).

[91] I shall avoid the question of Pliny's "true feelings" or "beliefs" here. He and his senatorial colleagues may have been convinced of the madness of Domitian's divine pretensions, but for a while at least, some of them must have been accomplices in those pretensions.

[92] Arnaldo Momigliano ("How the Roman Emperors became Gods," *American Scholar* [1986] 181–93; reprinted in idem, *On Pagans, Jews, and Christians* [Middletown, CT: Wesleyan University Press, 1987] 92–107) praises the clearheadedness of Caesar's successor: "Octavian was presenting himself as a restorer of the Roman republican traditions. There was a limit to the divinity of an alleged Republican leader. In Rome, therefore, he was satisfied with being the son of a god and being called Augustus, which was a borderline qualification between heaven and earth. Besides, he was a protégé of Apollo" (p. 99). In 13 BCE, the protégé of the sun god set up in the Campus Martius a huge sundial (*Horologium Solarium Augusti*), which cast a shadow onto a large inscribed area of the pavement below, indicating time of year and time of day. On the day of the equinox (the autumnal equinox was Augustus's birthday) the shadow followed a line down the center of the court, and moved directly up the front steps of the Ara Pacis (altar to Augustan peace). Thus the *Princeps* was connected with Apollo, as the Sun God led the celebration of the Augustan peace. E. Buchner (*Die Sonnenuhr des Augustus: Nachdruck aus RM 1976 und 1980 und Nachtrag über die Ausgrabung 1980/1981* [Kulturgeschichte der antiken Welt, Sonderband; Mainz: von Zabern, 1982]) has excavated portions of the pavement, and reconstructed the arrangement; see also idem, et al., *Augustus und die verlorenen Republik* (Mainz: von Zabern, 1988).

[93] Pliny recognizes that he is stressing Trajan's humanity, and he says confidently: "Indeed there is no danger that when I speak of his humanity he will think that I reproach him for haughtiness" (*Pan.* 3.4).

that under a new emperor, everything including praise should be different: "The difference of time should mean a difference in our speeches" (2.3). Pliny had learned from experience that once an emperor began to receive and to expect divine honors in his lifetime, he was not going to be limited by the confines of proper ritual observance (what Bickerman calls "principles of Roman religion."[94] In the *Panegyricus*, Pliny seeks to reinforce Trajan's reluctance to accept such honors.

Indications exist that Trajan, too, sensed the need to be moderate, and that he was severe in his avoidance of divine honors: "You do not allow, Caesar, thanks to be given with similar reverence to your genius as to the deity of Jupiter Optimus Maximus" (*Pan.* 52.6). Sacrifice to the *genius* of an emperor is usually said to be an acceptable form of offering in Rome,[95] but according to Pliny, Trajan insisted that honors to his genius should not resemble those offered to Jupiter. He seemed to want to separate himself even from the forms of divine honors which were permitted. This tendency to avoid allusions to divinity might also explain Trajan's refusal to accept the cognomen *Optimus* when it was offered by the Senate. To encourage Trajan's caution, Pliny emphasized the humanity of the living emperor, using pointed reminders throughout the *Panegyricus*. "Indeed the life of all is brief and fragile, as with other human beings, so with the *principes*, even those who perceive themselves to be gods" (*Pan.* 78.2).

In the next Chapter, I shall discuss the extent to which Pliny's message of caution is reflected in the course of Trajan's reign, but for now one piece of evidence should be mentioned. After the conclusion of the Dacian wars in 106 CE and Trajan's triumph in 107,[96] Pliny wrote to Caninius Rufus who planned to write a poetic history of the conflict. Pliny supported the idea, and joked that his friend should follow poetic convention and invoke the help of the gods in his work. Pliny also suggests that he should invoke "among the gods (*inter deos*), the one of whose deeds, acts and judgment you are telling" (*Ep.* 8.4.5). Pliny was dealing with his friend's inquiry on a humorous level, but given his insistence in the *Panegyricus* that Trajan should never be called a god (*Pan.* 2.3), it is striking that he would do so even in jest. It could be that nine years into the reign it was obvious that Trajan was committed to a cautious policy about divine honors, and therefore, Pliny felt comfortable joking about it. Sherwin-White chooses this perspective when he says that

[94] Bickerman, "Consecratio," 9–10.

[95] "On the Western side the cult of the ruler's *genius* became especially acceptable" (Momigliano, "How Roman Emperors Became Gods," 99). Momigliano continues, "I wish we really knew what a *genius* was, a sort of guardian angel."

[96] That the letter is to be dated after the second war is demonstrated by the reference to the death of the Dacian leader Decebalus (*Ep.* 8.4.2).

"the hailing of the emperor in verse as a deity had been a harmless convention."[97] On the other hand, the period immediately following the second Dacian war was in many ways the height of Trajan's power, as evidenced by the extensive building projects financed by the Dacian spoils. It is possible that Trajan had become less than cautious about divine honors, and that by the time this letter was written it was common to refer to the living emperor as *inter deos*. In this case Pliny's remarks could be read as a sarcastic response to these developments, or as a sign that he had overcome the anxiety he demonstrates in the *Panegyricus* about calling the emperor a god, and had become acclimated to the idea. These suggestions about later developments remain speculative, but in Chapter Four, closer examination of other portrayals of the relationship between Trajan and the gods will provide further evidence.

The Emperor's Relationship to the Gods Is Extraordinary

While commenting upon the process by which Trajan came to be adopted, Pliny suggests that, in making such an important choice, it was right for Nerva to extend the search beyond his own children:

> Would you not have looked completely through the population, and judge as the one closest to you, the one joined to you, the one whom you found most to resemble the gods? (*Pan.* 7.5)[98]

The idea that Trajan was selected to rule on the basis of his similarity to the gods seems to contrast with Pliny's emphasis on Trajan's humanity. I believe it makes sense, however, as part of Pliny's effort to persuade Trajan to see himself in a balanced power relationship with the gods and thereby with his subjects. Instead of separating Trajan from all divine connections, Pliny wanted to show that, as emperor, he was in an extraordinary and mutual relationship with the gods. Not surprisingly he also wanted the emperor to

---

[97] Sherwin-White, *Letters*, 452; he refers to Vergil *Georgics* 1.24; and Horace *Carm.* 3.5.2.

[98] This statement is ironic, since Nerva probably did not have much choice in whom he selected to rule with him and eventually to succeed him. Pliny prays elsewhere (*Pan.* 94.5) that Trajan will have a successor born of him and formed by him, "or if this is denied by fate," that he will select a successor worthy to be adopted in Jupiter's temple. Trajan did not have a child, and neither did Pliny, although he wanted one (*Ep.* 8.10, 11). In *Pan.* 7.4, Pliny criticizes previous emperors (Augustus and Tiberius) for allowing their wives to influence their choice of heirs. While Pliny's attitude toward women is generally negative, there is valuable information on women's roles in society (esp. imperial women) in his writings. Much of this is covered in Hildegard Temporini, *Die Frauen am Hofe Trajans: ein Beitrag zur Stellung der Augustae im Principat* (Berlin: De Gruyter, 1978).

undertake a similarly extraordinary and mutual relationship with the Senate. By means of this parallel Pliny attempted to legitimate his ideal social order, and he did this first by emphasizing Trajan's unique relationship with the gods.

Pliny explains that although Nerva received deification because of his crucial act of adopting Trajan, the gods were in fact responsible for Trajan coming to power. "Indeed the gods have claimed this glory for themselves. Theirs was the work, theirs the command. Nerva was just a servant" (*Pan.* 8.2).[99] Chapter one of the *Panegyricus* makes it clear that Trajan was "a gift of the gods" (*Pan.* 1.3). It was by none other than Jupiter, that Trajan "openly and publically was found and chosen" (*Pan.* 1.5).

Pliny maintains that even if there was a debate about the divine origin of rulers,[100] "it is clear, however, that our *princeps* is divinely constituted" (*Pan.* 1.4).[101] According to Pliny, Trajan's adoption was divinely ordained (*Pan.* 5.1), and this fact set Trajan apart from his predecessors. "Is it possible that nothing was to differ between the emperor whom human beings made, and the one whom the gods made?" (*Pan.* 5.2). Indeed, Pliny claims that Trajan exceeds his wildest dreams for an ideal *princeps*.

> Meanwhile when I have tried to fashion and form in my mind a *princeps* to whom a power equal to the immortal gods is appropriate, I never, not even in prayer, thought to express anything like this one whom we see now. (*Pan.* 4.4)

Pliny outdid himself in finding ways to express the divine basis upon which Trajan's rule was founded. This tendency indicates that Pliny held a high regard for the gods, and viewed their support and approval as an important source of *potestas* for the emperor. Momigliano has suggested that "people were finding it easier to call exceptionally powerful men gods because they were losing faith in the existence, or at least in the effectiveness, of their

[99] The gods' role is reinforced by locating the adoption in the temple of Jupiter Optimus Maximus (*Pan.* 8.1), and by the laurels brought from Pannonia "at the instigation of the gods" (*Pan.* 8.2).

[100] Fears ("PRINCEPS") traces the development of the concept of divine election throughout his book. He points out that Pliny, in two of his letters, mentions the idea that the gods have brought Trajan to power (p. 150). The first is *Ep.* 10.1, where Pliny congratulates Trajan on his accession, and asserts that the gods were responsible for the great event: "The immortal gods have hastened to move your virtue to the governance of the country, which you had already taken up." The second is *Ep.* 10.102, where Pliny celebrates the anniversary of Trajan's accession, and gives thanks "to the gods, the source of your authority."

[101] See also *Pan.* 56.3 where Pliny states: "The gods handed over supreme power to you." The omen described in *Pan.* 5.2 is also interpreted by Pliny to be an indicator of the gods' selection of Trajan.

traditional gods.''[102] For Pliny at least, the gods continued to be effective, and it was not necessary to supplement their effectiveness by deifying an exceptionally powerful human being.[103]

The resemblance which Trajan had to the gods is traced primarily to one factor, his character. The description of Trajan's character in the *Panegyricus* can be divided into two related aspects: his virtuous life which is praised in the document, and his modesty which makes such praise difficult.[104] From the beginning of the *Panegyricus*, Trajan's exemplary character was closely tied to his selection as emperor by the gods:[105] "What could be a more remarkable or lovelier gift of the gods than a pure and virtuous and god-like *princeps*" (*Pan.* 1.3). The virtue of Trajan not only elevated him above other human beings, but it also kept him firmly grounded in the real world: "You stand out and excell as do honor and power, which on the one hand are superior to human beings, but yet are human qualities" (*Pan.* 24.4).[106]

Preeminent among these qualities was Trajan's moderation, which was demonstrated even before he became *princeps*, during his obedient service as Nerva's coruler: "But by what temperament, good gods!, you moderated your power and your fortune." (*Pan.* 10.3). When he finally did enter the city as emperor, Trajan again demonstrated his moderation proceeding on foot instead of riding in a litter. In this way he walked with his subjects, instead of towering over them: "The ground where the footsteps of a *princeps* are shared and confused with ours, has elevated you to the stars" (*Pan.* 24.5). The expression *sidera tollit* ("raised to the stars") may be reminiscent of Pliny's description of Trajan's role in Nerva's consecration,[107] and indicates that Trajan could look forward to deification if he continued his

---

[102] Momigliano, "How Roman Emperors Became Gods," 95. It is unclear to whom Momigliano would attribute this attitude. Immediately before, he mentions Rome, and afterward he discusses the provinces. In any case, the idea has been advocated by others. See E. R. Dodds, *Pagan and Christian in an Age of Anxiety* (Cambridge: Cambridge University Press, 1965). Price (*Rituals and Power*, 14–15) describes the emphasis of many scholars on "the decline of the pagan cults" as a "Christianizing" motif, and recommends alternative views.

[103] Pliny specifically mentions that in the past deceased emperors have been divinized as "an insult to the gods" (*Pan.* 11.2).

[104] Fears has studied the virtues mentioned in the *Panegyricus* as part of his larger consideration of "The Cult of Virtues and Roman Imperial Ideology" ANRW (1981) 2/17.2, 913–17. While his description of the importance of virtues in the *Panegyricus* is helpful, I disagree with his assessment of the document as "imperial propaganda" (p. 913) and with his attempt to connect it with other "imperial propaganda."

[105] The same is true of his selection by Nerva (*Pan.* 7.5).

[106] Pliny's virtues were even extended to the behavior of his family: "You are much more worthy of praise because while you yourself are optimus, you make all those around you to be like you" (*Pan.* 83.3).

[107] See *Pan.* 11.2: "You placed your father among the stars" (Tu sideribus patrem intulisti).

moderate ways. Of course Pliny is especially proud of the moderate relations (*temperamentum*) which Trajan has established with the Senate (*Pan.* 55.5), and he tells Trajan that his acceptance of only modest honors will go down in history (55.1).[108]

Pliny does not stop with his own happiness over Trajan's moderation, nor even with that of posterity. As has been seen repeatedly, the favor of the gods is the decisive factor. In order to affirm Trajan in his moderation, Pliny declares that it is this attitude that has won him divine approval. "Thus it is that the gods have kept the highest position among human beings for you (*tibi*[109]), since you do not seek after their own position" (*Pan.* 52.2). Pliny emphasizes that Trajan's paramount virtue—his refusal to accept divine honors—is responsible for his ultimate honor: to be the chosen as emperor by the gods.

Fears maintains that the picture of Trajan as the chosen of the gods proves his theory that the *Panegyricus* "is an instrument of imperial and not senatorial propaganda."[110] It seems to me that just the opposite is true. A dual emphasis is present in Pliny's argument: Trajan was elected by the gods, but he was elected by virtue of his moderation. It was this moderation which demonstrated that the emperor was both uniquely endowed by the gods, and uniquely dependent on them. For Pliny, Trajan's election by the gods made him accountable to them (just as the hope for divinization was supposed to make him accountable to the Senate). Pliny was happy to affirm Trajan's divine election, and to describe him as godlike, if by doing so he might increase the chance that the moderation of Trajan's early reign would continue. He was even willing to grant that in some ways Trajan's benefactions for the empire exceeded those of the gods. In response to the emperor's emergency shipments to Egypt, Pliny remarks, "Even heaven never has such generosity, so that it nourishes and supports all lands at the same time" (*Pan.* 32.2).[111]

Pliny articulated the reciprocal relationship between Trajan and the gods in order to encourage the virtues which Trajan had demonstrated, and to hold

[108] Pliny explained that refusing all honors is merely courting favor, but accepting the lowest is true modesty (*Pan.* 55.5). He goes on to cite the voting and erecting of bronze statues (instead of gold or silver) as an example of such modest honors.

[109] *Tibi* ("for you") is not found in the manuscripts representing the *M* tradition. While the addition enhances the structure of the sentence, the meaning can be supplied even if *tibi* did not appear.

[110] Fears, *PRINCEPS*, 153.

[111] See also *Pan.* 40.4, where Pliny applauded Trajan's cancellation of debts which were accumulated under previous laws, saying, "Not even the gods are permitted to intervene in the past"; and *Pan.* 65.2 where he asks, "For to who more than to Caesar would they (the gods) pay attention?"

him accountable to the heavens. In the process, Pliny went to the extreme point of suggesting that Trajan's love for his subjects was so great that the people of Rome should pray that "the gods should imitate Caesar" (*Pan.* 74.5). This statement was both the ultimate flattery, and the ultimate reminder of the great expectations which Trajan's new reign had aroused in Pliny and the other senators. These were expectations which included the other side of the mutual relationship. The gods were to imitate Trajan's love for Rome, but they were also supposed to love Trajan to the extent that he loved the people.[112]

> Above all we have made this prayer, that thus the gods will love you as much as you love us. Who would say this either of himself or of a *princeps* who loved moderately? (*Pan.* 74.4).[113]

In Pliny's presentation, the relationship between the emperor and the gods was dependent upon two things: first, that the emperor did not claim to be a god, and second, that the emperor continued to show immoderate affection for his subjects. Pliny quotes Trajan as adding the line, "If he has ruled the state well and for the benefit of all" (*Pan.* 67.4) to the prayers for the emperor's *salus* ("well-being"). This line is reused repeatedly by Pliny, sometimes in different forms,[114] in order to make even more clear to Trajan that the support of the gods, and therefore the happiness of his reign, depended upon the continuation of his virtues and moderation.

In the conclusion of *Rituals and Power* , Price compares how the relationship of the emperor to the divine realm is presented in Pliny's *Panegyricus* with its portrayal in the fourth century *Panegyrici Latini*.[115] Price feels that the latter's description of "a Jupiter close at hand, visible and present . . . a Hercules who was not a stranger, but the emperor" would have been "unimaginable in Pliny's speech" in which "the emperor was simply under the protection of Jupiter." Price's observation is helpful, and I certainly agree that Pliny would not have been comfortable with the more explicit identifications found in the fourth century CE documents.[116] I think it is clear,

---

[112] Shochat ("Change in Roman Religion," 326–27) is right to point out the importance of *amor* ("love") in the *Panegyricus*. His thoughts on the source of this idea need modification, and his notion that Pliny's ideas represent a radical change in Roman religion exaggerates the influence of both Pliny and the *Panegyricus*.

[113] See also *Pan.* 85.5: "Therefore you love since you are loved" (spoken in the context of restoring the *amici principis* ["friends of the emperor"]).

[114] *Pan.* 67.6, 7, 8; 68.1, 3, 4; 72.1.

[115] Price, *Rituals and Power*, 246–47. See also Sabine G. MacCormack, *Art and Ceremony in Late Antiquity* (Berkeley/Los Angeles/London: University of California Press, 1981).

[116] The closest he came was in describing how Jupiter had handed over to Trajan administration of justice on earth (*Pan.* 80.4).

however, that Pliny's picture of the relationship between the emperor and the gods in the *Panegyricus* can in no way be classified as simple. Pliny went to great length laying out his picture of a relationship in which ritual acts served to remind Trajan that the affairs of the earth were only a microcosm for the macrocosm of heaven. The opportunity for deification after death is held out as the ultimate realization of that parallel universe. Trajan is repeatedly warned of the consequences of trying to achieve that connection during his lifetime. If he were to accept or demand divine honors, he would be guilty of *adrogantia* ("claiming powers that one does not rightfully have") the same evil displayed by the worst of his predecessors.[117] Finally, the actual relationship between the emperor and the gods is described not in simple terms of Jupiter protecting Trajan, but in terms of mutual support and responsibility, which holds the emperor accountable if he were to forget that he is not a god, or to rule in a less than virtuous fashion. That the relationship is so complex reflects Pliny's commitment to encourage the positive signs he has seen in Trajan's young reign. In the next Chapter, I shall consider evidence for other portrayals of the relationship between Trajan and the gods, and compare those portrayals with the images from Pliny's writing.

---

[117] *Pan.* 2.7; 11.4; 22.11; 76.7.

4

Other Images of the Relationship between Trajan and the Gods

Introduction

In the *Panegyricus*, Pliny presents a picture of the connection between the emperor and the gods featuring a balanced and mutual connection in which both parties maintain a share of power and responsibility. In this presentation, Pliny intended to use the images of the emperor's relationship with the gods to affirm the positive developments of Trajan's early reign and to encourage the maintenance of a similarly mutual relationship between the emperor and the Senate. Now that Pliny's presentation of the relationship between the emperor and the gods has been examined in its own right, it is possible to compare it with other evidence for how the relationship was portrayed during Trajan's reign. This evidence includes Trajan's responses to Pliny's letters and an assortment of numismatic, architectural, and artistic evidence. Almost all of this evidence could be described as official, and indicative of Trajan's policy, but it will become clear that the degree of connection to Trajan must be judged individually.

Traditional Perceptions of Trajan's Reign

There is a pervasive and persistent scholarly view that Trajan was in many ways the model emperor, who retained modest and positive relationships with all elements of society. Kennedy suggests that Pliny's efforts in writing the *Panegyricus* were successful and that "his speech may have contributed to the fact that Trajan remained true to his liberal principles and was honored throughout the empire as the best of rulers."[1] Liebeschuetz maintains that "The accession of Nerva or, more strictly speaking, Nerva's adoption of the distinguished soldier Trajan as his son and successor, was the beginning of the most harmonious years of the Roman empire."[2] An equally idealized picture of Trajan's reign is presented by Albino Garzetti who, in speaking about the situation in 100 CE asserts, "The actions of another two years had finally confirmed the promise of the reign and bore out the universal conviction that internal security had now been attained under the liberal and enlightened rule of an ideal Princeps."[3] These glowing appraisals of Trajan's tenure as emperor have been influenced, in large part, by the positive reporting of Pliny. The *Panegyricus* is a valuable source for information on Trajan's early years, but it was not intended to be an historical report, and it should not be read as a commentary on the full duration of Trajan's reign. Given these qualifications, the positive picture of Trajan's reign presented by Kennedy, Liebeschuetz, and Garzetti, should be open to further discussion and evaluation.

Challenge to the Traditional Perception: K. H. Waters

In addition to arguing that Domitian's reign was not as uniformly bad as the sources state, Waters has questioned whether the view of Trajan's reign as the best of times might also be an historical distortion. He contends that the two emperors were "committed to an almost identical policy . . . increasing autocracy."[4] According to Waters, the exaggerated view of Trajan's virtues is due at least in part to the *Panegyricus*, which he describes as "a compost of wishful thinking, extravagant flattery, and distortions of recent history."[5] While I would agree with Waters's contention that one must go beyond literary material to determine the true nature of Trajan's reign, I must object to his characterization of the *Panegyricus*. The discussion in Chapters Two and Three above reveals that Pliny's motivations are too complex to dismiss

---

[1] Kennedy, *Art of Rhetoric*, 545

[2] Liebeschuetz, *Continuity and Change*, 182

[3] Garzetti, *From Tiberius to the Antonines: A History of the Roman Empire AD 14–192* (London: Methuen, 1974) 310. Cf. Mattingly, *BMC*, lxvi n. (All references in this Chapter are to *BMC* vol. 3 unless otherwise noted.)

[4] Waters, "Traianus Domitiani Continuator," 385. Waters's argument is weakened by his uncritical use of terms like "autocracy" and "totalitarian." More specific definition of his categories relative to the practices of other emperors is required. I did not become aware of the major piece by Kenneth Hugh Waters ("The Reign of Trajan, and it's Place in Contemporary Scholarship [1960–72]" ANRW [1975] 2/2, 390–431) until this work was in publication.

[5] Ibid., 398.

summarily as "wishful thinking" or "extravagant flattery." Waters reads Pliny's use of Trajan's most famous title, *optimus princeps*, as "merely a somewhat empty phrase on which not much weight should be placed,"[6] but Pliny's motivations for using the title cannot be understood without careful attention to issues of language and timing in the *Panegyricus*.[7]

Waters is correct to emphasize that the *Panegyricus* and other literary testimonies to the reign of Trajan should be read more critically,[8] but he is wrong to dismiss those works as irrelevant flattery. Pliny's writings are not to be dismissed, but neither are they to be regarded as reflecting historical reality. Instead, they reveal Pliny's particular view of reality, and his hope for the continuation of the enlightened administration he perceived during the early years of Trajan's reign. Waters emphasizes that this enlightenment should not be generalized as the final, conclusive judgment on the character of Trajan's reign.[9] On the contrary, his survey of other sources of evidence leads him to conclude that, far from being enlightened, Trajan's reign is an extension of the Flavian autocracy.

Waters's conclusions rest on several points. He sees a continuity of imperial advisors and other prominent administrators retained from the reign of Domitian to that of Trajan.[10] In addition, Waters cites Trajan's continued adlection of provincials to the Senate.[11] Regarding imperial titles, Waters

---

[6] Ibid., 386.

[7] The subtlety with which Pliny uses the title suggests that there is some disagreement between the Senate and the emperor involving the Senate's offer of the *cognomen "Optimus"* to Trajan, and the emperor's refusal to accept it. I would agree with Waters's contention that the title itself "cannot substantiate the belief that there was much to differentiate Trajan's policy from that of the Flavians in general or that of Domitian in particular" (ibid.). At the same time, it cannot be denied that this differentiation from Domitian is a central part of Pliny's argument throughout the document.

[8] Waters holds that, while Tacitus supports the picture of Trajan's noble character in the prologues of the *Agricola* and the *Historiae*, he becomes disenchanted with Trajan, and does not comment on his reign in later writings. Waters ("Traianus Domitiani Continuator," 386) cites Syme (*Tacitus*, 495–503) who is less certain. Syme (pp. 497–98) points out that "of Trajan not even the name stands anywhere in the *Annales*. Tacitus pays homage to the Imperator after his own fashion—and not without ambiguity." Waters ("Juvenal and the Reign of Trajan," *Antichthon* 4 [1970] 63) also suggests that the fact that Juvenal does not include Trajan in his satirical writing means that he "lived and wrote under an unmistakably totalitarian regime."

[9] A kind of circular reasoning has allowed commentators to label Trajan as the ideal emperor based only on the literary evidence.

[10] Waters, "Traianus Domitiani Continuator," 388–90. He suggests that the resistance Pliny encountered in trying to prosecute Publicius for the death of the younger Helvidius under Nerva is an indication of that continuity (*Ep.* 9.3).

[11] Waters, "Traianus Domitiani Continuator," 392–93. Pliny himself advocates the adlection of Voconius Romanus from Spain (*Ep.* 10.4.1; cf. 2.13; 6.6.3).

argues that there is an inconsistency in the way that the adoption of Republican titles by emperors has been viewed. Domitian's emphasis upon his own possession of Republican magistracies is considered to be "in accordance with his autocratic nature,"[12] but Trajan's use of titles like *consul* and *consul designatus* is said to "imply honour for the Senate and People of Rome."[13] In Waters's opinion, the emphasis placed on Republican titles by both men is further evidence that Trajan is continuing the policies of Domitian rather than breaking with them.

Waters also stresses that, when the first Dacian conflict broke out, Trajan's initial approach was to follow Domitian's example and try to settle without creating a new province. It was not until the end of the second Dacian war that Trajan annexed the area.[14] In the east as well, Waters sees Trajan continuing the Flavian impetus for "strengthening the eastern frontier" by means of forts and roads, and eventually capitalizing on this foundational strength to launch his attack on Parthia.[15] Waters notes in the building programs of both Domitian and Trajan a similar combination of "ostentatious" constructions ("intended to magnify the prestige of the princeps") and other projects of a more utilitarian nature.[16] Finally, actions taken by both emperors affecting agriculture in Italy are seen by Waters to have been "imperial interference, which whether intentionally or not acted repressively upon the normal operations of the agricultural community."[17]

With regard to the relationship between the emperor and the gods, Waters again finds connections with Domitian. As with most of his conclusions, the discussion of the relationship between the emperor and the gods is based

[12] Mattingly, *Coins of the Roman Empire in the British Museum*, vol. 2: *Vespasian to Domitian* (London: British Museum, 1930) lxxxv; cited by Waters, "Traianus Domitiani Continuator," 393.

[13] Waters, ibid., 393 (citing *BMC* 3. xxvi). He (ibid., 394) observes that "Trajan's coin legends are the longest of any emperor's, ranging up to fifty letters on the obverse, in the anxiety to include as many titles as possible, and often continuing on the reverse to an almost equal length."

[14] "Not withstanding the eventual change of frontier policy, we have to recognize in this case too a gradual progression, not a sudden reversal" (ibid., 400).

[15] Ibid., 401. Waters posits that Domitian was also interested in Armenia, an area that Trajan annexed in 114 CE (p. 402).

[16] Ibid. This category of "utilitarian projects" is especially vague, and would seem to be applicable in some degree to every emperor. The only specific connection mentioned is that Domitian (the Flavian Amphitheatre), Trajan (baths), and Hadrian (Temple of Venus and Rome) all built over parts of the incomplete Golden House of Nero.

[17] Ibid., 404. He is referring to Domitian's edict of 92 restricting vine growing outside of Italy, and the *alimenta* instituted by Nerva and continued under Trajan under which landowners took a forced loan from the emperor and paid the interest to their towns for the support of poor children (cf. *Pan.* 26).

upon a small sample of the evidence. Waters describes Trajan's attempts to identify with Hercules as one link with Domitian.[18] Unfortunately Waters does not cite any specific evidence for this identification by Domitian, and for Trajan he refers only to a discussion by Beaujeu.[19] According to Waters, Trajan also followed and went beyond Domitian "in attempting an assimilation to, if not an equation with, the highest deity of the Roman pantheon, Iuppiter Optimus Maximus."[20] Evidence for this "assimilation" includes the sestertius reverse type on which Trajan is pictured holding a thunderbolt (fig. 1.A), and the sestertius reverse type featuring a triumphal arch on which is inscribed *IOM* ("Jupiter Optimus Maximus"; fig. 1.C).[21] As will be seen below, however, the reverse type of Trajan holding the thunderbolt is representative of a limited issue,[22] and the reverse featuring the IOM arch commemorates an unidentified monument[23] and implies nothing about Trajan's identification with Jupiter. It is on this very weak evidence that Waters bases his conclusion that Trajan "went further than Domitian in suggesting a close relationship between himself and the gods."[24] In fact, it seems unwise to base any theory about Trajan's portrayal of the relationshp of the emperor to the gods on such limited data. The other evidence offered by Waters is an undocumented statement that Trajan continued the practice of depicting himself in a radiate crown on some coins,[25] and the observation that "Trajan was likewise keen to consecrate or elevate his relatives."[26]

Although some of the examples adduced by Waters are thought provoking, his case could only be sustained with a more careful definition of terms, a wider spectrum of evidence, and a thorough investigation of each piece of evidence he cites. In this Chapter, I shall examine the question of how the relationship between the emperor and the gods is portrayed in images that are

[18] Waters, "Traianus Domitiani Continuator," 395.

[19] Beaujeu, *La religion* , 80–87.

[20] Waters, "Traianus Domitiani Continuator," 395.

[21] Ibid. See p. 15, n. 82 and p. 12, n. 65 above.

[22] See pp. 109–10 below. The type with Domitian holding the thunderbolt is attested in great number (see p. 13, n. 70 above).

[23] See p. 12, n. 65 above.

[24] Waters, "Traianus Domitiani Continuator," 395.

[25] Ibid., 395–96. Trajan's obverse portrait is often radiate; see, e.g., *BMC*, pp. 186–92, nos. 878–913 (dupondii). Waters argues that Nero had introduced the depiction of radiate heads for the living emperor, but that it had been limited to dupondii. "Domitian issued a reasonable proportion of radiate heads and busts, but the unpretentious laureate head predominated . . . Nerva made no change here and Trajan continued the policy." This does not constitute evidence that Trajan "went further in suggesting a close relationship between himself and the gods" ("Traianus Domitiani Continuator," 396).

[26] Ibid., 397.

to a greater or lesser degree related to Trajan. Literary evidence for Trajan's portrayal will be considered first, followed by numismatic evidence, and then several examples of monumental construction and sculptural images.

Literary Evidence

The literary evidence that can be attributed directly to Trajan is limited, and of the available material little deals with the relationship of the emperor to the gods.[27] One potential literary source is the collection of Trajan's responses to Pliny's letters. This material might be especially helpful since the majority of the letters date from around 111 CE, and therefore could provide a clue to the situation ten years after Pliny had expressed his hope for Trajan's reign in the *Panegyricus*.[28] There has been much debate about the extent to which Trajan was responsible for authoring this correspondence,[29]

[27] Some would include the *Orationes* on kingship by Dio Chrysostom as part of the literary evidence for Trajan's attitude on the relationship between the emperor and the gods (Fears, *PRINCEPS*, 158). While these are informative treatises which were part of the intellectual climate of Trajan's time, I would not include them with literary evidence for Trajan's portrayal of the relationship between the emperor and the gods. My reasoning for this is the same as for the *Panegyricus*. Both documents should be read as the product of the stated author, not as imperial propaganda statements. While Fears is careful to explain that Dio did not know Trajan at the time the essays were composed, he ends his discussion of Dio by saying, "Thus in a series of speeches, Dio, like Pliny, an intimate friend of the emperor, proclaimed divine election to be the true basis of imperial power" (ibid.). Waters ("Trajan's Character in the Literary Tradition," in J. A. S. Evans, ed., *Polis and Imperium: Studies in Honour of Edward Togo Salmon* [Toronto: Hakkert, 1974] 236–38) claims that there is no evidence that Dio was intimate with Trajan. Elsewhere he ("Traianus Domitiani Continuator," 398) comments that the *Orationes* on kingship are not as offensive as Pliny's work, but that Dio's speeches are "something between sermons and political propaganda," and therefore "as a historical source they should be used with caution."

[28] Of the 121 letters, 1–14 are written before Pliny leaves for Bithynia. The latest of these seems to be a congratulatory note (10.14) sent by Pliny on the occasion of one of Trajan's victories over the Dacians (102 or 106 CE). Of the first fourteen letters, only three are from Trajan to Pliny (10.3b, 7, 9).

[29] Sherwin-White (*Letters*, 536–46) discusses various arguments for Trajan's involvement in answering Pliny's requests. The uniform "chancery style" of the responses (p. 537), the tendency to repeat short phrases from Pliny's letters in the response (pp. 537–38), and "the formality by which grants of privilege are notified" (p. 538) are taken as signs of a secretary's hand. At the same time, Sherwin-White does see signs that Trajan actually participated in the process of corresponding. "The onus of proof is on those who would maintain that Trajan's replies were concocted by the secretariat without reference to the emperor" (p. 541). At the same time Sherwin-White does not claim to be able to discern Trajan's influence in all cases. "The influence of professional advisers and the share of the Princeps in the final decisions is to be detected and determined, if at all, only by the analysis of style and content together" (p. 546). See also Millar, *Emperor and the Roman World*, 219–28.

but even if Trajan's letters were drafted in large part by advisors and secretaries, it is safe to say that the letters were still indicative of policy decisions made by Trajan. In terms of decisions involving the gods, or the relationship between the emperor and the gods references in the correspondence are sparse but intriguing.

Trajan expresses appreciation for Pliny's reports that he and others in the province—including soldiers and native officials—have renewed their *sollemnia vota* ("yearly vows") for the emperor's safety (*Ep*. 10.35–36, 101), have celebrated the anniversary of his accession (10.53, 103), or have rejoiced on his birthday (10.89; see 10.17a.2). In each case, however, Trajan's acknowledgment is extremely brief and formal.[30] These votives are accepted without fanfare, and there is certainly no indication of any desire for additional or extraordinary honors. The same is true for situations in which Pliny enquires about other honors for Trajan. The emperor allows his statue to be set up in a temple which Pliny proposes to build in Tifernum.[31] Trajan insists that although normally he is against such honors, he grants permission lest he quench Pliny's loyalty:

> It is permissible that the statue of me be set up in the place which you have chosen. Although I do not usually allow this sort of honor, I do not want to appear to impede the course of your loyal acts to me. (*Ep*. 10.9)

Except for the fact that the statue is to be set up along with others of former emperors (*Ep*. 10.8.1, 4), there is no indication of where the statue of Trajan will be placed. One would expect that Pliny followed his own directive that imperial statuary was "to stand guard before a temple and to adorn the doorpost" (*Pan*. 52.2).[32]

Trajan continues to take a modest approach when confronted with other honors. When Pliny asks if a bequest from a citizen of Pontus should be used for either public buildings dedicated to Trajan or quinquennial games in

---

[30] He mentions the "vows to the immortal gods" in *Ep*. 10.36 and 101, and he applauds the "scrupulousness and joy" with which the *dies imperii* were observed (*Ep*. 10.53 and 103).

[31] *Ep*. 10.8–9; see *Ep*. 3.4 for the laying of the foundation stone, and *Ep*. 4.1 for the dedication of the structure which Sherwin-White (*Letters*, 264) dates to the summer of 104 CE.

[32] This is stated in response to Domitian who is accused of setting up his throne (and presumably statues) "in the midst of the gods" (*Pan*. 52.1). The placement of Trajan's statue in the Temple of Zeus Philios and Trajan in Pergamum offers an exception to Pliny's principle. The reverse of a coin of Pergamum (Vienna E36) shows a standing emperor next to a seated Zeus inside the temple (Fig. 1.D). Nock ("SYNNAOS THEOS I," 24 = *Essays*, 221) suggests that such a partnership can run into identification." Price (*Rituals and Power*, 156) suggests a very different relationship saying that "Zeus is enthroned in majesty, while the figure of Trajan, in military dress, is shown approaching him to do homage."

the emperor's honor, Trajan responds that he has no preference as long as the memory of the deceased donor is perpetuated (*Ep.* 10.75–76). The emperor also approves Pliny's plan to build a bath complex on an abandoned lot in Prusa and "to surround it with a hall and colonnades and to dedicate the structure to you [Trajan], for whose benefaction this will be a work tasteful and worthy of your name" (*Ep.* 10.7.3). Trajan shows some concern with Pliny's mention of an earlier plan to build a shrine (*templum*) dedicated to Claudius on the property. The emperor maintains that if this shrine (*aedes*) of Claudius had once been built "his sacredness occupies the soil" (*Ep.* 10.71). Trajan implies that it would be inappropriate to rededicate a structure built on that sacred soil to him. Unfortunately there is no further discussion of this intriguing situation.[33]

One final incident relating to the relationship of the emperor to the gods should be mentioned. In the letter reacting to Pliny's handling of the problems with Christians (*Ep.* 10.97), Trajan approves of the system that Pliny has devised to test those who claimed that they had never been Christians, or had ceased being Christians some time ago. At least, Trajan approves of half of the system when he acknowledges the test "by beseeching our gods" without mentioning that Pliny had included the emperor's image in the test as well (*Ep.* 10.96.5). While it is not possible to be sure of the reason for this omission, it would seem to correspond to the moderate and modest image of Trajan that is seen throughout these letters.

The moderate portrayal of the relationship between the emperor and the gods that is seen in Trajan's responses accords well with Pliny's presentation of Trajan's *moderatio* in the *Panegyricus*.[34] A modest picture of Trajan might be expected, since it was Pliny who collected most of the letters, even though his correspondence with Trajan was not published until after his death. it is possible that Pliny withheld or perhaps edited letters which presented Trajan

---

[33] In a similar situation, Trajan responds to a dilemma which Pliny encounters in Nicomedia (*Ep.* 10.49–50), where construction of a new forum necessitates rebuilding or relocating a temple to Magna Mater. Pliny asks Trajan if it would be possible to move the temple "without loss of sanctity" (*salva religione*). Trajan tells Pliny not to be concerned about the move since "foreign soil is not able to hold dedication which is made by our laws" (*Ep.* 10.50). In the case of the Claudius shrine in Prusa, Trajan implied the opposite idea: that the ground could hold a Roman dedication. Perhaps there is less at stake in the case of the Magna Mater temple. Sherwin-White (*Letters*, 659) feels that in the case of the shrine for Claudius, Trajan "is less concerned for legal technicality than for respect to the memory of Claudius," and probably for respect to all emperors, living and dead.

[34] Other parallels with the concerns expressed in the *Panegyricus* can be found. In responding to charges raised in Prusa against Dio Chrysostom, Trajan claims that it is his intention "not to acquire respect for my name from the hatred or fear of people, nor from criminal charges of maiestas" (*Ep.* 10.82.1); cf. *Pan.* 42.

in other than a moderate light. A more likely assumption, however, is that the collection is complete, and that until his death in ca. 111 CE, Pliny continued to approve of the course of Trajan's reign.[35] In any case, Trajan's correspondence provides no indication of a portrayal of the relationship between the emperor and the gods that differed from Pliny's portrayal in the *Panegyricus* in substantial ways.

Numismatic Evidence

The question of numismatic evidence commences the investigation of visual materials, and as such requires both introduction and a word of caution. The introduction is simply a reminder of the importance of nontextual material for study of the ancient world. On one hand, it is important because it may help to compensate for the paucity of textual evidence emanating directly from Trajan. Beyond this, however, visual evidence opens up a wide spectrum of ancient cultural developments that were accessible to those who did not have the ability or the leisure time to read or write textual material.[36] In speaking of the study of historical Christianity, Margaret Miles suggests that images are ''a significant piece of the discourse of christian communities that has not been systematically incorporated in the study of historical christian ideas. They are, however, a piece that is capable of changing our understanding of the whole discourse.''[37] The disciplines of numismatics and art history can provide an enhanced understanding, not only of historical Christianity, but of all aspects of ancient culture.

Issues in the Use of Numismatic Evidence

A cautionary note on the study of nontextual materials grows directly out of its unlimited potential. In the pursuit of enhanced understanding it is tempting to press visual images too far. This seems to be the case with some of

---

[35] Once Pliny went to Bithynia he would have had less immediate knowledge of Trajan's actions and attitudes in Rome. It seems likely that while in Bithynia, he continued to correspond with his associates in the capital, but unfortunately, only the correspondence with Trajan survives from this period.

[36] Not everyone who was able to read and write took textual material as seriously as Pliny, who describes the literary life he leads while on retreat in Tuscany (*Ep.* 9.36). His pace of work is relaxed compared to his description of the schedule of his uncle, the elder Pliny, who took time out from work for his daily bath, but either listened to something being read to him or dictated to his secretaries while receiving his rubdown and being dried off (*Ep.* 3.5.14).

[37] Miles, *Image as Insight: Visual Understanding in Western Christianity and secular Culture* (Boston: Beacon, 1985) 28.

Fears's arguments discussed in Chapter One, and also with the use of visual material—specifically coinage—by Waters. In fact, coins are a hybrid of literary and visual evidence, since they feature both pictorial images and textual notation.[38] For this reason they are especially popular with scholars such as Fears or Waters who wish to "illustrate" theories of imperial policy or ideology. There has been considerable progress, however, beyond the long-held position that coin types and legends were chosen solely by the *princeps* with the intention of influencing public opinion about his rule.[39] A variety of opinions now exist as to the proper understanding of numismatic evidence. It has been suggested that "in the eastern half of the Empire Latin legends meant nothing; even in the west the illiterate could not read the legends, the educated had something better to do; ancient authors do not comment on the message coins are thought to have carried."[40] With regard to coin types it is asked whether the "common man would care for the abstract 'virtues' excogitated by Greek intellectuals."[41] On the other hand, Toynbee has suggested that the language of visual imagery in coinage and other Roman art, "postulated in those to whom it was addressed keen eyes for visual detail, a highly-developed feeling for the past, imaginative intuition in delving beneath outward appearances."[42] The question cannot be decided one way or the other; in fact, Toynbee's appreciation for coin imagery can be enhanced by

[38] In discussing "Picture-language in Roman Art and Coinage," J. M. C. Toynbee comments, "Of all such documents the coins are the most servicable for our purpose. They are the most abundant of all monuments and form the most completely-surviving series of works of art which we have. Moreover, since their legends provide us with 'translations' of the language which we are studying, they are of basic value in building up its vocabulary and 'phraseology'" (in R. A. G. Carson and C. H. V. Sutherland, eds., *Essays in Roman Coinage Presented to Harold Mattingly* [Oxford: Oxford University Press, 1956] 221).

[39] Barbara Levick, "Propaganda and the Imperial Coinage," *Antichthon* 16 (1982) 104. Levick cites M. P. Charlesworth ("The Virtues of a Roman Emperor: Propaganda and the Creation of Belief," *Proceedings of the British Academy* 23 [1937] 105–33); C. H. V. Sutherland (*Coinage in Roman Imperial Policy 31 B.C.–A.D. 68* [London: Methuen, 1951]); and M. Grant (*Roman Anniversary Issues: An Exploratory Study of the Numismatic and Medallic Commemoration of Anniversary Years, 49 B.C.–A.D. 375* (Cambridge: Cambridge University Press, 1952) as representative of the traditional view.

[40] Levick ("Propaganda," 105) is here summarizing the arguments of A. H. M. Jones, "Numismatics and History," in Carson and Sutherland, *Essays in Roman Coinage* 13–33 (reprinted in P. A. Brunt, ed., *The Roman Economy* [Oxford: Blackwell, 1974] 61ff; T. V. Buttrey, "Vespasian as Moneyer," *Numismatic Chronicle* 12 (1972) 89–109; Gian Guido Belloni, "Significato storico-politico delle figurazione e delle scritte delle monete da Augusto a Traiano," ANRW (1974) 2/1, 997–1144, esp. 1018–21. Belloni's article includes an extensive discussion of Trajan's coinage (1076–1138).

[41] Levick, "Propaganda," 105; citing A. Wallace-Hadrill, "Galba's Aequitas," *Numismatic Chronicle* 21 (1981) 20–39.

[42] Toynbee, "Picture-Language," 226.

a more nuanced understanding of the process by which coin types and legends were determined.

Buttrey suggests that a mint master might have been tempted to reissue types that had been especially popular in the past.[43] Levick adds that the rationale for producing various types of coinage was not limited to informing or indoctrinating the public about the "merits, achievements, and policies" of the *princeps*. Rather, it included the desire of mint officials to present "their employer to himself in the most favourable aspect through designs that they found the most appealing and effective for the purpose."[44] This suggestion presents a number of possible explanations for coin types and legends beyond the usual understanding that the emperor or his associates chose them for propaganda value.[45] Jones suggests that the modern analogy for "the varying types and legends of Roman imperial coins" should be postage stamps, which are issued by the government, but are not accurate indicators of official policy. "No serious historian would use them as a clue which revealed changes of government policy, even if other evidence were totally lacking."[46] Even if Jones is overstating his case,[47] caution is needed in citing numismatic findings as evidence of official imperial policy.[48]

Metals and Meaning

With this caution in mind, it is possible to gain some important insights from the numismatic evidence of Trajan's reign. I shall consider numismatic evi-

---

[43] Buttrey, "Vespasian as Moneyer"; cited by Levick, "Propaganda," 105.

[44] Levick, "Propaganda," 106, 108. She suggests that her hypothesis explains instances such as the minting of coins promoting the adopted grandsons of Augustus as *principes* five to six years after they had died, and after there was no longer any apparent propaganda value in their images.

[45] Brunt ("Divine Elements," 173) contends that although there is literary evidence (Suetonius *Div. Aug.* 94; *Nero* 25) that emperors did select coin types in some cases, this does not mean that they normally did. "How can we be sure that officials did not sometimes or often select slogans and symbols which no doubt were designed to please their masters but which might betoken excessive adulation?"

[46] Jones, "Numismatics and History," 15–16.

[47] C. H. V. Sutherland has illustrated the potential value of coins for historical study in *Roman History and Coinage, 44BC–AD 69: Fifty Points of Relation from Julius Caesar to Vespasian* (Oxford: Clarendon; New York: Oxford University Press, 1987), which assesses the historical value of 50 coins dating from Julius to Nero. Sutherland maintains that "the imperial coinage was, fundamentally, a government-controlled economic instrument which also said things, and usually illustrated them. This much is beyond question or denial" (ibid., pref.). See also idem, "The Intelligibility of Roman Coin Types," *JRS* 49 (1959) 46–55; and idem, "The Purpose of Roman Imperial Coin Types," *Revue Numismatique* 25 (1983) 73–82.

[48] Fears (*PRINCEPS*, 200–201) acknowledges the need for caution, but I do not think he heeds it in his own use of numismatic materials.

dence from the time of Trajan, both as it relates to the relationship between the emperor and the Senate, and to the relationship between the emperor and the gods. Within these categories, I shall recognize a distinction between gold and silver coinage on the one hand, and *aes* (copper and bronze) coinage on the other. I shall not, however, follow the standard practice of including separate discussions for each metal group. This practice has been based on the idea that the emperor was responsible for coinage minted in gold and silver, while the Senate was in charge of coins made of copper or its alloy bronze.[49] Even Mattingly, however, in the first edition of *Coins of the Roman Empire in the British Museum*, raises the question of how firmly this division can be made.[50] He concludes, that although the emperor might have been involved in some *aes* issues,[51] it is best to "retain our old rule [senatorial prerogative for *aes*], while adding the necessary qualifications."[52] More recent consideration has cast even more doubt on the sharp distinction of responsibility based on metal type.[53]

Talbert emphasizes that there is no evidence other than the coins themselves to indicate that the Senate was involved in the minting of bronze coinage.[54] While the prominence of the legend S C (*Senatus consulto*) on most bronze types argues that the Senate was responsible for the issue, Talbert's assertion that "from the beginning of the Principate financial control and initiative indisputably passed to the emperor" makes it difficult to find a satifactory explanation of what the body's responsibility might have entailed.[55] Talbert's questions lead him to conclude that "it is possible that in time bronze coinage came to carry the legend SC or EX SC purely out of a sense of tradition."[56] Given this possibility, it is advisable to avoid excessive dependence on the assumption that bronze coinage can be tied only to sena-

---

[49] This view allows a separation of senatorial intentions from those of the emperor. Fears ("Jupiter," 84) points out that the minting of bronze coinage was "traditionally a senatorial prerogative." He is arguing, however, that Trajan's "magic" was his ability to make use of the "senatorial media." Is "senatorial" an accurate description of the bronze coinage if the emperor is able to "make use" of it?

[50] Mattingly, *BMC*, xciii–xciv. See idem, *Roman Coins* (2d ed.; London: Methuen, 1967) 102.

[51] This is a concession based on the work of Strack, *Untersuchungen*, 7–10.

[52] Mattingly, *BMC*, xciv.

[53] K. Kraft, "S(enatus) C(onsulto)," *Jahrbuch für Numismatik und Geldgeschichte* 12 (1962) 7–49.

[54] Talbert, *Senate*, 380.

[55] Ibid.

[56] Ibid., 383. "It must be acknowledged that we are quite unable to fathom the nature of the senate's involvement with the issue of coinage, or the nature of its relationship with the emperor in this sphere" (ibid.).

torial prerogative. This does not preclude the possibility that some coins reflected senatorial influence. Discussion of the varying levels of involvement of the emperor in the determination of coin types and legends leaves the process open to a number of different influences.

The Relationship between the Emperor and the Senate

Early in Trajan's reign, there is numismatic evidence that coheres well with Pliny's picture of an enlightened co-existence between the Senate and the *princeps*. The most obvious example is an exceptional issue made of silver (five denarius piece) which features the head of Trajan, laureate, on the obverse, with a legend IMP CAES NERVA TRAIAN AUG GERM.[57] The absence of PP in the legend indicates a date early in 98–99 CE before the title *Pater Patriae* was accepted.[58] On the reverse a togate figure standing, l., and a figure in military dress (Trajan) standing, r., are clasping hands, and supporting a globe between them (fig. 2.A). The reverse legend, PROVIDENTIA SENATUS, suggests that the togate figure represents the Senate and that the scene commemorates the foresight of the Senate's acclamation of Trajan, and its willingness to share with him the burden of ruling the empire. A similar design is taken from a Sestertius of Nerva, the reverse of which shows the emperor, laureate, facing a senator. The two are holding a globe between them, and the legend reads PROVIDENTIA SENATUS SC.[59] Trajan's adoption of this type from Nerva's coinage can be taken as a symbol of peaceful coexistence and cooperation between the Senate and Trajan.[60] It is also possi-

---

[57] *BMC*, p. 38 *. Gnecchi Collection (Rome). F. Gnecchi, *I Medaglioni Romani*, (Milan, 1912; reprinted Bologna, 1968) i. p. 44 (Trajan), no. 2. The piece may have been a medallion.

[58] *Pan.* 21.1. See Mattingly, *BMC*, lvii–lviii. The following chart summarizes Mattingly's dating scheme for Trajan's reign:

COS II IMP	98–99
COS II IMP PP	98–99
COS III IMP PP	100–101
COS IIII IMP II PP	101–102
COS IIII IMP III (IIII) DACICUS PP	102–103
COS V IMP IIII DACICUS PP	103–104
COS V IMP V DACICUS PP	104–106
COS V IMP VI DACICUS PP	106–112
COS VI IMP VI DACICUS PP	112–114
COS VI IMP VII DACICUS OPTIMUS PP	114–115
COS VI IMP VIII DACICUS OPTIMUS PARTHICUS PP	115–117

The *imperator* designations are included in this chart, but in most cases IMP is not numbered on the coinage. Thus, there are long stretches (esp. 103–12 CE) during which the consular number stays the same, and exact dating of issues is difficult.

[59] *BMC*, p. 21 *.

[60] Reverse types under Nerva showing only clasped hands (*BMC*, p. 1, nos. 4 [aureus, pl. 1. 2],

ble to interpret the reverse image as depicting the Senate handing over control of the empire to Trajan.

The idea that power is transferred, rather than shared, is more explicit in a similar denarius reverse type in which the togate figure is clearly handing the globe to Trajan (fig. 2.B).[61] It appears, therefore, that the sense of mutuality in holding the globe has been diminished. The same tendency is suggested by the change of legend from PROVID(ENTIA) SEN(ATUS) on the sestertius of Nerva and the five denarius coin of the time of Trajan simply to PROVID(ENTIA) on the denarius of Trajan. Perhaps the exceptional issue of the five denarius piece was presented very early in the reign as an assurance of Trajan's good relations with the Senate (the same good relations which Pliny encouraged in the *Panegyricus* and which Nerva apparently enjoyed). The regular denarius issue, including the PP legend, should therefore be dated after the acceptance of the title *Pater Patriae*.[62] Thus the later "globe passing" type without SENATUS could be evidence for a reduced emphasis on the Senate's role in this relationship. Perhaps the initial importance of mutuality and interdependence between the emperor and the Senate diminished after Trajan felt assured that he was in solid control of the situation in Rome.[63]

The reverse type of the Senate passing a globe reappears on a sestertius reverse of 101–102 CE.[64] In this case, Trajan is wearing a toga, not his

---

5 [aureus], 6 [denarius, pl. 1. 3]), or clasped hands holding a legionary eagle set on a prow (p. 2, nos. 7 [aureus, pl. 1. 4], 8 [denarius, pl. 1. 5], 9 [denarius]; p. 14, no. 86 [sestertius, pl. 4. 1]) with the legend CONCORDIA EXERCITUUM probably reflect an unsuccessful attempt to stabilize the precarious relationship between Nerva and the armies (Mattingly, *BMC*, xxxvii).

[61] *BMC*, p. 38, nos. 53–54, 55 pl. 10. 3. Mattingly (*BMC*, lxvii) suggests that in this instance the togate figure should be understood to be Nerva, not the Senate, and that the scene refers to Trajan's adoption by his predecessor. He points out that in this case the togate figure "holds roll, not sceptre, the characteristic attribute of Emperor, not of Senate" (ibid.). Of course it is Trajan who carries the sceptre in the five denarius coin.

[62] The date still should be 98–99, however, since the coinage from 100 CE begins with the title COS III. Mattingly (*BMC*, lvii–lviii) does present an argument for including the TR P COS II PP types before the death of Nerva, but it is a forced interpretation.

[63] Considering the lengths to which Pliny went to affirm Trajan's improved relationship with the Senate, it is striking that he does not mention something so memorable as the silver five denarius piece. Even if these were minted in limited quantities, one would expect that a person in Pliny's circle would have been familiar with them. It seems that the sentiment of the coin would have accorded very well with Pliny's presentation, and would have been a further reflection of Trajan's *moderatio* that Pliny was trying to encourage. This possibility would seem to lend support to the argument of Levick and others that ancient authors did not recognize or make use of the messages which modern readers ascribe to coins.

[64] *BMC*, p. 157 *; cf. Cohen, *Description historique des médailles frappées sous l'Empire romain* (2d ed.) 642.

military gear, and is receiving the globe from a togate senator. There is no mention of PROVID or SENATUS in the legend, only the titles TR POT COS IIII P P and the notation SC. Mattingly argues that, given the dating during the first Dacian war, it might be best "to say that Trajan is leaving the government in the hands of the Senate while he does his duty as a soldier in the field."[65] This interpretation would be more convincing if Trajan were wearing military gear, as on the denarius pieces mentioned above.[66] Furthermore, Mattingly's description of the coin states that Trajan is "receiving a globe from a Senator."[67] If one posits senatorial influence on the design (whether or not the SC indicates senatorial issuance), it is possible to regard the reappearance of the type as an attempt to reassert the role of the Senate as essential to Trajan's powerbase. This fits the timing well, since Trajan is in the process of demonstrating the formidable military aspect of his power against the Dacians—an aspect which Pliny tried to minimize in the *Panegyricus*. What better reminder of the emperor's mutual ties to the Senate than the renewal of this globe-passing type, with the emperor pictured in senatorial attire.[68] Admittedly, given the emperor's capability to influence bronze coinage, this type also could be viewed as Trajan's attempt to portray his commitment to the importance of the Senate's role, even as he was absent from the city while involved in the Dacian campaign.[69] This view is supported by an aureus reverse, probably from the end of the second Dacian war, that shows Trajan in military dress presenting a kneeling Dacian prisoner to the Senate, which is pictured as a male figure, togate, standing and holding a scroll (fig. 2.C).[70]

The *Providentia* legend returns to Trajan's coinage on a reverse type from the end of Trajan's reign. In this case, *Providentia* is pictured, draped, holding a vertical sceptre in her left hand, and resting her left elbow on a column.

[65] Mattingly, *BMC*, xcvii.

[66] Cf. a sestertius from sometime in 98–100 CE (*BMC*, p. 154, no. 742 A, pl. 26. 2) featuring Trajan, togate, clasping hands over a burning altar with an officer in military dress while three soldiers look on. The legend proclaims FIDES EXERCIT, a reference to the loyalty of the troops.

[67] Mattingly, *BMC*, p. 157.

[68] In commenting on Trajan's second consulship, held while he was still on the Dacian frontier, Pliny applauds Trajan for "display of arms no more than of the toga to restrain the enemy terror" (*Pan.* 56.7).

[69] In this case the question would arise as to why this would be the last issue portraying such a message. Fears (*PRINCEPS*, 227) argues that at least the gold and silver issues of this type are part of Trajan's attempt to portray his power as derived from the Senate at the expense of Nerva, with whom he was trying to sever connections.

[70] *BMC*, p. 65, no. 244, pl. 13. 14. Mattingly is unsure that the object held by the senator is actually a scroll.

With her right hand she points down to a large globe at her feet (fig. 2.D). The scene appears on aureus, denarius, and sestertius reverses from 115–116 CE (COS VI with OPTIMUS)[71] and from 116–117 CE (COS VI with OPTIMUS and PARTHICUS).[72] On all of the coins from 115–116 CE the reverse legend includes PRO(VIDENTIA) AUG(USTI) left and right of the figure in the field. The denarii from the following year changes to PRO VID(ENTIA) in the field, while the sestertius legend from 116–117 c.e. spells out PROVIDENTIA AUGUSTI S P Q R. Mattingly has suggested that the idea of *Providentia Augusti* reflects a concern with selecting a successor for Trajan.[73] If this is the case, or if it refers to more general forethought and care for the empire, the emphasis is on the emperor's action without any reference to the Senate in word or image other than the standard S P Q R.[74] It could be said that the *Providentia Senatus* from the beginning of the reign was replaced by *Providentia Augusti* at the end.

The description of Trajan as *optimus princeps* on the coinage is also a relevant issue for discussing the relationship between the emperor and the Senate. Mattingly speaks in glowing terms about the significance of the sudden appearance of S P Q R OPTIMO PRINCIPI on reverses of "all coins in all metals" for the period beginning in late 103 CE or early 104, and extending until 111.

> We can only infer that, shortly after the victorious end of the first Dacian war, the Senate, as representative of the Roman people, passed a resolution conveying to Trajan in the most formal style its homage, its devotion, and its gratitude for virtues that entitled him to be ranked only just after Jupiter Optimus Maximus as the 'optimus' *par excellence* among many—the perfect Emperor, under whom the perfect state, the 'optimus status rerum' of which Cicero and Augustus had dreamed, had become a fact.[75]

This statement would seem to go far beyond the available evidence, and to take for granted answers to several perplexing questions.[76] There are

[71] *BMC*, p. 114, no. 582, pl. 19. 15 (aureus); p. 114, no. 583 (denarius); p. 219 *, pl. 42. 1 (sestertius).

[72] *BMC*, p. 119, no. 607, pl. 20. 8; nos. 608–11 (denarii with PARTHICO on obverse [for aureus see n. on no. 607]); pp. 123–24, nos. 639, 640 (pl. 20. 20), 641–44 (denarii with PARTHICO on reverse); p. 222, nos. 1041–42, pl. 42. 9 (sestertius); p. 224 † (dupondius from Munich).

[73] Mattingly, *BMC*, lxxxv.

[74] The PRO VID issues would seem to stress divine providence without allusion to the emperor. "It is no longer the 'Providentia' of the Emperor, but the wider Providence of the gods, of which that is a part" (ibid.).

[75] Mattingly, *BMC*, lxx.

[76] Mattingly (ibid.) himself admits that "no record of this act of homage has been preserved in our pitiful literary tradition."

difficulties in connecting the legend S P Q R OPTIMO PRINCIPI to the *cognomen "Optimus,"* and it is possible that the legend S P Q R OPTIMO PRINCIPI was some sort of compromise by Trajan who would not accept the title *"Optimus"* which the Senate had offered at least three years earlier. If the most likely reason for his refusing the title *"Optimus"* was a desire to avoid its potential connection with Jupiter Optimus Maximus, then it is probably best not to associate the legend S P Q R OPTIMO PRINCIPI with a ranking "only just after" the god. The superlative comparison with previous *principes* is a more likely explanation. In this regard, the translation of *optimus* as "best" is preferable to Mattingly's enthusiastic "perfect."

While the assurance with which Mattingly posits a senatorial decree for the legend is probably justified, his analysis of what that decree and the resultant coin legend meant needs further examination.

> But we may reasonably find in the formula a statement of the general theory of the imperial administration ... The ultimate authority in Rome is the 'Senate and people of Rome'—they are the Roman state, and from them all legitimate power derives. But when the Senate and people of Rome finds its perfect Emperor, by a voluntary act of devotion it places everything in his hands, confident that its interests are best secured there. Trajan, for his part, set the greatest store on the voluntary co-operation and obedience of the Senate. As long as his essential powers were not questioned, he would go to almost any length to conciliate the Senate and to find the most flattering form under which he could receive the authority it delegated.[77]

Mattingly is idealizing the picture of the relationship between the emperor and the Senate for Trajan in particular, and the entire Principate in general. Pliny's even-tempered chiding of Trajan for refusing senatorial offices and honors indicates that even the *optimus princeps* could ignore authority delegated by the Senate just as easily as he could "find the most flattering form" in which to receive it. Mattingly stresses that granting of the legend S P Q R OPTIMO PRINCIPI is a voluntary act of devotion on the part of the Senate. Given the complete saturation of the coinage with this legend, it is unlikely that Trajan did not play some part in its adoption (perhaps only by giving his approval). On the other hand, the ubiquity of the legend also raises the possibility that it was Trajan who initiated the idea, or, at least, publicized the devotion of the Senate and People to an unprecedented extent.

The devotion of the Senate and People is also represented on the reverse of an aureus type from the end of the reign.[78] It features a figure that

---

[77] Mattingly, *BMC*, lxxi.

[78] The presence of OPTIMUS on the obverse puts the first aureus (*BMC*, p. 115. no. 587, pl.

Mattingly identifies as the Genius of the Senate, togate, pointing to a lighted altar (fig. 3.B).[79] A figure of the Genius of the Roman people is pouring the contents of a patera onto the altar, and holding a cornucopia in the opposite hand.[80] The legend describes the scene as VOTA SUSCEPTA, the offering of vows on behalf of the *salus* of the emperor. Mattingly considers this to be a reference to special vows offered every five years,[81] but since the type had not appeared previously at five-year intervals for Trajan, these coins were possibly a special commemoration of the annual vows.[82] Undoubtedly this type of devotion would have assumed extra importance when Trajan was engaged in the distant campaign against the Parthians. The Senate's role is pictured as supporting or perhaps overseeing, a ritual act of the Roman people. It is an important role, but it is also striking that at the end of the reign, the Senate is pictured in relation to the *Populus Romani*, as opposed to the relationship of shared responsibility with the emperor implied by the "globe passing" types from the earliest years of the reign.[83]

---

19. 18) in 115–116 CE, while PARTHICUS on the obverse of the second aureus (*BMC*, p. 120, no. 612, pl. 20. 9) places it in 117.

[79] This figure resembles others that are labeled as the Senate on the "globe passing" types (sestertius of Nerva [see n. 59 above]; five denarius piece of Trajan [fig. 2.A, see n. 57 above]), or assumed to be the Senate on the denarius type of Trajan (fig. 2.B, see n. 64 above) and the "captured Dacian" type (fig. 2.C, see n. 66 above). The only difference is that when the Senate figure is paired with the emperor in these other examples, the emperor carries a sceptre and the Senate figure carries a scroll. When paired with the Roman people in the sacrifice scene, the Senate is pictured with a sceptre. Mattingly gives no explanation as to why this figure is interpreted as "the Genius of the Senate," while the other occurrences are taken to be personifications of the Senate. Philip V. Hill ("Buildings and Monuments of Rome on the Coins of the Second Century, AD 96–192, Part 2" *Numismatic Chronicle* 145 [1985] 87) mentions a cult statue of the "Genius of the Senate" on coins from the reign of Antoninus Pius. No label is given, but the figure is described as "togate, holding a branch and a wand."

[80] The identification of the figures is confirmed by a type of Antoninus Pius from 141 CE (*BMC*, 2. p. 209 no. 207–9; cited in Hill, "Buildings and Monuments, Part 1," 40). On these reverse types a seminude male figure holding a cornucopia is labeled as GENIUS POP(ULI) ROMANI. In Trajan's coinage there are frequent attestations of an unspecified Genius, that Mattingly describes as naked, holding a patera in one hand, and downward-pointing corn ears in the other (e.g., *BMC*, p. 91, nos. 426–32; p. 104, no. 518, pl. 18. 9; p. 110–11, nos. 545–55; p. 117, nos. 595–99).

[81] Mattingly, *BMC*, lxxiv–lxxxv.

[82] Pliny *Ep.* 10.35. In the case of one aureus reverse type, Salus is pictured, draped, standing with her foot on a globe, sacrificing over an altar with a patera in her right hand, holding a rudder upright in her other hand (*BMC*, p. 87, no. 410, pl. 16. 1). The legend reads SALVS GENERIS HVMANI, and the coin must refer to sacrifice for the well-being of the world through the continued well-being of the world leader Trajan. This last type could be dated any time from 104–111 CE, but a time shortly after Trajan eliminated the Dacian threat to the empire's well-being (106–107) would make sense.

[83] Under Hadrian, an aureus reverse type is issued in which Roma is pictured joining together

Concern for Trajan's well-being while in the east also may be evidenced by the addition of the legend SALVS AUG at this time (115 – 117) to the frequently-used type of personified "Salus" ("well-being") sitting on a throne (or a backless chair) feeding a snake wrapped around a small altar from a patera held in her hand (fig. 3.A).[84] The images of Salus feeding a snake in her arms, or holding a patera, or sacrificing had all been used individually during the decades before Trajan,[85] but it was during his reign that these ideas combined into a single scene. This seems to be an attempt to portray the important role of sacrifice as an appeasement of the gods who provide for the ongoing welfare of Rome.

The Relationship between the Emperor and the Gods

Depictions of sacrifice provide a transition from the discussion of earthly relationships to the question of the relationship between the emperor and the gods. This is seen in the scenes of the *genii* of the Senate and people sacrificing, where the *Genius* as the personified spirit of a Roman person or institution participates in the principal means of communicating with the divine world, beseeching the gods for support of the earthly order. *Concordia* and *Salus* appear (separately) often on the coinage of Trajan, holding a patera, or offering a sacrifice.[86] In addition, there are examples of *Vesta* holding a patera,[87] *Pietas* praying at an altar (fig. 3.C) or sacrificing,[88] and Hercules pouring a libation out of a cup (fig. 3.D).[89] Trajan's father is pictured seated holding a patera in his extended right hand (fig. 4.A).[90] Trajan himself is shown sacrificing (over a lighted altar) in only one type,[91] but

---

the hands of the emperor on the right and the "Genius of the Senate" on the left (*BMC*, p. 303, nos. 506 – 7, pl. 56. 17 – 18).

[84] *BMC*, p. 114, no. 585, pl 19. 17 [aureus]; p. 124, nos. 644 – 645, pl. 21. 1 [denarii]; p. 223 * [Cohen, 333; sestertius]). Cf. many examples of this type without the SALVS AUG legend, e.g., *BMC*, p. 33 *, denarius of 98 – 99 CE from the Lavenham Hoard, p. 198, no. 934, pl. 36. 6 (sestertius).

[85] E.g., holding snake: *BMC* 2. p. 47, nos. 264 – 66, pl. 8. 5 – 6 (aureus and denarii of Vespasian); holding patera in extended hand (sceptre in other hand): *BMC* 2. 207, no. 827, pl. 40. 3 (sestertius of Vespasian); and sacrificing (Fortuna figure with legend SALVS GEN HUMANI): *BMC* 1. pp. 314 – 315, nos. 38 – 45, pl. 52. 18, 20 – 21 (aureus and denarii of Galba).

[86] For *Salus*, see nn. 84 – 85 above; for *Concordia* see, e.g., *BMC*, p. 32, nos. 4 – 6 (denarii); p. 148, nos. 714, 717 (sestertii). There are many more examples of each.

[87] *BMC*, p. 31, no. 2, pl. 9. 2 (denarius); p. 35, nos. 25 – 28, pl. 9. 13 (denarius).

[88] *BMC*, p. 150, nos. 724 – 25, pl. 25. 9. Ibid., p. 85, no. 404, pl. 15. 18 (aureus).

[89] *BMC*, p. 69, no. 263, pl. 14.1 (aureus).

[90] *BMC*, p. 101, nos. 500 – 504, pl. 17. 20 (denarii).

[91] *BMC*, p. 191 * (dupondius cited in Cohen, 513 [Paris]). Cf. the sestertius reverse with Trajan clasping hands with an officer over a lighted altar (see n. 66 above), and the sestertius with Trajan as a priest, veiled, togate, ploughing with two oxen (*BMC*, p. 175, no. 829, pl. 30. 7 [fig.

otherwise the coinage consistently reinforces the traditional importance of
sacrifice in the relationship between the emperor and the gods. Such rein-
forcement is not obvious, however, regarding the importance of the emperor
honoring his deceased predecessor.[92]

Divus Nerva

Pliny commended Trajan for displaying proper devotion toward Nerva. This
devotion is said to have included temples, altars, couches, a priest, and tears
(*Pan.* 11.1, 3),[93] but such devotion does not appear to have included coins
dedicated to *divus Nerva* until well into Trajan's reign. Such dedications
would be expected for a consecrated emperor, given the practices of some of
Trajan's predecessors.[94] Yet *divus Nerva* is found in the extant coinage only
on three examples of imperial aurei (fig. 4.C) restored by Trajan (probably
around 107 CE),[95] and on an aureus reverse type from 112–113 that features

---

4.B]). Mattingly (ibid., c–ci) interprets this type as depicting Trajan ploughing the *sulcus primi-
genius* ("original furrow") of a new colony—Dacia. Trajan also struck a denarius issue reviving
a Republican coin from ca. 170 BCE which featured a bust of Vesta on the obverse, and a
sacrificial knife, *simpulum*, and axe on the reverse (*BMC*, p. 134, no. 682, pl. 22. 17). What is
refered to by Mattingly ("The Restored Coins of Trajan," *NC* ser. 5, vol. 6 (1926) 232–78) as
Trajan's "restoration" of Republican and imperial coin types is discussed below.

[92] Mattingly (*BMC*, xcv) argues that the as reverse type from 98–99 CE showing "Pietas . . .
in prayer at the altar" (*BMC*, p. 152 * [Berlin], nos. 724–725, pl. 25. 9) should be understood as
"a spirit of piety towards the gods." He (ibid.) adds that "it need not exclude the thought of
'piety' to the memory of Nerva." Why not piety to *divus Nerva*? If either meaning is included,
it is certainly not explicit.

[93] No solid evidence for the temples Pliny mentions has been found. Strack (*Untersuchungen*,
147–49, 154) suggested that a sestertius reverse featuring an octastyle podium temple with visible pediment reliefs, roof statuary, and a standing togate figure (holding sceptre and cornucopia)
in the middle of the columns (*BMC*, pp. 181–82, nos. 857–59, pls. 32. 5–7) may represent the
temple of *divus Nerva*. Radice (Pliny, 2. 348) calls the identification as a temple to *divus Nerva*
"doubtful," and Strack (*Untersuchungen*, 154) admits that the identification is not certain, as
does Mattingly (*BMC*, cii). Hill ("Buildings and Monuments, Part 1," 35) argues that the octastyle building should be identified as the *templum Honoris et Virtutis*, an interpretation that
Strack (*Untersuchungen*, 149) explicitly rejected.

[94] Tiberius follows the precedent of Augustus in identifying himself on coinage as son of his
divine predecessor: TI(BERIUS) CAESAR DIVI AUG(USTI) F(ILIUS) from the beginning of his
reign (*BMC* 1. p. 120, no. 1, pl. 22. 1), and issued a series of DIVUS AUGUSTUS PATER coins in
aes (*BMC*, 1. pp. 140–42, nos. 141–60, pl. 25. 10–12, 26. 1–6) with the head of Augustus
radiate on the obverse. Similar honors are seen under Nero for Claudius (*BMC*, 1. pp. 200–1,
nos. 4–6, pl. 38. 7–8), under Titus for Vespasian (e.g., *BMC*, 2. pp. 243–46, nos. 112–35, pl.
47. 1–10 [gold and silver]; pp. 276–78, nos. 249–51 *, pls. 52. 10, 53. 1–2 [*aes*]), and under
Domitian for Vespasian (e.g., *BMC*, 2. 302, no. 21 [denarius; bust of Domitian with legend
including DIVI VESP F DOMITIAN]) and for Titus (*BMC*, 2. p. 313, no. 69, pl. 61. 12 [aureus
with head of Divus Titus, radiate]).

[95] *BMC*, p. 144, no. 706, pl. 24. 12; cf. p. 145, nos. 22–23. Dated by Mattingly.

facing busts of divus Nerva and Trajan senior with the legend DIVI NERVA ET TRAIANUS PAT (fig. 4.D).[96]

The absence of *divus Nerva* from any earlier issues accords with Mattingly's observation of a sharp break between the coinage of Nerva and that of his successor.[97] "The general celebration of it [Nerva's consecration] on the coinage was deferred for nearly ten years—a clear suggestion that his memory had been so unpopular that Trajan had not thought fit to obtrude it on the public till lapse of time had softened resentments."[98] It is not clear what public Mattingly is talking about. If Pliny's discussion in the *Panegyricus* and the letters is any indication, there was no resentment of Nerva by the Senators.[99] Mattingly admits that the sharp break with Nerva he observes in the coinage is "hard to reconcile with the smooth assurances of Pliny's *Panegyric*."[100] Surely it should not be reconciled.

While Syme agrees that there is a break in the coinage, he does not attribute it to Nerva's supposed unpopularity. He interprets the disappearance of Nerva's "Libertas" coinages under Trajan as indicative of the conditions under the new administration. "Although the proprieties are saved and respected, there is a breach in continuity between the 'principatus' of Nerva

---

[96] *BMC*, pp. 100–101, nos. 498–499, pls. 17. 18–19. Mattingly (*BMC*, lxxxi) classifies these coins honoring both adopted and natural fathers with a series of denarii and aurei featuring Trajan's father on the reverse with the legend DIVUS PATER TRAIANUS. These issues are dated to after 112 CE, because of the designation COS VI on the obverse. Mattingly (ibid.) suggests further that the reason for the prominence of Trajan senior at this time is the increasing threat from the east, and the desire to recall and repeat the triumph over the Parthians by Trajan's father in 77 CE (*Pan.* 14.1; cf. *ILS* 8970). Syme (*Tacitus*, 30) states that Trajan senior's resolution of a Parthian crisis was largely diplomatic. Hill ("Buildings and Monuments, Part 2," 91) suggests that "Trajan set up a statue to his father on the occasion of his consecration and that this statue was the model for the coin-type."

[97] "The noble father, Nerva, was succeeded in perfect loyalty and concord by the even nobler son Trajan. But there were ugly facts that could not be removed by a mere refusal to mention them. Nerva had lost respect, and all the piety of Trajan could not alter that fact" (Mattingly, *BMC*, lxix). Sutherland (*Roman Coins*, [New York: Putnam, 1974] 198) sees a significant change in coin portraiture early in Trajan's reign, but suggests a less dramatic explanation than Mattingly: "Perhaps it was because of the exhaustion of an idiom that had lost its flexibility that Trajan (98–117) introduced a totally new tradition—probably a totally new school—of portrait artists at the mint of Rome."

[98] Mattingly, *BMC*, xcii.

[99] *Pan.* 6–10, 88. The letters also reveal a positive attitude toward Nerva; see, e.g., *Ep.* 2.13.8; 7.33.9. Syme (*Tacitus*, 1. 12) is right to see that Pliny does not "disguise the gravity of the crisis" that precipitated Trajan's adoption, but this does not mean that Pliny or his fellow senators disapproved of Nerva. One of the few connections between the coinages of Nerva and Trajan is Trajan's adoption of the "globe passing" type featuring the Senate. It is perhaps significant that this type disappears from Trajan's coinage after 101–102 CE.

[100] Mattingly, *BMC*, lxix.

and the 'imperium' of Trajan. 'Libertas' recedes, the labels are discarded, and the new men surge forward.''[101] Trajan's decision to postpone coin dedications made to *divus Nerva* should be seen in the same realistic light. It was the result of Trajan's desire to distance himself from his senatorial predecessor, not of some supposed popular disenchantment with Nerva. While it may not be possible to understand fully why Trajan chose to postpone dedications to Nerva, certainly it was not done to appease Pliny and his colleagues. It is to the Senate's advantage to have the living emperor show proper devotion to his consecrated predecessor.

Restored Coins Featuring Other Divi Augusti

Trajan eventually honors Nerva as *divus* on coins as part of his series of "restored" Republican denarii and imperial aurei. These issues were probably associated with the collection of "all the obsolete coinage" which is mentioned by Dio Cassius (68.15). Although Dio does not mention that Trajan reissued some of the coin types, the evidence of so many restored issues and the Dio reference make it reasonable to assume that Trajan ordered the collection of much of the coinage that had survived to his day, and then reissued certain types from both the Republican and Imperial periods. Mattingly suggests two reasons for this practice: "(a) The withdrawal of obsolescent coins from circulation and the wish to preserve some record of what is being lost. (b) The desire to explain and commend current policy by linking it to the record of the great past.''[102] Thus Trajan restored coins which he or his mintmasters thought would present an interesting record of the past and a timely promotion of his own reign. He restored aurei from all the previous Caesars who had been deified, going back to Julius, as well as from Tiberius, Galba, and perhaps Vitellius, three emperors who were not consecrated.[103]

All of the "restored" aurei carry the legend IMP CAES TRAIAN AUG

---

[101] Syme, *Tacitus*, 1. 12. This is a much more reasonable understanding than that of Mattingly, who (*BMC*, lxix, lxxvii) suggests that even though it does not appear on the coinage until at least 104 CE, *Libertas* was "the spirit of Trajan's régime" and was therefore not depicted earlier since "it could be taken for granted." The earliest evidence for *libertas* under Trajan has the legend SPQR OPTIMO PRINC, and must be from 104 or later (*BMC*, p. 74, nos. 312–14, pl. 14. 13 [aurei]). It may be significant that the only other evidence for *Libertas* under Trajan comes from restored Republican coins of Brutus (*BMC*, p. 135, no. 684, pl. 22. 21) and Cassius (*BMC*, p. 140, # 24), and on a restored imperial aureus of Galba (*BMC*, p. 143, no. 701, pl. 24.2).

[102] Mattingly, "The Restored Coins of Trajan," *NC* (1926) 232; see also idem, *BMC*, lxxxvii. Mattingly (p. lxxxviii) also suggests that there might have been some hope of profit for the mint in melting down the heavier, finer Republican coins and producing more debased "restored" denarii.

[103] *BMC*, pp. 142–45, nos. 696–706.

GER DAC P P REST on the reverse. Mattingly claims that these titles are consistent with the date which he thinks Dio assigns to the recall of old coinage, 107 CE[104] but why would the "restorations" take place at this time? These titles would be consistent with any date after the awarding of "*Dacicus*" and before the long-delayed acceptance of "*Optimus*," in other words between 102 – 114. It is certainly possible that Dio might not have placed the event in proper chronological order, and that it could make more sense in another context. One suggestion is an earlier dating to the time after the first Dacian war.[105] In this case, it would be possible to tie the "restoration" issues to the beginning of the S P Q R OPTIMO PRINCIPI legend. This connection makes sense, since the restoration would have served as a reminder of the virtues of the great Roman leaders of the past, and a vivid background for the proclamation of Trajan as *optimus princeps*.[106] In contrast to this glorification of past leaders, it is striking that Pliny highlights the achievements of Trajan by focusing upon the negative aspects of previous *principes*, not the positive.[107] While it is impossible to be certain, given his generally poor opinion of Trajan's predecessors, it seems unlikely that Pliny would have been impressed by the "restoration" issues of the *optimus princeps*, even if he would have approved of the virtues that it promoted.

Virtus

The positive portrayal of the moral tone of Trajan's reign which was seen in Pliny's *Panegyricus*[108] is also present in the coinage. Personifications of various virtues[109] are employed to demonstrate that Trajan's reign is a time

[104] Mattingly, *BMC*, lxxxvii. In fact, Dio includes the recall among a number of activities that took place following Trajan's return to Rome after the second Dacian war, with no attempt at precise dating, and in fact Ernest Cary (*Dio's Roman History* [9 vols.; LCL; Cambridge: Harvard University Press, 1968] 8. 389 – 90) dates the preceding and following events to 110 CE.

[105] If there was any hope for financial gain from melting down the old coinage, it would make more sense to place the venture after the first conflict, when the cost of the war and repeated *alimenta* might have placed a strain on the economy. After the second war, the booty taken from Dacia apparently eased any financial tensions, and provided the abundance of resources that were then channeled into extensive building projects (see Dio 14).

[106] Of course the "restoration" issues would have provided this background even if they were released later in the reign. Mattingly (*BMC*, xciii) suggests that "the legendary glories of the Republic descend through the line of great Republican generals and statesmen and after them through the 'good' Emperors to the 'optimus princeps' who guarantees the 'optimus status rerum', which had been the dream of the Roman patriots of all ages."

[107] *Pan.* 45.1; 53.2. Pliny makes positive comparisons only with Pompey (*Pan.* 29.1), *divus Titus* (*Pan.* 35.4), and *divus Nerva* (*Pan.* 35.4; 88.6; 94.4 – 5).

[108] "Indeed, the rewards of virtue under the Principate are the same as in the time of freedom" (*Pan.* 44.6); cf. 70.2.

[109] The reverse types of *Pietas*, *Concordia*, *Genius*, *Libertas*, *Providentia*, and *Salus* have been

of right thinking, peace, and security.[110] Mattingly supports the picture of a promising opening to Trajan's reign with his interpretation of an early reverse type showing a woman seated on a curule chair that has cornucopiae as arms, holding a vertical sceptre (fig. 5.A).[111] Mattingly reads the image as representing *Iustitia-Astraea*, the spirit of the Golden Age, "who marked its close by taking flight to heaven."[112] Accordingly, the return of the goddess would signify that Trajan's reign was instituting a new Golden Age.[113] Mattingly does not provide any parallels for this image identified as *Iustitia*,[114] and although his suggestion is helpful, it cannot be regarded as final. Strack

---

mentioned above. Also emphasized are *Abundantia/Annona* (e.g., *BMC*, p. 206, no. 973 and n. [sestertius]; p. 56, nos. 169–73, pl. 12. 13 [denarius]; p. 57, no. 174, pl. 12. 14 [aureus]), *Aequitas* (*BMC*, p. 56, nos. 166–68, pl. 12. 11–12 [denarii]; p. 72, nos. 288–293, pl. 14. 7 [denarii]), *Aeternitas* (*BMC*, pp. 81–82, nos. 373–77, pl. 15. 11 [denarii]; p. 87, no. 411 A [denarius]; p. 95, nos. 465–67, pl. 17. 5 [denarii]), *Felicitas* (e.g., *BMC*, p. 59, nos. 192–99, pl. 12. 18–19 [denarii]; p. 219, nos. 1027–28, pl. 42. 2 [dupondii]), *Fides* (*BMC*, p. 59–60, nos. 200–202, pl. 12. 20 [denarii]; p. 130 [hybrid]; pp. 229–30, nos. 1080–82, pl. 44. 5 [sestertii with Plotina on obv.]), *Fortuna* (e.g., *BMC*, p. 32, no. 7, pl. 9. 4 [aureus]; p. 35, nos. 31–33, pl. 9. 15 [aurei]; p. 40, no. 66, pl. 10. 8 [aureus]; p. 60, nos. 203–204, pl. 13. 1 [denarii]; p. 219, no. 1026, pl. 41. 8 [sestertius]), *Pax* (e.g., *BMC*, pp. 74–75, nos. 315–318 *, pl. 14. 14 [denarii]; p. 189, nos. 891–92, pl. 34. 3 [dupondii]), *Securitas*(?) (*BMC*, p. 33 † [denarius]), *Spes* (e.g., *BMC*, p. 75, nos. 322–24, pl. 14. 16 [denarii]; p. 198, no. 935, pl. 36. 7 [sestertius], and *Victoria* (e.g., *BMC*, p. 50, no. 139, pl. 11. 14 [gold quinarius]; p. 87, no. 411, pl. 16. 2 [denarius]; p. 172, nos. 812–16, pl. 30. 1 [sestertii]).

[110] This emphasis on the quality of the age is seen in Trajan's order that Pliny not accept anonymous accusations against Christians "for it is the worst example and not fitting for our age" (*Ep.* 10.97.2). Likewise, Pliny thinks obeying the Senate's request for his services "to be most in accord with your [Trajan's] peaceful age" (*Pan.* 10.3 A). In *Ep.* 10.55 Trajan claims that forcing loans on people in order to fund public works "is not in accord with the justice of our times."

[111] *BMC*, pp. 32–33, nos. 9–13, pl. 9. 6 (denarii); p. 36, nos. 36–37, pl. 9. 17 (denarii); p. 37, no. 47 [denarius]; p. 40, no. 68, pl 10. 10 (denarius); p. 41, ‡ (Cohen, 596; denarius); p. 44, no. 98 (denarius); p. 149, nos. 719–23, pl. 25. 6–8 (dupondii); p. 151 * (Cohen, 57; as); p. 159 * (Cohen, 173; dupondius); p. 160, nos. 762–64, pl. 27. 8 (dupondii); p. 162 * (Cohen, 643; dupondius); p. 188, no. 890, pl. 34. 2 (dupondius); cf. p. 554. Most of these examples are from the first years of Trajan's reign, and only the last dupondius must be dated in 104 CE or later, given its SPQR OPTIMO PRINCIPI legend.

[112] Mattingly, *BMC*, lxvi. He calls the type rare, as it appears only under Trajan and in one instance under Antoninus Pius (ibid.).

[113] This is a common claim at the beginning of the reign of an emperor. Mattingly describes an aureus reverse of Hadrian, featuring a male figure naked to the waist, standing in an oval frame, holding a phoenix on a globe (*BMC*, p. 278, no. 312, pl. 52. 10). Since the legend includes SAEC(ULUM) AUR(EUM) in the exergue, Mattingly (*BMC*, cxxxi) takes the figure to be the "Genius of the Golden Age." *Astraea/Iustitia* also "returned" during Augustus's reign (Vergil *Eclogue* 4).

[114] He mentions one parallel on an aureus of Hadrian (*BMC*, 3. p. 332, no. 731, pl. 61. 8), identified as *Securitas*.

reads the figure as *Annona* with a suggestion of *Securitas* in her pose,[115] but this interpretation also would suggest an attempt to portray a propitious opening to Trajan's reign.

Throughout the reign, the coinage features images of *Virtus* herself wearing military dress (fig. 5.B), with her foot on a helmet, carrying a spear and a *parazonium* ("dagger").[116] In one case, Mattingly interprets a similar figure as *Roma* with attributes of *Virtus*,[117] and in other instances Trajan is shown holding the spear and *parazonium* as he is being crowned by Victory (fig. 5.C).[118] The attributes of *Virtus* are also present on an issue dated late in the reign (116–117 CE), which shows Trajan holding the spear and *parazonium* standing between reclining figures of the Tigris and Euphrates river-gods— representing Mesopotamia—and a reclining personification of Armenia (fig. 5.D).[119] The legend describes Trajan's resolutions of crises in these two provinces: ARMENIA ET MESOPOTAMIA IN POTESTATEM PR REDACTAE ("Armenia and Mesopotamia returned to the authority of the Roman people"). The image must depict Trajan at the end of his reign as a virtuous ruler/conqueror.[120] It is interesting to note that *Virtus* does not appear on coinage before the civil war following the death of Nero in 68.[121] It then continues to appear under Vespasian,[122] and becomes common on *aes* coinage of Domitian (fig. 6.A).[123]

---

[115] Strack, *Untersuchungen*, 65–67.

[116] *BMC*, p. 63, no. 229, pl. 13. 10 [aureus]; pp. 63–64, nos. 230–35, pl. 13. 11 [denarii]; p. 93, no. 444, pl. 16. 17 [denarius]; pp. 111–12, nos. 559–64, pl. 19. 10 [denarii]; p. 118, nos. 600–601, pl. 20. 4 [denarii]; p. 122, nos. 631–33, pl. 20. 17 [denarii]). *Virtus* does not appear alone on *aes* coinage, but does share sestertii reverses with *Felicitas* (*BMC*, p. 205, 225 n. [both coins in Vienna]). The *Virtus Felicitas* combination also appears on an aureus (*BMC*, p. 103 [Cohen, 653]). Mattingly (*BMC*, lxxx) describes *Virtus* as the "constant companion of Victory."

[117] *BMC*, p. 104, no. 517 * [Cohen, 111; denarius].

[118] *BMC*, p. 48, nos. 131–34, pl. 11. 10 [aurei]; p. 53, no. 154, pl. 12. 4 [denarii]; p. 64, nos. 236–41, pl. 13. 12 [denarii].

[119] *BMC*, pp. 221–22, nos. 1033–40, pl. 42. 6–8 [sestertii].

[120] The same idea is portrayed by the REX PARTHIS DATUS issue (*BMC*, p. 223, nos. 1045–49, pl. 43.1 [sestertii]) on which Trajan is crowning king Parthamapates with his right hand, and holding a *parazonium* in the left. Mattingly argues that a reverse type showing a naked male figure erecting a trophy (*BMC*, p. 48, no. 135, pl. 11. 11) might represent *Virtus Augusti* as depicted by Galba (*BMC*, 1. p. 316, no. 50), with "the conception of 'manliness' overriding the feminine gender of the noun 'Virtus' " (*BMC*, 3. lxix). I do not find this argument compelling.

[121] E.g., *BMC*, 1. 293, no. 14 rev., pl. 50.4 (denarius from Spain, obverse features female head with the legend BONI EVENTUS); *BMC*, 1. p. 351, no. 234 rev. (denarius of Galba).

[122] E.g., *BMC*, 2. pp. 104–5, nos. 499–501, pl. 18. 9 (denarius).

[123] E.g., *BMC*, 2. p. 383, no. 384, pl. 76. 1. This is an example of Trajan's continuity with Domitian which Waters did not mention.

The Gods on Roman Imperial Coinage Under Trajan

While the gods who are portrayed on Trajan's coinage are many and various, only a few appear frequently. Images of Neptune, Venus, Saturn, Apollo, Nemesis, Mercury, and Janus are found only among the Republican denarii and imperial aurei that Trajan restored.[124] Others, including Diana, Minerva, and Sol, appear in the restored coinage, and in one or two other places.[125] Silvanus, or what Mattingly describes as the "great native deity of the wood-lands of Illyricum" with the attributes of Silvanus, appears on two *aes* coin reverses.[126]

The goddess Vesta appears more frequently. She is present early in the reign, draped, wearing a crown and a veil, and holding a patera in one hand and a torch in the other (fig. 6.B).[127] This figure is common on the denarii through 101 – 102 CE, after which it disappears.[128] Mattingly describes this type as " '*Vesta P. R. Quiritium*,' the goddess of the old state worship, not the new imperial cult of Vesta, founded by Augustus for the imperial family on the Palatine."[129] According to Mattingly the latter Vesta is represented on a series of coins starting after 102 CE,[130] in which Vesta is seated holding a palladium and a sceptre (fig. 6.C).[131] That Vesta in this pose is to be

[124] Neptune: *BMC*, p. 137, no., 693, pl. 23.14; p. 140 # 17b. Venus: *BMC*, p. 139 # 13; p. 141 # 31. Saturn: *BMC*, p. 139 # 8a (cf. *BMC*, p. 196 ‡). Apollo: *BMC*, p. 134, no. 680, pl. 22. 14; p. 137, no. 691 obv., pl. 23. 12 (Diana on rev.). Nemesis: *BMC*, p. 142, no. 696, pl. 23. 17. Mercury: *BMC*, p. 133, no. 678 obv., pl. 22. 13. Janus: *BMC*, p. 138 # 1, pl. 22. 1.

[125] Diana (restored issues): *BMC*, p. 137, no. 691 rev., pl. 23 (Apollo on obv.). 12; p. 140 # 23 a and b; p. 141 # 34 a. Diana (other): *BMC*, p. 225, no. 1057 rev., pl. 43. 6 (quadrans). Minerva (restored issues): *BMC*, p. 139 # 11 c; p. 145 # 20 rev. (with Mars). Minerva (other): *BMC*, p. 107 * rev. (R.It., 1902, p. 17; gold quinarius with Plotina on obv.); p. 225, no. 1057 obv., pl. 43. 6 (quadrans); p. 226 * (Cohen, 342; quadrans); p. 227 * (Stefano Johnson Coll., Milan; quadrans). Sol (restored issues): *BMC*, p. 134, no. 681 obv., pl. 22. 16; p. 141 # 34 a obv. (Diana on rev.). Sol (other): *BMC*, p. 117, nos. 592 – 93 rev., pl. 20.1 (denarii); p. 121, nos. 621 – 25 rev., pl. 20. 12 – 14.

[126] *BMC*, p. 196 ‡ (Cohen, 364; dupondis); p. 213 ‡, pl. 39. 10 (Vienna; as). See Mattingly, *BMC*, xcix.

[127] E.g., *BMC*, p. 31, no. 2, pl. 9. 2 (denarius from the first year of the reign, 98 – 99 CE). The bust of Vesta appears on the obverse of two restored Republican denarii (*BMC*, p. 134, no. 682, pl. 22. 17; p. 135, no. 685, pl. 22. 22). Cf. *BMC*, p. 131, no. 671, pl. 21. 20.

[128] The same pose is found on the reverse of a restored aureus of Claudius and a restored aureus from the time of the civil wars (Mattingly suggests Galba) with a bust of Jupiter on the obverse (*BMC*, p. 145 nos. 9, 11).

[129] Mattingly, *BMC*, lxv.

[130] All of the coins with Vesta in this pose are labeled COS V, COS V DES VI, or COS VI. As such they all can be dated between 103 and 113 when the OPTIMUS cognomen is added. The series might be best dated near the end of this time frame since there are more examples with COS V DES VI (111 CE) and COS VI (112 CE) in the legend.

[131] Mattingly, *BMC*, lxxvi, lxxix, lxxxii. Examples of the type include *BMC*, p. 71 * (Cohen,

associated with the imperial family is supported by her appearance on coins with obverses featuring Plotina.[132] According to Mattingly, in the coinage, the Vesta of the people was superceded by the Vesta of the imperial family.

Divine Military Imagery

The military successes of Trajan's reign are also emphasized on coins using divine imagery. The goddess Roma frequently appears helmeted, in military dress holding a Victory in one hand and a spear in the other.[133] The source of the victory is depicted on sestertii reverses from 103 CE. In the scene, Roma, seated with her spear, receives the Victory figure from the outstretched hands of Trajan (fig. 6.D).[134]

Of all divinities associated with war, the figure of Mars appears most frequently on Trajan's coinage. The most common pose shows Mars, naked except for a helmet, walking with spear in one hand and trophy over the other shoulder (fig. 7.A). The type appears first on reverses of denarii and sestertii with COS IIII designations, meaning a date of 101–102 CE.[135] This would place it during or shortly after the first Dacian war. The same reverse type continues to be used until the end of the reign.[136] The image of Mars standing with his spear and resting on his shield is also found,[137] along with an adaptation on which the shield rests on top of a small figure of a Dacian.[138] In Trajan's coinage, the gods are often invoked to symbolize the military successes of the régime.

64; denarius); p. 86, nos. 405–9, pl. 15. 20 (denarii); p. 98, nos. 482–83, pl. 17. 12 (denarii).

[132] *BMC*, p. 106, no. 525, pl. 18, 12 (aureus); p. 106, nos. 526–28, pl. 18. 13–14 (denarii).

[133] E.g., *BMC*, pp. 70–71, nos. 271–80, pl. 14. 4–5 (denarii). Mattingly would date this issue to shortly after the second Dacian war 106–107. A similar design (holding Victory and *parazonium*) is found on an aureus rev. type from the beginning of the reign (*BMC*, p. 31, no. 1, pl. 9. 1; p. 34 † (Cohen, 204). Various poses of Roma holding the Victory and spear are also seen on the reverses of *aes* coinage (e.g., *BMC*, p. 187, nos. 881–83, pl. 33. 7 [dupondii]). The end of the Dacian conflict is made clear in a reverse type in which a small figure of a Dacian is kneeling below a much larger standing Roma emploring her for mercy with outstretched hands (e.g., *BMC*, p. 164, nos. 772–74, pl. 28. 1 [sestertii]), or in scenes where a seated Roma, still holding Victory and spear, has her foot on the head of a Dacian (e.g., *BMC*, p. 165, 778 [sestertius]).

[134] *BMC*, pp. 159–60, nos. 757–59, pl. 27. 4; p. 161 * (Cohen, 600).

[135] *BMC*, p. 43, nos. 94–97, pl. 10. 17 (denarius); p. 156, no. 743, pl. 26. 7 (sestertius).

[136] It is found on denarii with the PARTHICO legend from 115–117 CE (*BMC*, pp. 120–21, nos. 616–20, pl. 20. 11).

[137] *BMC*, p. 55, nos. 158–60, pl. 12. 7–8 (denarii); p. 153, nos. 737–39, pl. 26. 5 (as); p. 154, no. 742 A (as). In another case, Mars stands holding spear in right hand and trophy in left (*BMC*, p. 102 * [aureus]).

[138] *BMC*, p. 55, nos. 161–62, pl 12.9.

Hercules

While there is no obvious attempt to make any direct connection with
Trajan's military accomplishments in the Hercules imagery, the implication
is that Trajan's efforts are comparable with the labors of Hercules.[139] The
type of Hercules standing on a low statue base with the lion skin over his
head (or draped over his arm), holding his club downward (fig. 7.B), is found
primarily on issues with COS III or COS IIII legends, which can be dated
between 100–102 CE.[140] In addition to this statue type, the bust of Hercules
also appears on the obverse of quadrans types from 102 CE.[141] Mattingly suggests that Trajan's birthplace in southern Spain accounts for his special
interest in Hercules Gaditanus, who drove the cattle of King Geryon to Italy
from the island near Gades.[142] The image serves an additional purpose, however, according to Mattingly, who sees Trajan placing Hercules on the
coinage to promote himself "as the imperial Hercules whose labours for the
world will one day win him immortality."[143] It is probably not possible to be
as certain about Trajan's intentions as Mattingly is here. While Hercules is
an important figure on Trajan's coinage, the use of Hercules imagery falls
within a fairly limited time frame. There are no examples before the period
100–103 CE and only a few after. Did the image prove unpopular for some

[139] Pliny makes this comparison as well (*Pan.* 14.5).

[140] *BMC*, p. 38–39, nos. 56–58, pl. 10. 5 (aurei); p. 39, no. 59 (denarius); p. 42, nos. 81–85,
pl. 10. 14 (aurei); pp. 42–43, nos. 86–92, pl. 10. 15 (denarii); p. 43, no. 93, pl. 10. 16 (silver
quinarius). There is one example of a denarius (*BMC* , p. 51, † [Cohen, 597]) with COS V designation which runs through 111 CE. Since it does not have the SPQR OPTIMO PRINCIPI legend it
is probably from 103 CE. One later denarius (COS VI, 112–117 CE) and an as have a similarly
posed Hercules (*BMC*, p. 89 * [Cohen, 382]); p. 213 *). Cf. the reverse of an undated quadrans
(*BMC*, p. 225, no. 1058, pl. 43. 7). Hill ("Buildings and Monuments, Part 2," 82) points out
evidence of the statue on aureus and denarius types from 107 CE that are omitted from *BMC*: a
denarius from the Pyrford hoard, now in the British Museum, and an aureus from the Bourgey
sale, 27 March 1912, 290.

[141] Dated by Hill, "Buildings and Monuments, Part 2," 82. *BMC*, pp. 226–27, nos.
1062–67, pl. 43. 10–12 (boar on rev.); p. 227, nos. 1071–74, pl. 43. 14–15 (club on rev.).
There is also one example of a bust of Hercules with the legend COS VI (*BMC*, p. 225, no. 1060
n. [Cohen, 338]) which would date to 112–113 CE. A bust of Hercules is also found on a
restored Republican issue (*BMC*, p. 132, no. 674, pl. 22. 7). Examples of Hercules sacrificing
(*BMC*, p. 54, no. 156 A n. [denarius]; p. 69, no. 263, pl 14. 1 [aureus]) have already been mentioned (see p. 99, n. 95 above).

[142] Mattingly, *BMC*, lxx. Hill ("Buildings and Monuments, Part 2," 82) suggests that the
image represents the statue associated with the *Ara Maxima Herculis Invicti* ("great altar of
unconquerable Hercules") which was located in the Forum Boarium ("cattle-market") of
ancient Rome where Hercules slew the giant cattle thief Cacus.

[143] Mattingly, *BMC*, lxx. Cf. Strack, *Untersuchungen*, 95–104; and Beaujeu, *La Religion*,
80–87.

reason, or was it perhaps simply superceded by the images of Mars and other types more directly tied to the military achievements of Trajan's reign?

Jupiter

When viewed in context of the rest of Trajan's coinage, Jupiter's appearances are not as predominant as Fears has implied in his theory of Trajan's "Jovian theology."[144] In some cases, images of Jupiter were used in the same way as were those of Roma and Mars to emphasize the military efforts of Trajan. Jupiter is found seated (fig. 7.C), holding a Victory and sceptre much as Roma was.[145] One reverse type of restored denarii shows Jupiter riding in a quadriga, and another type shows Victory in the same pose.[146] Hill interprets the image of an octastyle temple with colonnades right and left and a seated statue (holding a sceptre) between the columns as a depiction of the temple of Jupiter Victor (fig. 7.D).[147] The image is found on the reverse of sestertii that Hill dates to Trajan's decennalia in 105–106 CE.[148] This dating would also correspond with the projected or realized end to the second Dacian war, and again serve as a celebration of the military successes of Trajan.[149]

The most frequently attested image of Jupiter shows the god holding a thunderbolt over a much smaller figure of Trajan (fig. 8.A). It appears on reverses of coins of all metals with the legend CONSERVATORI PATRIS PATRIAE ("to the preserver of the father of the country").[150] Mattingly

[144] Fears, "Jupiter," 77–85.

[145] *BMC*, p. 54 ‡; p. 69, no. 264, pl. 14. 2 (aureus).

[146] Jupiter: *BMC*, p. 139 # 8a (head of Saturn obv.); p. 140 # 25. Victory: *BMC*, p. 139 # 4 (Roma rev.). Cf. p. 138 # 1 (Janus obv.), in which Jupiter holds a thunderbolt and a sceptre and rides in a quadriga driven by Victory. Busts of Jupiter also appear on the obverse of restored coinage (*BMC*, p. 133, no. 676, pl. 22. 9 (denarius); p. 145 # 11, pl. 24. 3 (restored aureus from the time of the civil wars, Mattingly posits it as a coin of Galba). An undated quadrans depicts Jupiter Ammon on the reverse (*BMC*, p. 222 * [Vienna]).

[147] Hill, "Monuments and Buildings, Part 2," 49–50. Mattingly (*BMC*, 182, no. 863 n.) also admits that the seated figure is probably Jupiter.

[148] *BMC*, pp. 182–83, nos. 863–66, pl. 32. 8–9; p. 193 †; p. 202, no. 958, pl. 37.8.

[149] Another coin image associated with Jupiter is the archway structure (with the IOM inscription) which is pictured on reverses of sestertii dated by Hill to between 104 and 107 CE. Mattingly (*BMC*, ci, 177) calls this a triumphal arch, but Hill ("Buildings and Monuments, Part 1," 42–43) argues that it should be seen as the entry gate to the temple of Jupiter Optimus Maximus on the Capitoline, even though there is no record of Trajan having done any work on such a monument.

[150] *BMC*, p. 100, nos. 493–94, pl. 17. 16 (aurei); p. 100, nos. 495–97, pl. 17. 17 (denarii); p. 103, no. 513, pl. 18. 6 (aureus); p. 104, nos. 514–17, pl. 18.7–8 (denarii); p. 108, no. 533, pl. 18. 19 (aureus); p. 109, nos. 534–35, pl. 18. 20 (denarius); p. 203 § (Cohen, 48; sestertius); p. 215 * (Vatican; sestertius); p. 217 * (Cohen, 49; sestertius).

believes that this type should be connected to Trajan's miraculous escape from an earthquake which caused great loss of life in Antioch in 114 CE.[151] This is a reasonable suggestion, but it raises one problem with regard to date. All of the "*conservatori*" types bear the designation COS VI with the cognomen OPTIMUS, but not PARTHICUS. These suggest a dating after 114 CE when OPTIMUS was added and before the addition of PARTHICUS in 115, and as such they could fit as a response to the earthquake which occurred in early 115. Two examples of this type, however, do not have OPTIMUS among Trajan's titles,[152] and it is hard to imagine that these can be related to the earthquake in 115 when the OPTIMUS title would have been well established. That the issue with Jupiter as protector could have appeared when Trajan left for his eastern campaign in 113 CE, is certainly possible; it may have been continued, or renewed after the miraculous rescue two years later.

In looking at the portrayal of the relationship between the emperor and the gods one final coin type should be considered. It is the reverse type from sestertii dated to 104 – 111 CE, on which Trajan is depicted as being crowned by a Victory while holding a spear in his left hand, and a thunderbolt in his extended right hand (fig. 1.A).[153] This reverse type is actually an adaptation of the Victory crowning type in which Trajan holds a spear and a *parazonium* (fig. 5.C).[154] The difference in the objects held by Trajan is significant, however, since the thunderbolt carries significant meaning as an undeniable attribute of Jupiter.[155] This scene, in which Trajan holds the thunderbolt, is a revival of a similar type of Domitian, but while it was widespread as a coin type under Domitian,[156] it survives in only two types from Trajan's reign. It is significant that Trajan revived the image, since it does not seem to fit with the picture of the modesty of Trajan's reign observed elsewhere.

Mattingly tries to explain this difficulty by blaming the Senate. "Now the passion of the Senate to confer praise overrides the decent modesty of Trajan."[157] It has already been stated, however, that the emperor was not entirely removed from the minting of *aes* coinage. If Pliny is any indication, it can also be said that at least some members of the Senate would have frowned upon such a representation of Trajan as Jupiter. Because this type

---

[151] Mattingly, *BMC*, lxxxii; cf. Dio 58.24 – 25.

[152] *BMC*, p. 100, nos. 494 – 97; p. 203 §.

[153] See p. 15, n. 82 above.

[154] See p. 105, n. 118 above.

[155] The reverse of a coin of *divus Vespasianus* restored by Trajan, features a winged thunderbolt on a throne (*BMC*, p. 143, no. 703, pl. 24. 7).

[156] See p. 13, n. 70 above.

[157] Mattingly, *BMC*, c. He continues, "To attribute the thunderbolt of Jupiter directly to the Emperor is to step very near the line that divides homage from adulation" (ibid.).

survives in only a few examples of one metal, it is probably safe to say that this was a limited issue, one that was not repeated to any extent. Whether Trajan or one of his mint-masters was responsible for the idea of reusing this type from the coinage of Domitian cannot be known with certainty. It can be surmised, however, that at some point of military success in the reign, most likely after the second victory over the Dacians, the image of Trajan being crowned while holding the thunderbolt was released as the ultimate expression of Trajan as the victorious general. Apparently it did not meet with much success, and when Jupiter imagery was next called for, it was the god who held the thunderbolt, with Trajan standing in much smaller scale under its protection.

Observations and Conclusions on Coinage

This investigation of imperial coinage under Trajan has produced several separate conclusions. For some of the coin types considered, the portrayal of Trajan's reign and his relationship to the gods is compatible with the picture presented by Pliny. There is evidence to illustrate both sides of the mutual relationship between the emperor and the gods that Pliny had presented. On the one hand, the gods are honored for acting on behalf of the emperor: Mars going off to battle, or Jupiter protecting Trajan. In response, Trajan is pictured offering sacrifice, or presenting a Victory to Roma. The personification of Salus feeding the snake wrapped around the altar, and the image of the Genius of the Senate affirming the sacrifice of the Genius of the Roman people are both symbolic of the important part that traditional sacrifice plays in maintaining the mutual relationship. All these images would fit well into the picture of the proper relationship between the Senate, the emperor, and the gods which Pliny presents in the *Panegyricus*.

Other images from the coinage, however, do not fit as well with Pliny's picture. One of the most prominent themes of the imperial coin reverses is divine responsibility for Trajan's military successes. This is not surprising during the reign of a general who continued to be a successful soldier after becoming *princeps*. It is clear, however, that while Pliny understood the need for successful military action, his preference was for the nonmilitary qualities and achievements.[158] As a realist, Pliny includes praise in his revised *gratiarum actio* for what he expected to be Trajan's victory in the first Dacian conflict (*Pan.* 16.5 – 17.3), but his picture of the ideal reign of Trajan and the proper relationship between the emperor and the gods did not

[158] *Pan.* 16.1. Cf. *Ep.* 10.14.

include the extensive emphasis on military matters that is predominant in the coinage.[159]

The "globe passing" coinage of Nerva, that was continued in the early years of Trajan's reign, coincided with Pliny's picture of the Senate sharing with the *princeps* in the administration of the empire. The fact that this type disappeared after 103 CE should not be overemphasized: it could simply have fallen out of fashion after Trajan's accession. On the other hand, its disappearance might be indicative of a decrease in the Senate's participation in the reign. Likewise, too much meaning should not be given to the failure to honor *divus Nerva* on the coinage until the middle of the reign. Yet it must be recognized that Pliny put a great deal of emphasis upon the proper relationship between Trajan and his divinized predecessor, while this emphasis is almost completely absent from the range of reverses on coins issued by the imperial mints during Trajan's reign.

Trajan's use of Hercules imagery would not have raised problems for Pliny,[160] but it is likely that he would have objected to the use of the image of Trajan holding the thunderbolt.[161] Even if Pliny did not object, there must have been resistance from some quarter, since the type was so short-lived.

What emerges from examination of the imperial coinage, then, is a mixed picture of Trajan's reign and a variegated portrayal of the relationship between the emperor and the gods. Scholars such as Kennedy, Liebeschuetz, and Mattingly who try to present Trajan's rule as a time of pure enlightenment, must account for evidence of a more authoritarian style of rule: perhaps suggested by the absence of *Libertas* types until well into the reign, and the attempt to downplay the memory of his predecessor. At the same time, others such as Waters, who would paint Trajan's reign as a period of increasing despotism, must admit that the evidence is not unequivocal. There are indications that the reverse imagery on imperial coinage under Trajan is more modest than under Domitian. This is seen especially in the very limited evidence for identification of Trajan with Jupiter by portraying the emperor holding the thunderbolt. Trajan's coinage portrays him as a strong leader and a virtuous general who is mindful that he is indebted to the gods for his successes. It also makes clear that his subjects are indebted to the gods for their ruler. The picture is not simple, then, and must not be treated as if it were. When Pliny presents his *gratiarum actio* at the beginning of Trajan's

---

[159] This is one example of why Pliny's picture should not be accepted as representative of the entire reign.

[160] While he would have understood an implied connection between Trajan and Hercules, he would not have shared the extreme interpretation of Mattingly (*BMC*, lxx).

[161] Under no circumstances was the emperor to be considered as being a god (*Pan.* 1.3).

reign, he is not trying to give a complete picture, but rather a perspective of the positive aspects and promise of that reign that he would like to encourage. The presentations on the coinage of Trajan presumably were meant to do the same. The positive aspects of Trajan's character and achievements that the coinage emphasizes are not exactly the same as Pliny's, but neither are they very different. If one considers the evidence of Pliny and the coinage as independent, but complementary sources, it is possible to obtain a fuller and more complex picture of Trajan's reign.

Monumental Art and Architecture

Other nonliterary sources for perspectives on Trajan's reign and the relationship between the emperor and the gods come from monuments, buildings, and sculptural reliefs. As with coinage, there has been a tendency among scholars to postulate a category of "official monuments" which can be used as evidence of the "policy" of the ruler.[162] While some monuments may be accurate reflections of imperial policy, it is necessary to use the same care as with coinage to determine the extent to which the emperor was involved in a particular building project. In discussing "Imperial Building in the Eastern Roman Provinces," Stephen Mitchell has explored the problems inherent in discerning the level of imperial involvement in financing construction projects.

> A subject that at first sight might seem easy to investigate, a simple matter of emperors paying for the erection of public buildings, following a well-ordered and predictable pattern of aristocratic liberality, turns out to be far more involved. The model by which we should interpret imperial generosity must be a complex one, corresponding to the complicated role that the emperor played in the life of his subjects.[163]

Mitchell cites one illustration of the uncertainty of this process found in the Augustan market building at Lepcis Magna. The inscription above one doorway reads [Imp. Caesar divi f. Augustus] cos. XI imp. XIIII trib. pot. XV pont. M[axi]mus. If this restoration is correct, one would assume that Augustus had sponsored the construction of the building. Additional text has survived, however, which makes it clear that funds for the building came from a local priest.[164] Another example concerns the city walls at Nicaea.

---

[162] Fears ("Jupiter," 58), when he adapts A. D. Nock's distinction between the "working theory of the principate" and "the metaphorical language used by men of letters," includes "official monuments" as one of the indicators of "what the princeps officially says or does."

[163] Mitchell, "Imperial Building in the Eastern Roman Provinces," *HSCP* 91 (1987) 333–65.

[164] Ibid., 343.

An inscription at the West Gate credits Claudius Gothicus with constructing the fortifications. The South Gate features an inscription stating that the city dedicated the walls to the emperor.[165] These two examples argue for caution about claiming official status both for imperial monuments and for inscriptions. It could be argued that Mitchell's examples come from the provinces, and that since there was more official control of building projects in Italy and Rome, it is possible to make definite determinations about imperial involvement in projects close to home. Even near the capitol, however, it is not always easy to determine the extent to which the emperor influenced a building project.

The Arch of Beneventum

For example, the "Arch of Trajan" still stands in the town of Beneventum, approximately halfway between Rome and the southern Italian port city of Brundisium (Brindisi). The arch marks the beginning of the *via Traiana*, a new roadway built by Trajan between Beneventum and Brundisium.[166] The inscription (*CIL* 9. 1558), identical on both sides of the arch (figs. 9 and 10), reports that it is the Senate's dedication to Trajan:

IMP(eratori) CAESARI DIVI NERVAE FILIO/NERVAE
TRAIANO OPTIMO AUG(usto)/GERMANICO DACICO
PONTIF(ici) MAX(imo) TRIB(unicia)/POTEST(ate)

---

[165] Ibid., 342

[166] An inscription (*ILS*, 5866) found on the road between Beneventum and Aequum Tuticum records Trajan's support for the project:

> Imp. Caesar divi Nervae f. Nerva Traianus Aug. Germ. Daci[c.] pont. max. tr. pot. XIII imp. VI cos. V p.p. viam et pontes [a] Benevento Brundisium pecunia sua [fecit];

> "Emperor Caesar, son of the god Nerva, Nerva Trajan Augustus, triumphant over Germany and Dacia, Chief Priest, Tribunician power for the thirteenth time, imperium for the sixth time, Consul for the fifth time, Father of his Country, constructed the road and bridges from Beneventum to Brundisium from his own funds."

The indication of the thirteenth tribunician power dates the inscription and some stage of the road's construction to 108–109 CE. On the question of imperial wealth see Millar, *Emperor*, 189–201.

The *via Traiana* is also commemorated on coinage featuring a reverse type of a reclining female figure holding a wheel (*BMC*, p. 98, nos. 484–85, pl. 17. 13 [aurei]; pp. 98–99, nos. 486–91, pl. 17. 14 [denarii]; pp. 208–9, nos. 986–89, pl. 39. 1 [sestertii]; pp. 211–12, nos. 998–99, pl. 39. 6 [dupondii]; pp. 214–15, nos. 1012–13, pl. 40. 7 [as]). The COS VI legend of these types would date them to 112–114 CE. Mattingly (*BMC*, p. 219 †) refers to one example with COS VI and OPTIMUS indicating a date in 114 CE. It is possible that the inscription from 108–109 CE notes an early stage in the project, while the coins celebrate the completion of the road.

XVIII IMP(eratori) VII CO(n)S(uli) VI (P)atri
P(atriae)/FORTISSIMO PRINCIPI SENATUS
P(opulus)Q(ue) R(omanus)

The Senate and People of Rome to the Emperor
Caesar, Son of the God Nerva, Nerva Trajan
Optimus Augustus, Triumphant over Germany and
Dacia, Chief Priest, Eighteen times Tribuni-
cian Power, Seven times Imperium, Six times
Consul, Father of his Country, Most Coura-
geous Princeps.[167]

The presence of the cognomen *"Optimus"* coupled with the designation of
the eighteenth tribunician power allows the inscription to be dated to sometime in 114 CE. This seems quite straightforward, but there has been a great
deal of debate about how the inscription and its date relate to the construction
of the arch and to the scenes depicted on its relief panels.

Franz Josef Hassel posits that the inscription should be taken to mark the
completion of the arch in 114 CE. In turn Hassel suggests that the design of
the arch including the reliefs was planned five years earlier in 109 CE,[168] and
that all of the events depicted on the arch took place before that date. Others
have countered that the inscription of 114 CE reflects the Senate's initial
decree for the construction of the arch, not its completion.[169] If this were the

---

[167] Cf. *Pan.* 53.4, where Pliny points out that Trajan's modesty is evidenced by the fact that the
Senate no longer had to spend hours debating enormous arches and inscriptions that were too
long for the architrave on which they were to be inscribed.

[168] Hassel, *Der Trajansbogen in Benevent: Ein Bauwerk des römischen Senates* (Mainz: von
Zabern, 1966) 8–9. Hassel feels that the Senate was moved to vote the arch in 109 because of
the recent completion of the *via Traiana.* As noted above, however, there is no certainty on
when the road was finished. Cf. Frank Lepper, "Review of Hassel, *Der Trajansbogen in
Benevent,*" *JRS* 59 (1969) 252. Erika Simon ("Die Götter am Trajansbogen zu Benevent,"
Trierer Winckelmannsprogamm 1 [Mainz: von Zabern, 1981] 3) accepts Hassel's chronology of
the arch. Fears (*PRINCEPS*, 229, n. 74) argues for a completion date in 114 on the basis of
parallel inscriptions on the column and aqueduct of Trajan. He claims that in the case of the
other two monuments, references in the *Fasti Ostienses* confirm that the date of the inscription is
the date of dedication (column: *CIL* 6. 960 and *Fasti Ost.* 22. 54; aqueduct: *CIL* 6. 1260 and *Fasti
Ost.* 22. 11). Even if this connection is true for other monuments, it cannot be applied with certainty to the arch. There is ample evidence of other honorific structures that were voted by the
Senate, but not completed until much later. Hill ("Buildings and Monuments, Part 1," 39) refers
to an altar of *Pietas* in Rome which was vowed by the Senate in 22 CE but not erected and dedicated until 43 CE under Claudius. In regard to the arch, Trajan's absence from the city in 114
makes a dedication at that time improbable.

[169] See Ian Richmond, "The Arch of Beneventum," in idem, *Roman Archaeology and Art:
Essays and Studies* (London: Farber & Farber, 1969) 229–30; Frank Lepper, "Review of
Hassel," 252–53; Werner Gauer, "Zum Bildprogramm des Trajansbogens von Benevent,"
Jahrbuch des Deutschen Archäologischen Instituts 89 (1974) 312–13.

case, the arch was constructed and decorated in the closing years of Trajan's reign, when the emperor was absent from Rome on the eastern campaigns from which he would not return alive.[170] Those who adhere to this later dating scheme hold that the arch might not have been completed until after Trajan's death. Different authors suggest various degrees of influence exerted by Hadrian on the relief panels,[171] but the clear appearance of Hadrian in several of the scenes (figs. 13.B, 15.B, 8.B [closeup of 15.B])[172] would seem to be incontrovertible evidence that his succession in 117 CE did play a part in determining the final scheme.

While this dispute over dating and responsibility for the arch cannot be resolved here, the involvement of the Senate and the potential influence of Hadrian make it difficult to cite the reliefs on the arch as evidence for Trajan's personal portrayal of the relationship between the emperor and the gods.[173] The arch does, however, present an interesting collection of images

[170] Trajan died in Selinus in Cilicia 11 August 117 CE (Dio, 68.33.1–3; *SHA Hadrian*, 4.6–7).

[171] At the end of the last century, A. von Domaszewski ("Die politische Bedeutung des Trajansbogens in Benevent," *Österr Jh* 2 [1899] 173–92) had argued for clear Hadrianic influence on the arch. Gauer ("Bildprogamm," 329, 332) detects three phases of construction, the last of which entails Hadrian adapting parts of the relief program "seinen eigenen umstrittenen Herrschaftsanspruch zu legitimieren" (ibid., 332). Lepper posits an unsettled time experienced by those (presumably senatorial authorities) who are planning the monument in Rome. They must adjust first to the initial success of Trajan's eastern campaign which makes references to Dacian triumphs planned for the arch seem out of date. Then the difficulties in the east, Trajan's death, and Hadrian's accession would have in turn influenced the designs of the reliefs (Lepper, "Review of Hassel," 259). In support of his theory, Lepper sees evidence of breakage that could indicate a removal and reworking of some of the attic panels (ibid., 260). Richmond ("Arch," 237–38) goes the farthest in asking whether in 114 CE the Senate commissioned a structure identical to the Arch of Titus, with reliefs only in the passageway, and Hadrian later added the outer face reliefs to present both an affirmation of his place as the successor to Trajan, and a confirmation of the aspects of Trajan's reign which he was emphasizing: peace, beneficence, and nonexpansion.

[172] K. Fittschen ("Das Bildprogramm des Trajansbogens von Benevent," *Archäologischer Anzeiger* [1972] 742–88) claims that the bearded figure is not Hadrian but Romulus. Gauer ("Bildprogramm," 315, 327) rejects this claim. Hassel accepts Hadrian's presence in the scenes, but claims that his actions were depicted as part of the imperial court before 109 CE. Richmond ("Arch," 229–30) is clear that the arch represents "an epitome of Trajan's achievements as seen through Hadrianic eyes."

[173] This is the approach taken by Fears who uses the arch in his article and book to support his theory of a developing "Jovian Theology" under Trajan. There are several difficulties with Fears's use of the arch and its images. He highlights the reliefs on the arch as an "official image" of what he calls Trajan's "divine election" (*PRINCEPS*, 234; "Jupiter," 84). Given the questions about the involvement of the Senate and Hadrian in the project, however, surely the idea of an "official image" should be qualified. In the book, Fears raises the issue of Hadrianic influence, but dismisses it without explanation "on clear stylistic and historical grounds" (*PRINCEPS*, 230, n. 76). In the article he avoids any reference to Hadrian or the dating controversy.

portraying aspects of that relationship that contribute to our understanding of the use of divine imagery at this time. While the interpretations of the reliefs, offered by various commentators, and the theories of how the reliefs are related cannot be repeated here, a brief discussion of the panels follows. On the north and south face of the arch two reliefs are found on each side of the passageway, and one relief on each side of the attic inscription (figs. 9 and 10). The six reliefs on the north side of the arch (facing the country) are representative of Trajan's activities in regard to the provinces (fig. 9), while those on the south (city) side are related to Trajan's actions in and around Rome (fig. 10). The reliefs on either side of the passageway interior refer to events in the city of Beneventum itself (figs. 11.A and 11.B).

Beginning with the interior passageway reliefs, the panel on the right side (when viewing from the city) shows Trajan offering benefactions to the people of Beneventum (fig. 11.A). Four city goddesses stand nearby, one holding a now lost object, one holding a small child, and another pushing a small boy forward to receive the emperor's offering. The left passageway relief (fig. 11.B) pictures a sacrificial scene probably commemorating the opening of the *via Traiana*.[174] Trajan is featured sprinkling [incense] on a portable altar, while *popae* ("sacrificial attendants") are seen to the left in the act of slaughtering a bull with a second bull waiting its turn.

The country side lower left relief (Fig. 12.C) portrays Trajan making peace with the barbarians while Jupiter looks on.[175] On the right-hand lower panel (Fig. 12.D), Trajan is pictured facing a group of men one of whom is wearing a lion skin. The interpretation of this latter figure as Hercules seems natural,[176] but while Gauer thinks the figure is leading a group of Roman soldiers,[177] Richmond claims that the group should be taken as a peace delegation of the Parthians for whom Hercules was the patron deity.[178] The middle

---

In his review of *PRINCEPS*, Brunt ("Divine Elements," 173) mentions the investiture scene on the arch "which *contra* Fears should surely be attributed to Hadrian."

Fears ("Jupiter," 83, n. 410) does inform the reader that his interpretation of the imagery is defended in the book, but given the pivotal place of the arch in the Jupiter article, he definitely strengthens his argument by not citing dissenting viewpoints. Fears cannot entertain the possibility that the reliefs are to some degree the work of Hadrian since they play such a critical role in his picture of Trajanic ideology.

[174] Richmond, "Arch," 235–36.

[175] Ibid., 232. Richmond suggests that the barbarians are Germanic, harking back to Trajan's first triumph. He also identifies Jupiter as Jupiter *Feretrius*, the god of treaties.

[176] Simon ("Götter," 5) follows Fittschen ("Bildprogramm," 754) in seeing that in this scene, the lion skin signifies not Hercules, but an army standard bearer. She calls this panel "the only one on the arch without a divine figure" (ibid.). Standard bearers wearing lion skins are depicted on Trajan's column (fig. 18).

[177] Gauer, "Bildprogramm," 319.

[178] Richmond, "Arch," 232. He relies on a story told by Dio (68.18.2).

reliefs on the country side feature on the left Mars Ultor presenting a recruit to Trajan (fig. 12.A), and on the right *Abundantia* standing between Trajan and Mars *Pater* who are presenting two small children to Roma who is carrying a plow (fig. 12.B).[179] The implication of both of these panels is that Trajan in conjunction with Mars has expanded the Empire and provided for the future of Rome both soldiers and general population.

Controversy abounds about the interpretation of both attic reliefs on the country side. On the right attic relief, a female figure kneels before Trajan, who stands in front of a group of men of whom the second from the left appears to be Hadrian (fig. 13. B). At the bottom of the relief left and right are two figures of river gods. Given the provincial connections on this side of the arch, the scene can be taken to refer to a province begging for mercy from Trajan. However, which province is it? Hassel and those who want to date the completion of the arch before any Parthian campaign argue that the figure must be Dacia.[180] Interpreters who accept a later dating see the figure as Mesopotamia surrounded by the Tigris and Euphrates.[181] Gauer sees definite characteristics for neither province and asks if the scene might be intentionally ambiguous to include both possibilities.[182]

The left attic relief on the country side is preserved only in part (fig. 13.A), and therefore is again open to differing interpretations. The part of the relief that remains pictures the divinities Liber (with *thyrsus*), Libera (with torch), Diana (wearing quiver), and Silvanus (with a flowering branch), collectively signifying the deities of the Danube provinces.[183] Most commentators agree that an image of Trajan originally stood with these divinities on the lost portion of the relief. If true, this relief would symbolize Trajan's efforts for peace in the northern provinces.[184] Fears stands alone in arguing that the lacuna should be filled with an image of Jupiter holding out a thunderbolt similar to the one in the corresponding panel on the opposite face of the arch (fig. 15.A).[185] In his book Fears does not mention that his interpretation goes

---

[179] Ibid., 232–33. He identifies the plow carried by Roma as symbolic of colonization; cf. the coin reverse with a veiled Trajan plowing (fig. 4.B).

[180] Hassel, *Trajansbogen*, 18.

[181] Richmond, "Arch," 231. Lepper ("Review of Hassel," 255) is not convinced that the kneeling figure is Dacia, but he cannot prove it to be Mesopotamia. Cf the sestertii reverses with ARMENIA ET MESOPOTAMIA IN POTESTATEM PR REDACTAE (see p. 105 above).

[182] Gauer, "Bildprogramm," 321. Simon ("Götter," 8–9) rejects the provincial connection and contends that the kneeling figure represents Italy. She cites an aureus reverse type showing a similar scene with the Legend REST ITAL (*BMC*, p. 85, no. 404, pl. 15. 19; cf. p. 186 *).

[183] Richmond, "Arch," 231. He associates Liber and Libera with Dacia, Diana with Moesia, and Silvanus with Illyricum; cf. Hassel, *Trajansbogen*, 17.

[184] Simon ("Götter," 9) reconstructs the scene with Trajan shaking hands with Diana. Cf. Hassel, *Trajansbogen*, 17; Richmond, "Arch," 231; Beaujeu, *La religion*, 434–35.

[185] Fears, *PRINCEPS*, 233. Parallelism with the other face is the only reason Fears gives for

against the near unanimous opinion of scholarship, and in his article he avoids any suggestion of doubt that Jupiter belonged in the lacuna: "Again Jupiter, now missing from the relief, was portrayed in the act of extending the thunderbolt towards Trajan."[186]

The city side of the arch contains another set of six panels: those portraying some aspect of Trajan's reign involving Rome. The bottom panels which are especially worn portray the first *adventus* ("arrival") of Trajan into the city. On the left he is greeted by the Senate, and the *Genius* of the Roman people (fig. 14.C),[187] and on the right the *praefectus urbi* ("city magistrate") motions Trajan to enter one of the city gates (fig. 14.D).[188] The middle registers on the city side portray the beneficent Trajan. The left panel is taken to be the offering of land to veterans who are escorted to the emperor by *Virtus* (fig. 14.A). Lepper mentions two possibile interpretations for the complementary panel on the right (fig. 14.B) in which Trajan is handing something to a group of three men (usually called merchants) while three divinities (Portunus,[189] Hercules, and Apollo) look on.[190] Lepper cites suggestions that the scene is set in the *Forum Boarium* in Rome, where all three divinities had temples, or that the setting is Ostia where Trajan's Harbor improvements would certainly have benefited the Roman merchants.[191] Erika Simon suggests that the small scale of the three figures before the emperor is intended to portray Trajan's care for the young men of Rome (*iurenes*) for whom Hercules was a patron deity. She cautions that neither her analysis, nor the accepted view of the men as merchants can be proven based on existing evidence.[192]

Finally, the interpretation of the city side attic reliefs offer the best-known imagery from the arch. On the right Trajan is pictured returning to Rome (fig. 15.B). He is greeted by Hadrian (fig. 8.B) in military attire, Roma, two smaller togate male figures representing the consuls, and two divine male figures taken to be either the Penates, or the Dioscuri.[193] Hassel holds that the

---

this suggestion, but it is obviously tied to his desire to show the arch as the pinnacle of Trajan's "Jovian Theology."

[186] Fears, "Jupiter," 84. He mentions in a footnote (p. 83, n. 410), that his interpretation of the reliefs is defended at length in the book, but that is not true in this case, and the reader of the article would have no reason to suspect that a defense was called for.

[187] Cf. the Senate and *Genius* of the people on the VOTA SUSCEPTA issue (pp. 97–99 above).

[188] Gauer, "Bildprogramm," 321; Richmond, "Arch," 234.

[189] Portunus, god of harbors, is identified on the far left by the partial anchor surviving near his left shoulder. Portunus is often equated with Palaemon.

[190] Lepper, "Review of Hassel," 257–58; Richmond, "Arch," 235.

[191] The latter idea is supported by Hassel (*Trajansbogen*, 16–17).

[192] Simon, "Götter," 9.

[193] Gauer, "Bildprogramm," 323.

scene must reflect Trajan's triumphal return to Rome after the Dacian war.[194]
Gauer supports the opinion that at another level of meaning (part of the
Hadrianic third phase of the design) the scene could be the return of the
deceased and divinized Trajan to the city as a post mortum *adventus* from the
Parthian conflict.[195] This suggestion would have obvious implications for the
connection with the relief on the opposite side of the inscription, where
Jupiter stands among a group of other deities and holds out his thunderbolt in
a gesture of passing it across the inscription to Trajan (fig. 15.A; cf. fig. 10).
Fears and others have seen this as the ultimate expression of Trajan's divine
election for earthly rule.[196] If, however, one follows Gauer's later dating
scheme and sees the image as a symbolic return to the city of the deceased
Trajan, the passing of the thunderbolt then could be taken as the empowering
and honoring of *divus Trajan*, while his earthly successor Hadrian looks on in
admiration.

One final panel on the arch is found in the least conspicuous place but
holds one of the more intriguing reliefs. At the top of the inner passageway,
the scene shows Trajan standing in military dress being crowned by Victory
(fig. 8.C). Fears sees this depiction as completing the theme of the attic
reliefs. He describes Trajan: "In his left hand he carries a spear, in his right
he wields a thunderbolt."[197] A quick glance at the illustration reveals that in
fact both arms of the Trajan figure are missing from the elbow down.[198] In
his book, Fears includes a photo of the relief, and admits that his restoration
of the thunderbolt is based on parallel representations on coins.[199] While
there is a similarity between the two scenes (figs. 1.A and 8.C), the differ-
ences are also obvious.[200] It would seem to be just as likely that Trajan's

---

[194] Hassel, *Trajansbogen*, 18–19.

[195] Gauer, "Bildprogramm," 322, 332. Lepper ("Review of Hassel," 259) thinks that the
scene should be read as a *Profectio* ("departure") scene presumably depicting Trajan's departure
for the Parthian campaigns. He asks why Trajan would be dressed in a toga (and Hadrian in military attire) if he were returning triumphant from battle?

[196] Fears, *PRINCEPS*, 229–33.

[197] Fears, "Jupiter," 95.

[198] It is not possible to glance at the scene in the "Jupiter" article since Fears does not include
a photograph of this relief as he does with the attic panels.

[199] Fears, *PRINCEPS*, 232, pl. 5, 19. The reverse type of Trajan holding the thunderbolt is discussed above (see 109–10 above, fig. 1.A); also mentioned is the relative rarity of the type and
the possibility that it was not a popular issue.

[200] While trying to accentuate the positive in his argument for the "Jupiter" article, Fears
("Jupiter," 95) mistakenly says that in the relief Trajan carries a spear in his left hand and a
thunderbolt in his right. This is the arrangement in the coin type, but the opposite is true in the
vault relief. The left hand is the one that could be carrying a thunderbolt, but couldn't it also
carry a patera or some other object?

missing left hand contained not a thunderbolt, but a *parazonium*, and that the scene was an adaptation of the Virtus reverse type which is abundantly attested on gold and silver imperial coinage under Trajan.[201]

Several observations can be made about this review of the program of relief sculptures on the Arch of Beneventum. In the first place there seems to be good evidence that the work should be seen as reflecting the influence of Hadrian. To whatever extent Hadrian did influence the final design of the reliefs, it makes perfect sense that he retained the senatorial inscription of 114 CE. In that way, his presence as successor to Trajan was given monumental as well as senatorial approval.[202] As concerns the relationship between the emperor and the gods, it is striking that divinities are present in almost every relief; in many cases they are depicted in some sort of mediating role between Trajan and the people, or Trajan and other deities (such as Roma on the country side middle left relief, fig. 12.A). The divine figures are usually in the center of the composition, or else looking on with approval.[203] The sense of mutuality which was seen in Pliny's *Panegyricus* is repeated here, with a strong affirmation of the place of the gods at the center of earthly activity. While Trajan's deeds are honored on the arch, it is clear in every scene that he did not act on his own.

One final point is that although some connection with Trajan's military success can be found in almost every relief, there is a subtlety about the way it is handled. Unlike the coin reverses where Victory was ubiquitously and often graphically portrayed, the arch recognizes Trajan's military successes in a subdued fashion.[204] Richmond feels that Trajan's military successes are intentionally downplayed by Hadrian who chose not to follow Trajan's path of expansion but to withdraw from some areas (Mesopotamia) and to strengthen the empire's existing boarders.[205] Whether or not Hadrian was responsible for the design of the arch, the tendency of the reliefs to portray the results of Trajan's military actions, but not the conquests themselves, is in striking contrast with the relief programs associated with Trajan's Forum and Column in Rome.[206]

---

[201] See pp. 104–5 above.

[202] Lepper, "Review of Hassel," 259.

[203] The significance of Hadrian's position in the center of the city side right attic relief (fig. 15.B) is not coincidental.

[204] There is continuous frieze depicting Trajan's Dacian triumphal procession running just below the attic on the arch (figs. 9 and 10).

[205] Richmond, "Arch," 237. He also notes that Hadrian had reason to defend his policies from critics who thought he was foolish to give up eastern territory which Trajan had conquered (ibid., 232; citing Fronto *Principia Historiae* 10; *SHA Hadrian*, 5).

[206] Richmond, "Arch," 237.

Trajan's Forum and Column

These monuments, completed in 112–113 CE, prior to Trajan's departure for the East, were more certainly constructed under the emperor's influence than was the arch.[207] Narrative of the Dacian wars makes up the total subject matter of the column (fig. 16), and of much of what survives of the sculpture from the forum.[208] This tendency to portray the graphic details of battles is in contrast to the relief program on the Arch of Beneventum which ignores the actual fighting of the wars, and focusses on the resulting peace and prosperity.

There is also a difference between the way the gods are treated on the Column of Trajan and their depiction on the Arch. The role of the gods in the Column relief is limited, so, therefore, is the portrayal of the relationship between the emperor and the gods. Near the beginning of the Column frieze,

[207] On the forum, see Paul Zanker, "Das Traiansforum in Rom," *AA* (1970) 499–544; Marc Waelkens, "From a Phrygian Quarry: The Provenance of the Statues of the Dacian Prisoners in Trajan's Forum at Rome," *AJA* 89 (1985) 641–53; and James Packer, "Numismatic Evidence for the Southeast (Forum) Facade of the Basilica Ulpia," in Lionel Casson and Martin Price, eds., *Coins, Culture, and History in the Ancient World: Numismatic and Other Studies in Honor of Bluma L. Trell* (Detroit: Wayne State University Press, 1981) 57–67. On the column there is abundant bibliography highlighted by Giacomo Boni, *Trajan's Column* (Proceedings of the British Academy, vol. 3; London: Oxford University Press, 1908); Karl Lehmann-Hartleben, *Die Trajanssäule* (Berlin: de Gruyter, 1926); Ion Miclea and Radu Florescu, *The Column*, (Cluj: Publishing house Dacia, 1971); Lino Rossi, *Trajan's Column and the Dacian wars* (J. M. C. Toynbee, trans. rev.; London: Thames and Hudson, 1971); Werner Gauer, *Untersuchungen zur Trajanssäule* (Berlin: Mann, 1977); Richard Brilliant, "The Column of Trajan and Its Heirs: Helical Tales, Ambiguous Trails," in idem, *Visual Narratives: Storytelling in Etruscan and Roman Art* (Ithaca: Cornell University Press, 1984) 90–123; and Frank Lepper and Sheppard Frere, *Trajan's Column* (Gloucester: Alan Sutton, 1988). See also Gerhard Koeppel, "Official State Reliefs of the City of Rome in the Imperial Age: A Bibliography," ANRW (1982) 2/12.1, 477–506, esp. 491–94; Giovanni Becatti, "La Colonna Traiana, espressione somma del ril revo storico romano," ANRW (1982) 2/12.1, 536–78; and Alain Malissard, "Une nouvelle approche de la Colonne Trajane," ANRW (1982) 2/12.1, 579–606.

[208] Waelkens ("From a Phrygian Quarry," 645–48) includes a list of forty-five "presently known statues of Dacian prisoners which can be connected with the Forum." Many are fragmentary. Zanker ("Traiansforum," 513–17) describes the so-called Great Frieze associated with the Forum or the Basilica Ulpia. Four panels now lining the central archway and outer sides of the Arch of Constantine are associated with the Great Frieze. Zanker indicates that the original location and extent of the Frieze in the Forum cannot be determined. The subject matter of the surviving panels is Trajan leading his troops in a fierce battle against the Dacians (fig. 20), along with a scene of Trajan being crowned by Victory while Roma looks on (fig. 21). See also Anne-Marie Leander Toueti, *The Great Trajanic Frieze: The Study of Monument and the Mechanisms of Message Transmission in Roman Art*; Koeppel, "Official State Reliefs," 494–96; idem, "The Grand Pictorial Tradition of Roman Historical Representation during the Early Empire," ANRW (1982) 2/12.1, 507–35.

the river god Danube looks on as Roman troops cross the river (figs. 17 and 18).[209] In the first battle scene, Jupiter appears in the sky preparing to throw something (presumably a thunderbolt) down onto the Dacian troops (fig. 19).[210] Lepper and Frere are unable to resolve whether or not Jupiter's presence should be interpreted as symbolizing a thunderstorm which occured during the battle.[211] In a later battle scene, a female figure in the sky above the fray is taken to be the goddess of night, who helped the Romans surprise the Dacians in a night attack (fig. 22, upper left).[212] Victory writes upon a shield as the dividing point between the depictions of the First and Second Wars (fig. 23).[213] Finally, one additional goddess appears in the sky over the scene of the final battle of the Second War (fig. 24).[214]

The depictions of divinities on the Column differ from those on the Arch in several respects. In the first place, on the Arch, the gods are pictured as an integral part of almost every scene. On the Column, divine figures appear only five times in some 150 scenes. In the second place, when they do appear on the column, the gods are consistently operating in a different sphere than the human beings. For instance, the river god is clearly separated from the troops marching over the bridge (figs. 18 and 19). On the Arch, one of the river gods in the country side right attic panel reaches up to touch Trajan (fig. 13.B). On the Arch, the gods are usually standing in the midst of the action interacting with the human participants. On the Column, the gods are in the sky, perhaps helping by means of thunder or night, but certainly working on another level. Finally, the gods on the Column do not really have any contact with Trajan, whereas on the Arch they are usually standing by his side, implying divine support and encouragement of his every action.

Divine support is acknowledged on the column by the prominent place given to sacrificial scenes.[215] By way of sacrifice, Trajan acknowledges his debt to the gods. This has been an essential part of the depiction of the relationship between the emperor and the gods in all other media examined.[216] Because depictions of the gods on the column, however, are relatively rare,

[209] Lepper and Frere, *Trajan's Column*, 50–51, pl. 6 scene 3 and pl. 7 scene 4.

[210] Ibid., 68, 71, pl. 19 scene 24.

[211] Ibid.

[212] Ibid., 85, pl. 29 scene 38.

[213] Ibid., 121–22, pl. 57 scene 78.

[214] Ibid., 182–84, pl. 110 scene 150.

[215] Ibid., 30, 51, 57–59, 91, 100–1, 157–59, pl. 10 scene 8, pl. 38 scene 53, pl. 62 scene 85 pl. 63 scene 86, pl. 66 scene 90 (fig. 25), pl. 72 scene 99, pl. 75 scene 102, pl. 76 scene 103 (fig. 26).

[216] Although there is only one coin reverse type which shows Trajan sacrificing (see pp. 99–100, n. 91).

the balance of this relationship is heavily on the side of Trajan and his actions as a pious emperor. The column delivers a message that responsibility for the Dacian victory lies firmly with the armies of Rome and the sacrificing emperor at their head. The gods appear only to furnish an occasional bit of supernatural assistance. This depiction of the emperor and the gods is especially important since the Column clearly can be associated with the emperor, and presumably it depicts most securely the relationship between the emperor and the gods which Trajan intended to portray. It is a relationship of support by both the sacrificing emperor and the gods in heaven. The connection is important, but not nearly as explicit as in either Pliny's *Panegyricus*, or the Arch reliefs in Beneventum.

Conclusion

I began this study with brief mention of Pliny the Younger and his problem with Christians in Bithynia. In attempting to gain some insight into that situation, and the many situations within which Christianity was developing in the early second century CE, I proceeded to consider different portrayals of the relationship between the emperor and the gods at this time. All the evidence I selected was connected in some way with the city of Rome. This may seem unusual given the provincial location of Pliny's problem, but as important as the provinces were becoming, the city of Rome remained the center point of the empire. When Pliny wrote to Trajan about the Christian problem, the Forum and Column were under construction in Rome, and were being widely portrayed on imperial coin reverses.[217] There is no reason to think that Trajan was not in or near Rome when he wrote his response to Pliny's inquiry. The way in which the relationship between the emperor and

---

[217] Column: *BMC*, lxxx, cii, cv, p. 86 * (denarius); p. 87 * (aureus); pp. 93–94, nos. 449–50, pl. 16. 19 (aureus); p. 94, no. 451–55, pl. 16. 20, 17.2 (denarii); p. 105, nos. 522–24, pl. 18. 11 (denarii); p. 106 #; p. 112, nos. 565–68, pl. 19. 11–12 (denarii); p. 128, no. 665, pl. 21. 15 (aureus with two reverses, forum on opposite side); p. 206, nos. 971–72, pl. 38. 3 (sestertius); p. 210, nos. 993–95, pl. 39. 4–5 (dupondii); p. 213, nos 1003–5, pl. 40. 1–2 (as); p. 216 § (dupondius); p. 218, nos. 1023–25, pl. 41. 6–7 (sestertii); p. 219 #, pl. 42. 3 (dupondius); p. 220 † (as). Forum: *BMC*, lxxx, lxxxi, ciii, p. 102, nos. 509–10, pl. 18. 3 (aurei); p. 208, nos. 984–85 (sestertii); p. 218 n. Basilica Ulpia: p. 99, no. 492, pl. 17. 15 (aureus); p. 185 *; pp. 207–8, nos. 982–83, pl. 38. 8 (sestertii). If one were to accept the earlier dating scheme of Hassel, then the Arch at Beneventum would also be under construction at this time. The fact that the Arch does not appear on the extant coinage from Trajan's reign is one more reason for dating its construction after 114 CE. Russell Meiggs (*Roman Ostia* [2d. ed.; Oxford: Clarendon, 1973] 231) mentions a carefully cut graffito found at Ostia that pictures the column of Trajan. He suggests that the drawing demonstrates "how spectacular this monument must have seemed to contemporaries."

the gods was being portrayed in Rome was relevant to any provincial setting.

The main discovery of this research has been that there was not any single portrayal of the relationship between the emperor and the gods, but several. Pliny's *Panegyricus* emphasized a mutual relationship in which Trajan recognized his indebtedness to the gods, and the importance of displaying that indebtedness by acts of piety. In Trajan's letters to Pliny, the emperor showed modest appreciation for acts of devotion to himself and concern for piety shown to deified predecessors, but he seemed uninterested in problems related to other ritual activity, except where it threatened good order. The reverse images of the imperial coinage emphasize the importance of ritual acts, bringing the gods directly into the picture with heavy dependence on a variety of divine military images acting to secure victory for Rome. On the Column of Trajan the divine images are less important than, and physically separated from, the acts—both heroic and ritual—of Trajan and his men. Finally on the Arch at Beneventum, the emphasis is again on the mutual responsibility of the emperor and the gods, but the gods are now portrayed as present and involved in the activities on a plane and scale equal with the emperor.

While the entire significance of these different portrayals of the relationship cannot be known, it is reasonable to suggest that this variety of images represented a larger ongoing discussion of how the gods were to be understood in relationship to the emperor, and to the state. If this discussion included such differing opinions in Rome, it can be assumed that there would have been even more variety in the provinces where local customs and beliefs remained strong. Since this discussion was going on in public visual media as well as in literature, the discussion would have been accessible to a greater spectrum of the population. Although the details of this discussion are inaccessible, it is not difficult to imagine that differing portrayals of the relationship between the emperor and the gods might have been confusing for some observers, especially those observers who were on the outside of the discussion, trying to survive in the Empire in spite of having radically different beliefs. I am speaking now particularly of Christians, who, although they did not have any sense of unified belief in the early second century, were in large part united in their rejection of the Graeco-Roman gods, and the worship of those gods through sacrifice.

For those Christians who shared this point of view, the relationship between the emperor and the gods would have been more than a scholarly curiousity. Pliny's testimony (*Ep.* 10.96) tells us that, while in the early second century, conflicts between Christians and imperial officials were rare (he had never been present at a trial), the consequences of those conflicts could be fatal for the Christian. It is natural, then, that some Christians wanted to know how they could continue to live in the Empire and retain their Christian beliefs. Evidence exists that at this time some Christians were trying to get along with the Empire, and that they did so by encouraging proper respect for, and even prayer for the emperor and other rulers.[218] Is it possible that some who felt this way were influenced by currents of thought that emphasized the virtuous human deeds of the emperor without dwelling on his relationship to the gods? This must remain an unanswered question, but long before the early second century, Christians thought that it was their god who empowered and supported the state (Romans 13:1–2),[219] and later on in the second century, Christian apologists addressed letters to the emperors and described the gods as unimportant secondary demons.[220]

This thesis has demonstrated that it is not practical to approach the question of Christian conflicts with the Empire with predetermined understandings of the relationship between the emperor and the gods. Price has elucidated the complex system of relationships on which the imperial cult in Asia Minor was based. In this thesis, I have not focused on the imperial cult, or any one way that the emperor could or could not receive honors, but I have found that, in Rome as well, the relationship between the emperor and the gods was portrayed in a variety of images and rituals which were connected with socio-political relationships. I hope that this insight can lead to further consideration of the relationship between the emperor and the gods, and the way in which that relationship affected the developing Christian communities.

Any such consideration will have to take into account different situations, different locations, and definitely different time periods. In the material covered by this thesis, the portrayal of the relationship between the emperor and the gods was not a static thing. The portrayal of the relationship changed from emperor to emperor, and even within the reign of a single emperor. It is advisable, therefore that study of the conflicts between Christians and the Empire be time specific, and avoid generalizing about what the Roman emperors thought, or how the Roman emperors were worshiped. To the extent that reasonable dating can be determined, Christian documents should be read in light of the attitudes and actions of one emperor in particular, rather than an imperial policy presumed to be consistent. It would be interesting to investigate the results of reading Christian documents with an eye to the images of the relationship between the emperor and the gods

---

[218] 1 Clem 21.6, 50.4–51.3; 1 Tim 2:1–2; and 1 Pet 2:13–15.

[219] Paul assumes that the rule of the emperors is moral, and a threat only to those who choose a path of immorality (Rom 13:3–5). This is not far from Pliny's picture of the new society of the virtuous ruler Trajan.

[220] Elaine Pagels, "Christian Apologists and the 'Fall of the Angels': An attack on Roman Imperial Power?" *HTR* 78 (1985) 301–25.

which were prevalent at the time of their writing. This could be attempted with Revelation and 1 Clement under Domitian, the *Epistles* of Ignatius and 1 Peter under Trajan, the Pastoral Epistles under Hadrian, and apologies addressed by Justin Martyr to Antoninus Pius and by Athenagoras to Marcus Aurelius. This dating scheme can serve as a working hypothesis for consideration of the documents in a certain time period, even if individual dating is disputed.

In the case of 1 Peter, there is sound scholarly opinion which places its composition during the reign of Trajan.[221] The letter also contains several tantalizing elements which seem to have great promise for study in light of my research on different portrayals of the relationship between the emperor and the gods during Trajan's reign. These are: its address "to the exiles of the Dispersion in Pontus, Galatia, Cappadocia, Asia, and Bithynia," its composite nature indicating different levels of conflict with Roman authorities,[222] and its very strong admonition to honor the emperor (2:17), to be subject to the power of the emperor as delegated to the governor (2:13),[223] and to extend that subordination throughout the social order.[224] Even a glance at these aspects of 1 Peter indicate that there is much to compare with what has

---

[221] Norman Perrin and Dennis Duling, *The New Testament, an Introduction*, (2d ed.; San Diego: Harcourt Brace Jovanovich, 1982) 376; Helmut Koester, *Introduction to the New Testament* (2 vols.; Foundations and Facets; Philadelphia: Fortress, 1982; Berlin/New York: De Gruyter, 1983) 2. 294. Arguments for an earlier date can be found in Bo Reicke, *The Epistles of James, Peter, and Jude*, (AB 37; 2d. ed.; Garden City/New York: Doubleday, 1964); John H. Elliott, *A Home for the Homeless: A Sociological Exegesis of 1 Peter, Its Situation and Strategy* (Philadelphia: Fortress, 1981). Elliott places the document from 69–96 CE, but he admits that any dating hypothesis is tenuous (pp. 84–85).

[222] Koester (*Introduction*, 2. 294) asks if 1 Peter 4:12–5:14 is "an appendix that was added when the situation suddenly changed and the persecution was intensified?" I am curious if the statement that "those who suffer according to the will of god put their souls in the hands of a trustworthy founder/creator" (1 Peter 4:19) might reflect the abundant honors which the emperor received as *ktistēs* ("founder") in the provinces (cf. *anthrōpinē ktisei* ["human institutions/foundations"] in 2:13).

[223] In the same spirit as Rom 13:3–5 that power is intended "to praise those who do good" (1 Pet 2:14).

[224] It was extended especially to slaves (2:18–21) and women (3:1–6). Elisabeth Schüssler Fiorenza (*In Memory of Her: A Feminist Theological Reconstruction of Christian Origins* [New York: Crossroad, 1983] 336) points out that in 1 Timothy, the section on the subordination of women (2:9–15) is preceded by an admonition to pray for the emperor in order to live in peace (2:1–4), and that therefore it is necessary to consider "the religio-political context" of the passage. The same is true of the arrangement of these topics in 1 Peter 2–3. Elliott (*Home for the Homeless*) makes use of Roman sources in his study of the sociological situation of 1 Peter, but his only citations from Pliny come from the letter about the Christians (*Ep.* 10.96), the letter about the fire fighters in Nicomedia (*Ep.* 10.33), and a letter about Pliny's attitude toward slaves (*Ep.* 8.17).

been learned from and about Pliny who was delegated with imperial power for his mission to Pontus and Bithynia, who wanted to see that the emperor was prayed for, but not prayed to as a god, who attempted to show that the relationship between the emperor and the gods had a definite impact on the socio-political order in Rome, and who for the first time on record, evaluated the innocence of accused Christians by requiring them to invoke the gods, and make an offering to the image of the emperor.

Appendix 1

CIL 5. 5262

C. PLINIUS L. F. OUF. CAECILIUS [SECUNDUS COS.]
AUGUR LEGAT. PRO PR. PROVINCIAE PON[TI ET BITHYNIAE]
CONSULARI POTESTA[T.] IN EAM PROVINCIAM E[X S.C. MISSUS AB]
IMP. CAESAR NERVA TRAIANO AUG. GERMAN[ICO DACICO P.P.]
CURATOR ALVEI TI[B]ERIS ET RIPARUM E[T CLOACAR. URB.]
PRAEF. AERARI SATU[R]NI PRAEF. AERARI MIL[IT. PR. TRIB. PL.]
QUAESTOR IMP. SEVIR EQUITUM [ROMANORUM]
TRIB. MILIT. LEG. [III] GALLICA[E] [X VIR STLI]
TIB. IUDICAND. THERM[AS ex HS. . . . .   ] ADIECTIS IN
ORNATUM HS CCC [. . . ET EO AMP]LIUS IN TUTELA[M]
HS. CC. T. F. I. [ITEM IN ALIMENTA] LIBERTOR SUORUM HOMIN.C.
HS. | XVIII | LXVI DCLXVI REI [P. LEGAVIT QUORUM INC]REMENT
        POSTEA AD EPULUM
[PL]EB URBAN VOLVIT PERTIN[ERE ITEM VIVU]S DEDIT IN
        ALIMENT. PUEROR
ET PUELLAR PLEB. URBAN. HS [D. ITEM BYBLIOTHECAM ET] IN
        TUTELAM BYBLIOTHECAE HS C.

Gaius Plinius Caecilius Secundus, son of Lucius of the tribe Oufentina, consul: augur: praetorian commissioner with full consular power for the province of Pontus and Bithynia, sent to that province in accordance with the Senate's decree by the Emperor Nerva Trajan Augustus, victor over Germany and Dacia, the Father of his Country: curator of the bed and banks of the Tiber and sewers of Rome: official of the Treasury of Saturn: official of the military Treasury: praetor: tribune of the people: quaestor of the Emperor: commissioner for the Roman knights: military tribune of the Third Gallic legion: magistrate on board of Ten: left by will public baths at a cost of . . . and an additional 300,000 sesterces for furnishing them, with interest on 200,000 for their upkeep . . . and also to his city capital of 1,866,666 2/3 sesterces to support a hundred of his freedmen, and subsequently to provide an annual dinner for the people of the city. . . . Likewise in his lifetime he gave 500,000 sesterces for the maintenance of boys and girls of the city, and also 100,000 for the upkeep of the library. . . .

(Translation, Radice, *Pliny*, 551)

Appendix 2

List of Figures

Figure 1A

Figure 1B

Figure 1C

Figure 1D

Figure 2A

Figure 2B

Figure 2C

Figure 2D

Figure 3A

Figure 3B

Figure 3C

Figure 3D

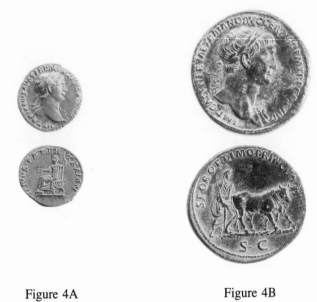

Figure 4A   Figure 4B

Figure 4C   Figure 4D

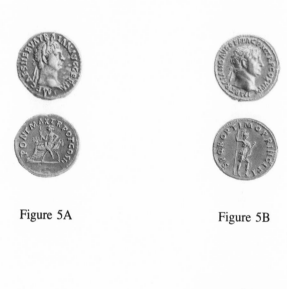

Figure 5A   Figure 5B

Figure 5C   Figure 5D

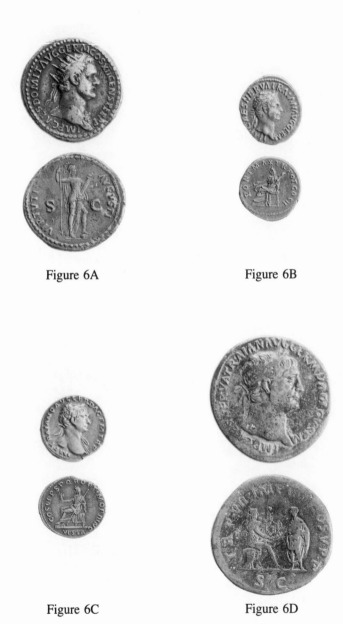

Figure 6A   Figure 6B

Figure 6C   Figure 6D

Figure 7A

Figure 7B

Figure 7C

Figure 7D

Figure 8A

Figure 8B

Figure 8C

Figure 9

Figure 10

Figure 11A

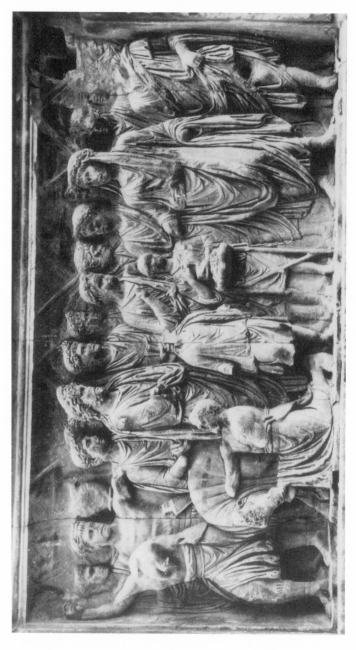

Figure 11B

Figure 12A

Figure 12B

Figure 12C

Figure 12D

Figure 13A

Figure 13B

Figure 14A

Figure 14B

Figure 14C

Figure 14D

Figure 15A

Figure 15B

Figure 16

Figure 17

Figure 18

Figure 19

Figure 20

Figure 21

Figure 22

Figure 23

Figure 24

Figure 25

Figure 26